MAX WEBER

MAKERS OF MODERN SOCIAL SCIENCE

MAX WEBER

EDITED BY
DENNIS WRONG

A SPECTRUM BOOK

Prentice-Hall, Inc.
Englewood Cliffs, New Jersey

PRENTICE-HALL INTERNATIONAL, INC. (*London*)
PRENTICE-HALL OF AUSTRALIA, PTY. LTD. (*Sydney*)
PRENTICE-HALL OF CANADA, LTD. (*Toronto*)
PRENTICE-HALL OF INDIA PRIVATE LIMITED (*New Delhi*)
PRENTICE-HALL OF JAPAN, INC. (*Tokyo*)

MAKERS OF MODERN SOCIAL SCIENCE

LEWIS A. COSER

GENERAL EDITOR

ÉMILE DURKHEIM, by Robert A. Nisbet, *with selected essays*, S–118
GEORG SIMMEL, edited by Lewis A. Coser, S–119
PARETO & MOSCA, edited by James H. Meisel, S–122
MAX WEBER, edited by Dennis H. Wrong, S–223

FORTHCOMING VOLUMES

KARL MANNHEIM, edited by Paul Kecskemeti
SIGMUND FREUD, edited by Harold Lasswell
KARL MARX, edited by Thomas Bottomore

CONTENTS

vii

PART THREE

SOCIOLOGY OF RELIGION

PART FOUR

BUREAUCRACY

PART FIVE

POLITICAL SOCIOLOGY

PART SIX

WEBER'S PHILOSOPHY OF HISTORY
AND POLITICS

MAX WEBER

MAX WEBER

DENNIS H. WRONG

ARISTOTLE HAS OFTEN been acclaimed as the last universal genius, the last thinker to have absorbed and mastered the total body of knowledge available in his time. With equal justice Max Weber deserves to be called the last universal genius of the social sciences. Originally trained as a student of law, his scholarship ranged across jurisprudence, political science, economics, sociology, comparative religion, the philosophy of history, and the histories of several nations and half a dozen civilizations, both ancient and modern. Although today he is chiefly regarded as a sociologist, his impact on all of these fields was a lasting one. With the exception of Freud and, more doubtfully, Marx, no other thinker has had so great an influence on modern social science. Yet Weber left no true descendants, not even in his native Germany. The same diversification and specialization of knowledge that long ago eliminated the possibility of a second Aristotle has taken place in the social sciences since Weber's death in 1920.

Weber was born in 1864 to a solidly established professional family of the Prussian middle class. He studied at the universities of Heidelberg, Goettingen and Berlin, continuing his studies at the latter after having qualified for legal work in the courts of the capital city. He accepted a full professorship in economics at Freiburg at the age of thirty, a remarkable achievement in the hierarchical, seniority-ridden world of German academic life. In 1896 he took a chair at Heidelberg, but little more than a year later he suffered a nervous collapse which, despite a partial recovery, prevented him for the rest of his life from assuming the full burden of an academic post. His life for the next eighteen years consisted of periods in which he could partially resume academic duties, weeks and months of intense intellectual productivity,

Material from my earlier article, "Max Weber: The Scholar as Hero," *Columbia Forum*, V, no. 3 (Summer, 1962), 31–37, has been revised and incorporated into the text of the introduction with the permission of the original publisher.

and relapses into enervating depression relieved only by frequent travel abroad.)

He supported his nation's cause in the First World War, but made frequent attempts directly to influence Germany's leaders, whose uncompromising outlook during both the war and the peace negotiations he bitterly opposed. His enormous reputation as a scholar and political thinker created a general expectation that he would play a major role in postwar German politics. Beginning in the 1880s as a nationalist liberal, a "realistic" supporter of the monarchy and national *Machtpolitik,* Weber had by 1918 become a constitutional democrat and a friend and adviser to influential socialists, though he never made their cause his own. He contemplated running for office under the Weimar Republic, but, like his previous political interventions, this came to nothing. He died rather suddenly in 1920, shortly after resuming full academic duties for the first time in years.

Hegel, Marx, Comte, Tocqueville, Mill, Spencer—this line of great nineteenth-century thinkers who aimed at universal interpretations of human history ends with Max Weber. We are still living off the intellectual heritage bequeathed us by these men. More than the sheer increase of knowledge accounts for the absence of comparable figures today: great leaps forward in our general understanding of man and society seem to require the simultaneous occurrence of major historical transformations. The social sciences are themselves part of the very situation they seek to transcend by seeing it in universal terms, in contrast to the physical sciences where the accumulation of knowledge proceeds more autonomously and is less dependent on the scientist's personal—or "existential"—involvement with the fate of his own time and place.

All of these giants of nineteenth- and early twentieth-century social thought were essentially trying to understand the emerging new society, no longer so novel to us today, created by the progress of science and industrial technology and the increased participation of majorities (or "the masses") in politics and the making of history. All of them were reacting to the historical convulsions of the French Revolution and its successors and the continuing Industrial Revolution. To be sure, social change has hardly come to a stop in the present century—it has, on the contrary, accelerated and become worldwide in scope. Yet much of contemporary reality was anticipated by the nineteenth-century thinkers. We still use the language they created in trying to understand our world: "bureaucracy," "alienation," "class struggle," "social revolution," "industrial society," "social leveling," "status groups," "power politics."

Social scientists have even recently fallen into the bad habit of describing the goal of the newly independent, underdeveloped nations as "modernization," which they broadly equate with attainment of the institutional forms of the "mature" societies of the West. Yet, short-sighted though it is to regard the Western world as free from the continuing tensions of historical change, it is hard—barring nuclear war—to envisage future transformations on the scale of the political and technical revolutions that created both the modern world and the intellectual disciplines of the social sciences with which we seek to understand it. For creative thinkers of the range and stature of the makers of modern social science, we shall perhaps in the future have to look to the "Third World" of the underdeveloped countries, now striving to attain the technological level of the West under conditions differing utterly from those of the premodern West.

Max Weber's earliest intellectual development was shaped by the profound historical consciousness and sense of the novelty of the present passed on to him by his nineteenth-century predecessors. Thus a concern with defining the distinctive qualities of his time was even more explicit in his work than in most of theirs. The desire to grasp what was central and unique about contemporary Western civilization and to discern the outlines of its future development led Weber to explore the religious conflicts of ancient India, the rise of the Hebrew prophets, the traditional structure of Chinese society, the agrarian problems of the classical Mediterranean civilizations, and the growth of cities in medieval Europe. Even his methodological reflections on the social sciences and his effort to develop a set of general and necessarily abstract sociological concepts were byproducts of his interest in understanding a particular "historical individual," the modern West. Contemporary American sociologists, who often picture Weber as a detached, impersonal scientist, chiefly concerned with building a scientific sociology comparable to physics in its powers of precise observation and abstract generalization, hold a distorted and one-sided view of both the man and his intellectual *milieu*.

If Weber was the last of the great nineteenth-century European social theorists, he was also one of the last of a more restricted breed of thinker as well as being one of its finest representatives: the university professor of Imperial Germany. In his essay on "Science as a Vocation," Weber himself gives a masterly analysis of the structure of the German university and the type of man most likely to succeed within it. Reflecting on what advice should be given to a talented young scholar, he at one point exclaimed, "One must ask every man: Do you in all conscience believe that you can stand seeing mediocrity after mediocrity, year after year, climb beyond you without becoming embittered?"[1] Perhaps this question needs to be put to all gifted men contemplating a career that will make them dependent for support and recognition on institutions specifically concerned with the grading and regulating of creative intellectual activity, whether they be universities, cultural and scientific foundations, publishing houses, or even literary coteries.

But if the university professor in Imperial Germany was at his worst a stiff, self-important pedant, overly deferential to the authority of State and Church, prejudiced in his exclusion of Jews and socialists from his ranks, and dangerously messianic in his readiness to turn the lecture hall into a rostrum for the propagation of conservative nationalist opinions, at his best he was a Kant, a Hegel, a Wilhelm Dilthey, a Leopold von Ranke. Capable of the most minute and careful investigations, German philosophers, social theorists, and historians never failed to be concerned with synthesizing and integrating their knowledge to achieve a comprehensive world view or *Weltanschauung* —a word with no exact equivalent in either English or French. When Max Weber was asked once what personal meaning his immense learning had to him, he answered: "I want to see how much I can stand!" He did not mean that he aspired to some sort of record for intellectual absorptive capacity; the reply expresses the intensity of his will toward intellectual and emotional synthesis—a force which he himself described as "demonic."

Far more acutely than most of his contemporaries, Weber experienced the tensions between past and present, individual freedom and the needs of social organization, the rationality of science and the irrationality of values, the life of contemplation and the call to political action to stave off impending historical disaster. Other men at the close of the nineteenth century—which ended in 1914 by historical time—felt as deeply as Weber what he called, following the poet Schiller, the "disenchantment of the world" and were as full of foreboding about the shape of the future. Today we hail the greatest of them as prophets and seers: Kierkegaard, Dostoevski, Nietzsche, D. H. Lawrence. But these men were chiefly literary artists or subjectivist philosophers, while Weber was preeminently a scholar and an uncommonly painstaking and rigorous one. His work thus expresses what two of his most perceptive critics, Hans Gerth and C. Wright Mills, have called the "pathos of objectivity."[2] Hence the sense of disciplined

---

[1] H. H. Gerth and C. Wright Mills, eds. and trans., *From Max Weber: Essays in Sociology* (New York: Oxford University Press, 1946), p. 134. This volume will be cited hereafter as *Essays.*

[2] Ibid., "Introduction," p. 27.

passion that pervades his writing, a passion that occasionally breaks through in passages of an overpoweringly tragic eloquence.

Weber was capable of protesting against the emptiness of modern culture and the cramping overorganization of modern society quite as savagely as the most splenetic of our present-day existentialist and romantic critics. Of those who in the jargon of today's fashionable social criticism would be called "organization men," he observed:

> That the world should know no men but these: it is in such an evolution that we are already caught up, and the great question is therefore not how we can promote and hasten it, but what can we oppose to this machinery in order to keep a portion of mankind free from this parcelling-out of the soul, from this supreme mastery of the bureaucratic way of life.[3]

And nearly half a century before laments about "conformism," "mass society," and "wasteful affluence" began to fill the air, in the closing pages of his most famous historical essay, *The Protestant Ethic and the Spirit of Capitalism,* Weber passed the following judgment on contemporary industrial civilization: "Of this last stage of cultural development, it might well be truly said: 'Specialists without vision, sensualists without heart; this nullity imagines that it has attained a level of civilization never before achieved.' " [4]

Yet Weber's enormous sense of responsibility toward the truth prevented him from indulging in "romantic protests" against modern life or nostalgic dreams of restoring the past. Nor did his analysis of historical trends allow for hopeful Utopian anticipations of the future. Such responses to the general "crisis of values" precipitated by industrial advance, the decline of religious faith, and the rise of the bureaucratic state too frequently amounted, Weber thought, to a form of sentimental escapism, an evasion of intellectual responsibility. The tension and subtlety of his outlook is illustrated by the following remarks on the alleged cold, dissecting spirit of modern science:

> To affirm the value of science is a presupposition for teaching in a university. I personally in my very work answer in the affirmative, and I also do so from precisely the standpoint that hates intellectualism as the worst devil, as youth does today, or usually only fancies it does. In that case the word holds for these youths: "Mind you, the devil is old; grow old to understand him." This does not mean age in the sense of the

---

[3] Max Weber, "Some Consequences of Bureaucratization," in *Sociological Theory,* ed. Lewis A. Coser and Bernard Rosenberg (New York: The Macmillan Company, 1957), p. 443.

[4] Max Weber, *The Protestant Ethic and the Spirit of Capitalism* (New York: Charles Scribner's Sons, 1930), p. 182. This volume will be cited hereafter as *Protestant Ethic.*

birth certificate. It means that if one wishes to settle with this devil, one must not take to flight before him as so many like to do nowadays. First of all, one has to see the devil's ways to the end in order to realize his power and his limitations.[5]

Weber was strongly imbued with Marx's sense of the limits to historical possibility. But against the vulgar Marxism that has become one of the most influential ideologies of our time, he saw no reason to leap forward and embrace the future simply because it *was* the future. (Of course, the Marxists have turned out to be largely wrong about the future into the bargain.) What Weber counseled was a stoical recognition of necessity which nevertheless refused to surrender values that appeared destined for what Leon Trotsky used to call "the dustbin of history." This is the source of Weber's "defensive pessimism" and the ever-present tension between rival perspectives that one feels in his work. "We are individualists and partisans of democratic institutions against the stream of material forces," he once remarked. "He who wishes to be the weathercock of an evolutionary trend should give up these old-fashioned ideals as soon as possible. The historical origin of modern freedom has had certain unique preconditions which will never repeat themselves." [6]

To show Weber's viewpoint in its full depth and complexity, I cannot resist quoting the magnificent closing peroration of his essay on "Politics as a Vocation," originally delivered before an audience of students at the University of Munich in the period of disorder and demoralization following the German surrender in 1918:

> Politics is a strong and slow boring of hard boards. It takes both passion and perspective. Certainly all historical experience confirms the truth—that man would not have attained the possible unless time and again he had reached out for the impossible. But to do that a man must be a leader, and not only a leader but a hero as well, in a very sober sense of the word. And even those who are neither leaders nor heroes must arm themselves with that steadfastness of heart which can brave even the crumbling of all hopes. This is necessary right now, or else men will not be able to attain even that which is possible today. Only he has the calling for politics who is sure that he shall not crumble when the world from his point of view is too stupid or too base for what he wants to offer. Only he who can say 'In spite of all!' has the calling for politics.[7]

These are not the words of a slavish worshipper of "the wave of the future." They are the words of a man, called by Albert Salomon "the *bourgeois* Marx," who understood, perhaps more deeply than their

[5] *Essays*, p. 152.
[6] Ibid., p. 71.
[7] Ibid., p. 128.

author, the truth of Marx's assertion that "men make their own history; but they do not make it just as they please; they do not make it under circumstances chosen by themselves, but under circumstances directly encountered, given, and transmitted from the past." [8]

Nor are they the words of a resigned or complacent conservative, contemptuous of efforts to change the world—for "man would not have attained the possible unless time and again he had reached out for the impossible." Comparing Durkheim and Weber, H. Stuart Hughes remarks that "Durkheim does not strike one as a particularly troubled individual," whereas "Weber, for all the intemperance of his polemical style, was hesitant, self-divided and enormously troubled." [9] In their basic attitudes towards time, change, and possibility in human life, one can with rough accuracy describe Marx as the great radical and Durkheim, Pareto, and Mosca as conservatives. Weber might be called a critical liberal, resembling Tocqueville and Mill most closely among the major social thinkers who immediately preceded him or were his contemporaries. But he lacks the serenity—essentially a conservative emotion—of the Frenchman and the benevolent innocence of the Englishman, who stood closer to the original spirit of the Enlightenment and was remote from the violence and furies of continental politics.

In its complexity and ambivalence, Weber's outlook most suggests that of the Freud who wrote in *Civilization and Its Discontents*: "My courage fails me . . . at the thought of rising up as a prophet before my fellow-men, and I bow to their reproach that I have no consolation to offer them; for at bottom this is what they all demand—the frenzied revolutionary as passionately as the most pious believer." [10] But then, after noting that the forces of Thanatos, of death and self-destruction, are rising in the world, Freud adds, "And now it may be expected that the other of the two 'heavenly forces,' eternal Eros, will put forward his strength so as to maintain himself alongside of his equally immortal adversary." [11] Though not conceived in psychological terms, Weber's sense of death and rebirth in history resembles Freud's: characterizing the modern economic order as an "iron cage," Weber asserts in the closing paragraphs of *The Protestant Ethic and the Spirit of Capitalism*, "No one knows who will live in this cage in

---

[8] Karl Marx, *The Eighteenth Brumaire of Louis Bonaparte* (New York: International Publishers, n.d.), p. 13.

[9] H. Stuart Hughes, *Consciousness and Society* (New York: Alfred A. Knopf, Inc., 1958), p. 288.

[10] Sigmund Freud, *Civilization and Its Discontents* (Garden City, N.Y.: Doubleday & Company, Inc., Anchor Books, 1958), p. 105.

[11] Ibid.

the future, or whether at the end of this tremendous development entirely new prophets will arise, or there will be a great rebirth of old ideas and ideals, or, if neither, mechanized petrifaction, embellished with a sort of convulsive self-importance." [12]

WEBER'S SOCIOLOGICAL METHOD

If Weber was the last great polymath of nineteenth-century social thought, one of the greatest academicians of Imperial Germany, and a pessimistic prophet who foresaw the burdens we now live under, it is as a sociologist that he remains most influential today. He was, in fact, the only truly great man we sociologists have a clear right to claim as one of our own. His methodological writings are probably his greatest achievement. Debate continues today over the similarities and differences in the approach and method of the social or cultural and the natural sciences; yet Weber's reflections on method are still uniquely successful in doing equal justice to our desire in social science on the one hand to discover uniformities in social experience, however restricted their application, and on the other to understand that experience in its full individuality. Weber shows why the attempt to build a social science similar to physics in precision, scope, and utility is bound to fail—without denying our ability to arrive at generalizations from history. Nor does he succumb to the subjectivism and irrationalism of those who assert so radical a contrast between man and the rest of the universe that the careful search for evidence which constitutes scientific method in its broader sense has no relevance to our understanding of human affairs. Here, as so frequently on other subjects, Weber was attempting to bridge the chasm between two extreme viewpoints representing rival intellectual traditions: the positivism of the natural sciences and German idealism and historicism.

Unfortunately, American sociologists, writing out of a different tradition, have often stressed Weber's positivist side while minimizing his insistence on the irreducibly individual and subjective character of our interest in social life. Or (like Talcott Parsons and Peter Blau in the selections included in this volume) they have treated Weber's historicism as an unfortunate prescientific residue of his neo-Kantian philosophical heritage. Science, to these writers, is identified with the natural sciences, and sociology is defined as a science-building enterprise which must aim at the abstract generality, formal logical structure, and practical importance of physics and strive to command the same degree of consensus among its practitioners. "Science" in the

[12] *Protestant Ethic*, p. 182.

English-speaking world has always meant natural science or technology and has become a much-coveted honorific label. While German thinkers ever since Kant were concerned with the differences between the natural sciences and our knowledge of human affairs, they were less inclined than we have been to measure the worth of the latter by the standards of the former. The German word *Wissenschaft* has a far broader connotation than "science"; the title of Weber's essay *"Wissenschaft als Beruf"* should be rendered in English as "scholarship" or "the pursuit of knowledge as a vocation" rather than, as is customary, "science as a vocation." In the body of that essay Weber treats aesthetics, jurisprudence, history, the social sciences, and even philosophy and theology as responsible disciplines, so far is he from confining his remarks to the natural sciences. Several of these disciplines would not be considered "sciences," even potentially, in England or America, yet Weber's essay is often read as a plea for the introduction into the study of man and society of more rigorous methods modelled on the procedures of the natural sciences.

Weber's idealist and neo-Kantian predecessors—Dilthey, Windelband, Rickert, and Eduard Meyer—regarded the distinction between the social or cultural sciences (*Geisteswissenschaft*) and the natural sciences as an absolute one necessitated by the radical contrast between the realm of mind and spirit studied by the former and the realm of nature investigated by the latter. They concluded, therefore, that different methods were appropriate to the study of these contrasting subject-matters. In rejecting their methodological position, Talcott Parsons is certainly correct when he maintains that "in a purely *logical* aspect there is no difference whatever" between the two groups of disciplines. But in accepting this as a warrant to proceed with the task of building a generalizing, "analytical" theory of society, Parsons does not do justice to the modification of the extreme neo-Kantian position developed by Weber and by Rickert, whose views greatly influenced Weber.

Weber did not take seriously either the neo-Kantian insistence on the ontological difference between the objects of investigation in the human and the natural sciences or the contention that they must pursue different methods. As H. Stuart Hughes points out, Weber argued that "in practice . . . the object of investigation *defined itself* through the very method that was directed towards it." [13] In other words, the sorts of questions we ask rather than differences in either their subject-matter or the logic of inquiry distinguish the human from the natural sciences. But this distinction, though a pragmatic one, is

[13] Hughes, op. cit., p. 309 (Hughes' italics).

still crucial. Extreme versions of the neo-Kantian metaphysical dualism and allied intuitionist methodologies have been so thoroughly discredited in American social science that it is important to examine more closely exactly how Weber and Rickert transcended the idealist position without, however, surrendering to the positivist view that science is a unity and that the more developed natural sciences present the social sciences with a picture of their own future.

It is not that what is sometimes called the "problem of the unique" or the "persistence of the particular" is a peculiar characteristic of human affairs that bedevils our efforts to create an abstract, generalizing science. Nor is it a matter of the "irreducible historicity" of human life, as the heirs of the neo-Kantians who remain committed to an antiscientistic view of social and historical studies are apt to put it. Uniqueness and historicity are, as Parsons observes, categories applicable to all phenomena, those studied by the natural as well as by the social sciences. No two peas in a pod are alike or have identical histories. What Weber and Rickert insisted on, however, was that our interest in human affairs is often precisely in those aspects of it that are concrete, individual, and understandable only in qualitative terms. As Barrington Moore, Jr., who has recently ably restated the Weber-Rickert view, remarks: "Goethe is not a lump of coal, whose only interest to us is the qualities it shares with other lumps of coal and whose properties can be expressed in the form of scientific generalizations. What we want to know and understand about Goethe is his unique contribution to human civilization. To some extent we can acquire this understanding only by uncovering a unique pattern of connections between unique events." [14]

Weber's concept of *Wertbeziehung,* or "value-relevance," takes fully into account the fact that our major interest in the subject-matter of sociology is often not abstract and quantitative to the degree that characterizes our interest in the physical world or even in economic phenomena. Positivist or "science-building" sociologists are inclined to forget that in seeing the objects of the social sciences as "constituted for us by our values," Weber did not have in mind merely the general properties or attributes of human actions to which we attach significance in the light of a "value-system" that is universalistic in its implications. (Although, particularly in his sociology of religion, he made an important contribution to a general typology of such value-systems.) Weber also regarded particular entities—*this* man, *this* institution, *this* nation, *this* economic system—as objects selected from the flux of reality by our acts of valuing in exactly the same way that the deifica-

[14] Barrington Moore, Jr., *Political Power and Social Theory* (Cambridge: Harvard University Press, 1958), p. 146.

tion of secular authorities may be selected as "relevant" to the universalistic values of transcendental religion or the facts of economic exploitation to the values of humanitarian socialism. In other words, *"historical individuals" are themselves values* and in part determine what constitutes relevant or significant knowledge in the social sciences. In Weber's own words:

> The "points of view," which are oriented towards "values," from which we consider cultural objects and from which they become "objects" of historical research, change. Because, and as long as they do, new "facts" will always be becoming historically "important.". . . This way of being conditioned by "subjective values" is, however, entirely alien in any case to those natural sciences which take mechanics as a model, and it constitutes, indeed, the distinctive *contrast* between the historical and the natural sciences. . . . The concept of the "culture" of a particular people and age, the concept of "Christianity," of "Faust," and also—there is a tendency to overlook this—the concept of "Germany," etc. are individualized *value-concepts* formed as the objects of *historical* research, i.e., by relation with value-ideas.[15]

The difference, then, between the study of human affairs and the natural sciences is not the result of inherent differences in the objects investigated by these disciplines or in the differing "methods" employed by students of human society and natural scientists. It lies, rather, in the different kinds of questions we ask, in what it is that we wish to know, and in the different degree to which idiographic as against nomothetic knowledge will satisfy our quest. The contrast, though one of degree, follows, of course, from the fact that in the study of human affairs man is both the subject and the object of inquiry. Social science is self-knowledge and man's relation to his own motives, beliefs, and customs is more intimate than his relation to stars, amoebas or molecules. Thus Weber argued that one of the major goals of social science—for him it was clearly *the* major goal—was to achieve *clarity*, clarity about the situations in which men select and act on their values, clarity that helps the individual, in Weber's words, "to give himself an account of the ultimate meaning of his own conduct." [16] It is obvious that one cannot simply take for granted the relevance to this goal of knowledge possessing the quantitative precision and the formal, logical structure of the physical sciences—or, more often, of what philosophers and logicians tell us the physical sciences are like. But if abstract, general propositions, or "laws," about human be-

---

[15] Edward A. Shils and H. A. Finch, eds. and trans., *Max Weber on the Methodology of the Social Sciences* (Glencoe, Ill.: The Free Press, 1949), pp. 159–60 (Weber's italics). See also pp. 84, 111. This volume will be cited hereafter as *Methodology*.
[16] *Essays*, p. 152.

havior resembling those of the natural sciences are *possible*—and few would deny this today—then why should not sociology adopt as its primary aim the search for such propositions and leave the study of historical individuals to historians and humanists? This is, in effect, the position taken today by the majority of American sociologists. The objection to it implied by Weber's methodological views is that, far from being too ambitious a goal for social science, to model sociology after the natural sciences is to impoverish it by neglecting the kinds of questions to which we most urgently seek answers. As Michael Polanyi observes:

> In relying for its own interest on the antecedent interest of its subject matter, science must accept to an important extent the pre-scientific conception of these subject-matters. The existence of animals was not dis-covered by zoologists, nor that of plants by botanists, and the scientific value of zoology and botany is but an extension of man's pre-scientific interest in animals and plants. . . . Admittedly, the pursuits of biology, medicine, psychology and the social sciences, may rectify our everyday conceptions of plants and animals, and even of man and society; but we must set against any such modification its effect on the interest by which the study of the original subject matter had been prompted and justified. If the scientific virtues of exact observation and strict correlation of data are given absolute preference for the treatment of a subject-matter which disintegrates when represented in such terms, the result will be irrelevant to the subject-matter and probably of no interest at all.[17]

But does not such a view "reduce" the sociologist to no more than a comparative historian, a "historical empiricist" bereft of general the-ory, as Parsons has argued? One might initially respond to such a charge by wondering what is wrong with being a comparative his-torian in the first place. Max Weber, as a matter of fact, at one time frequently described himself as a "comparative historian" and repu-diated the label "sociologist," claiming he didn't know what it meant.[18] Yet Weber's own immense work suggests that there is a task for the sociologist that makes him potentially more than simply a historian or at most a trained observer of contemporary society amassing data by means of special techniques of behavioral investigation that will be useful to the future historian. The sociologist, unlike the monographic historian, is committed to the systematic comparative study of historical and contemporary social structures. His goal, however, is not neces-sarily to compare in order to arrive at overarching general laws en-

---

[17] Michael Polanyi, *Personal Knowledge* (London: Routledge & Kegan Paul, Ltd., 1958), p. 139.
[18] I owe this information to a conversation with the late Albert Salomon, who was a member of Weber's circle at Heidelberg.

compassing the variety of social structures, but rather to illuminate the similarities *and* the differences between social structures.

Alexis de Tocqueville, a social thinker whom it is difficult to classify as either sociologist, historian, or political philosopher, wrote of his master work, *Democracy in America*:

> In my work on America . . . though I seldom mentioned France, I did not write a page without thinking of her, and placing her as it were before me. And what I specifically tried to draw out, and to explain in the United States, was not the whole condition of that foreign society, but the points in which it differs from our own, or resembled us. It is always by noting *likenesses and contrasts* that I succeeded in giving an interesting and accurate description of the New World . . . I believe that this perpetual silent reference to France was a principal cause of the book's success.[19]

The difference between Tocqueville and the modern sociologist is that for Tocqueville's "perpetual silent reference to France," the modern sociologist tries to substitute a systematic, explicit comparative frame of reference. Weber, more than any of the other founding fathers of contemporary sociology, has helped to shape this frame of reference. Whether the sociologist is concerned with the big issues that, in Moore's words, "history places on the agenda for us" [20]—"Why did Hitler come to power?" "Are the United States and the Soviet Union becoming more alike?" "Can the underdeveloped countries control their population explosions?"—or with more limited questions— "Why does the affluent United States have a high crime rate?" "Why does the middle class vote in greater numbers than the working class?" —no narrow historical analysis confined to particular events of one time and place can do full justice to these questions.

But if sociology is best defined *tout court* as the comparative study of social structures, it also concerns itself with transhistorical and universal questions about man and society: "How is social order possible?" (the Hobbesian question), "How do societies regulate group conflict?" (the Marxist question), "How is man's animal nature domesticated by society?" (the Freudian question). Yet our answers to these transhistorical questions do not easily cumulate into a set of scientific generalizations from which, given the initial conditions of a particular historical situation, we can work our way down deductively to an adequate explanation of that situation. And it is this that is the guiding ideal of the science-building sociologist, seeking a body of analytical

[19] Quoted by Reinhard Bendix and Bennett Berger, "Images of Society and Problems of Concept Formation in Sociology," in *Symposium on Sociological Theory*, ed. L. Gross (Evanston, Ill.: Row and Peterson, 1959), p. 109 (italics mine).

[20] Moore, op. cit., p. 113.

theory permitting deductive inference to a particular set of data. In part, we seek answers to these general questions for their own sake rather than to clarify individual historical situations. In part, the hallmark of the work of the great theorists of the recent past is to explore the subtle interplay between transhistorical problems faced by all societies and their embodiment in the structure of historical individuals rather than to derive the particular from the general by formal logical inference.

The theorists who are most successful in giving us the sense of this interplay—the essence of what C. Wright Mills called the "sociological imagination"—are those who were on the whole least interested in consciously emulating the abstract models of theory in the natural sciences. Today we still read and honor Marx rather than Spencer, Durkheim rather than Comte, Weber rather than Pareto, Cooley rather than Ward, Veblen rather than Giddings, Simmel rather than von Wiese. The first-named thinkers differ greatly among themselves and most of them were by no means indifferent to the scientific status of sociology, but collectively they stand in sharp contrast to the second-named thinkers in the degree to which such a concern had priority in their actual work over the substantive, historically specific questions they sought to ask and answer. Cooley and Simmel were unsystematic, aphoristic thinkers. Marx said the point was not merely to understand the world but to change it. Weber, as we have seen, was torn by strong political passions and all of his work expresses his intense concern over the fate of Western civilization. Veblen's writings were intended in part to be an ironic and critical commentary on his own society. Durkheim was far more of a self-conscious and programmatic science-builder than the other men, but his case-study approach to social phenomena brought him to grips with genuine substantive problems.

Weber's methodological reflections, therefore, do not deprive sociology of a perspective distinct from that of the historian studying a particular society in a particular age. Yet it is true that in his substantive work Weber was less directly concerned with transhistorical questions than, for example, Durkheim or Simmel. There is this much justice to the complaints of his critics that he neglects analytical categories (Parsons), mixes concepts with hypotheses (Blau), and that the enormous array of definitions in *Economy and Society* amounts to a gallery of discrete and static historical types (Antoni).

These limitations, however, are not inevitable consequences of Weber's views on the methodological distinctiveness of the social sciences with their roots in nineteenth-century German historicism. Moreover, scholars influenced by quite different intellectual traditions have recently arrived at conclusions almost identical to the Weberian position. Within American sociology itself, Herbert Blumer has argued that "sensitizing" rather than "operational" concepts are most typical of the social sciences. Our general concepts, he contends, cannot be more than sensitizing instruments because we are unable "to cleave aside what gives each instance its peculiar character and restrict ourselves to what it has in common with the other instances in the class covered by the concept." [21] Or, in Weberian terms, we cannot, or rather do not wish to, ignore the historical individuality of the phenomena we conceptualize.

In the philosophy of history—the analytical or "critical" rather than the "speculative" philosophy of history, to use W. H. Walsh's distinction[22]—what William Dray has christened the "covering law theory" of historical interpretation has become a major topic of debate in recent years. Dray has challenged the view that all historical interpretation necessarily involves at least implicit reference to a general law or universal proposition from which the explanation of particular historical facts can in principle be deduced.[23] Dray does not deny that all historians classify their data under general concepts—"revolutions," "wars," and "princes"—but he argues in terms highly reminiscent of Weber's long critique of Eduard Meyer[24] that historians are primarily concerned with establishing unique causal sequences of events and that their understanding of these sequences does not depend on their prior knowledge of general laws. Dray is an Oxford-educated analytical philosopher, although he has clearly been influenced by R. G. Collingwood, the British philosopher-historian, who was well versed in the writings of Dilthey, Windelband, and Rickert.

Like Weber, though by different intellectual paths, both Blumer and Dray see the autonomous concern with individuality that characterizes the human disciplines as the result of our capacity to achieve an inner "understanding" of the springs of human action in contrast to our "external" knowledge of physical events. Blumer is a "symbolic interactionist," in the tradition of John Dewey and George Herbert Mead —a tradition that owes nothing directly to Weber—which stresses the creative role of language or symbolic communication in enabling us to "take the role of the other" and interpret the meaning of his conduct —that is, the goals, motives, and assessments of the situation that guide

[21] Herbert Blumer, "What is wrong with Social Theory?" *American Sociological Review*, XIX (February, 1954), 8.

[22] W. H. Walsh, *Philosophy of History: An Introduction* (New York: Harper & Row, Publishers, Harper Torchbooks, 1960), pp. 16 ff.

[23] William Dray, *Laws and Explanation in History* (London: Oxford University Press, 1960), *passim.*

[24] *Methodology*, pp. 113–88.

him from within. Dray argues that we explain the conduct of historical
actors by understanding the intelligibility or "reasonableness" of their
concrete intentions, rather than by subsuming their actions under a
general law expressing relations that takes the form "if p, then q."
Like Weber, Dray regards a rational act, one in which the means are
appropriate to the end sought, as the prototype of "understandable"
human behavior and, again like Weber, his critics have accused him of
overestimating human rationality. The more general charge of "intuitionism" has also been leveled at him, as it was and still often is at
Weber.

Indeed, the whole debate over the nature of historical explanation
recently carried on by logicians and philosophers of the stature of Carl
Hempel, Karl Popper, Isaiah Berlin and others is concerned with essentially the same issues that sociologists have raised in connection with
Weber's methodological views in general and his concept of *Verstehen*
in particular. Unfortunately, there is little evidence that either the
philosophers or the sociologists have more than a fleeting acquaintance
with one another's writings. Since Weber's concept of *Verstehen* is the
link between his methodological reflections on the social sciences and
the general but substantive set of sociological concepts developed most
fully towards the end of his life in *Economy and Society,* I shall post-
pone a more detailed examination of what he meant by it until the
next section.

One of the methodological convictions for which Weber is most famous was his insistence on the distinction between objective knowledge
and the personal moral values of the knower. He strongly condemned
the practice of many of his academic contemporaries of turning the
classroom with its "captive audience" of students into a forum for
partisan pronouncements on the issues and controversies of the day.
These strictures have earned Weber the reputation of being the fore-
most exponent of "value-free social science," of a social science that is
ethically and politically neutral and eschews all concern with what
ought to be in favor of concentrating on what is. This position has
completely carried the day to the point of having become—at least
until very recently—an unquestioned dogma of contemporary social
science.

Yet I do not believe that Weber would have approved of the total
disjunction between knowledge and values that is often taken for
granted today. I am sure he would have agreed with one of his recent
critics, Leo Strauss, who complains that the determined avoidance of
value-judgments by modern scholars reminds him of "a childish game
in which you lose if you pronounce certain words, to the use of which

you are constantly incited by your playmates." Strauss remarks of accounts of the Nazi concentration camps that "every reader of such a description who is not completely stupid would, of course, see that the actions described are cruel." [25] As a matter of fact, Weber made it plain that he was not opposed "to the clear-cut introduction of one's own ideals into the discussion," [26] to a teacher's *stating* his values in the classroom or in a scholarly work provided he did not *preach* them, or fail to make clear when he was evaluating rather than describing or interpreting objective fact. All that Weber insisted on was that "the professor should not demand the right as a professor to carry the marshal's baton of the statesman or reformer in his knapsack." [27]

Weber was far from regarding values as arbitrary personal tastes or mere subjective sentiments. He was more sensitive than most men to the inevitable interaction between one's values and objective knowledge about the external world. He certainly believed that values were not immune to intellectual control, that they should constantly be re-examined, revised, and deepened in the light of the knowledge of man and society made available by the social sciences. Of the teacher who succeeds in helping the individual "to give himself an account of the ultimate meaning of his own conduct," Weber observed: "I am tempted to say of a teacher who succeeds in this: he stands in the service of moral forces." [28] It is doubtful that the man who said this would have viewed with equanimity the tendency of modern social scientists to define themselves as neutral experts, as technicians, eager to win public recognition for their profession so that they may barter their skills and services to help governments, business corporations, or political parties, to achieve *their* particular values, no matter what the content of these values. As Alvin Gouldner has argued with eloquence, Weber's espousal of a "value-free" social science was advanced in an entirely different intellectual and historical context.[29]

GENERAL SOCIOLOGY

Weber accepted from the neo-Kantians the notion that students of man and society are able to "understand" their subject-matter by identifying themselves with the human actors and imaginatively experiencing their intentions and motives. Such a procedure of *Verstehen*, or

[25] Leo Strauss, *Natural Right and History* (Chicago: University of Chicago Press, 1953), p. 52.
[26] *Methodology*, p. 60.
[27] Ibid., p. 5.
[28] *Essays*, p. 152.
[29] Alvin W. Gouldner, "Anti-Minotaur: The Myth of a Value-Free Sociology," *Social Problems*, IX (Winter, 1962), 199–213.

understanding, is clearly impossible in investigations of the physical world and of most living organisms. It has perhaps some restricted applications in studies of the higher animals, especially those resembling us most closely in their cognitive and emotional capacities.

Both the supporters and the critics of *Verstehen* have frequently seen it as a special method of gaining knowledge that is peculiar to the human disciplines. They have regarded it as essentially an intuitive mental process in which one feels one's way into another person's mind and emotions by trying to reproduce his thoughts in one's own mind and to empathize with his feelings. Since this process can never be a complete and reliable one—to be so one would have to *become* the other person—extreme intuitionists have stressed the essential incomprehensibility of other men or, as in the case of Oswald Spengler, other cultures committed to values differing from our own. Obviously, in an ultimate sense, this is true. We are all imprisoned in our own bodies and our own selfhood, forever victims of what James Joyce called the "soul's incurable loneliness." And if we are thus separated from our contemporary fellowmen, how much more difficult it is to bridge the gap between ourselves and men of different cultural traditions, or the dead who lived in an earlier historical era! Yet it may be unnecessary to acquire a total empathic understanding of others in order to achieve what Weber called a "causally adequate" explanation of their conduct —"one does not have to be Julius Caesar in order to understand him." [30]

The standard objection to *Verstehen,* and to all forms of intuitionism, is that at most it is a source of hypotheses, of "hunches," but that it provides no procedure of verification, no way of determining whether the intuited meaning of an action really corresponds to the actor's actual judgments and intentions. The most thorough criticism, by a sociologist, of *Verstehen* as a special method for obtaining valid knowledge is that of Theodore Abel.[31] In the analytical philosophy of history, William Dray's critics have similarly argued that to provide an "intelligible" or "meaningful" explanation of an action is at most to satisfy criteria of plausibility rather than of empirically verified truth.[32]

[30] Max Weber, *Economy and Society,* 3 vols., ed. Guenther Roth and Claus Wittich (New York: Bedminster Press, 1968), I, 5. This work will be cited hereafter as *E. and S.*

[31] Theodore Abel, "The Operation Called *Verstehen,*" *American Journal of Sociology, LIV* (November, 1948), 211–18.

[32] See, for example, the arguments of Carl Hempel, "Reasons and Covering Laws in Historical Explanation" in *Philosophy and History,* ed. Sidney Hook (New York: New York University Press, 1963), pp. 154–61. Several other contributors to this symposium argue along similar lines.

It cannot be said that Weber was always as clear as one might wish in his use of the concept of *Verstehen*. Some writers have charged him with straightforward intuitionism, while others (e.g., Hughes) attribute to him a position not very different from that of Abel, namely, that *Verstehen* is no more than an indispensable aid in framing hypotheses which will then have to be put to the test of empirical verification that is the basic method of all science. Yet there is another way of viewing the matter that is at least implicit in Weber's formulations. If *Verstehen* is seen as a directive to look for certain *substantive* aspects of human conduct rather than as a special *method* of acquiring knowledge, it appears in a somewhat different light.

To be specific, the postulate of *Verstehen* can be interpreted as directing us never to overlook the goals or ends-in-view in the mind of the actor, never to fail to find out how he himself "defines the situation," and to treat his purposes and judgments as causally relevant, or as key "variables," in explaining his action. Such a viewpoint is widely accepted in contemporary sociology—indeed, only programmatic neopositivists and behaviorists are likely to dissent from it. One prominent version of it is Parsons' conception of the "end-means schema," developed in his first book, where he argued that all interpretation of social action must take into account how the objective situation is viewed "from the point of view of the actor" as a constellation of possible ends, means, and conditions.[33] Another version is Robert M. MacIver's insistence that all efforts to discover social causation must include consideration of the actor's "dynamic assessment" whereby he selects from the total external world impinging upon him those features of it that are relevant to his values and goals.[34] Still another version is the symbolic interactionist argument that all human behavior is directed by the actor's developing self-conception.[35]

Ultimately, it is true that we are only able to know what goals and motives *are* because we ourselves are beings capable of purposive and motivated action and we have privileged access to our own inner lives. In this sense—but in this sense alone—*Verstehen* has an inescapably subjective reference. But it is going too far to conclude from this, as Abel seems to, that our understanding of others is limited to the scope of our own personal experience. It may take a thief to catch a thief,

[33] Talcott Parsons, *The Structure of Social Action* (New York: McGraw-Hill Book Company, 1937), esp. pt. IV.
[34] Robert M. MacIver, *Social Causation* (Boston: Ginn and Company, 1942), chaps. 11–12.
[35] See the essays by Herbert Blumer and Ralph H. Turner, among others, in *Human Behavior and Social Processes*, ed. Arnold M. Rose (Boston: Houghton Mifflin Company, 1962).

but surely a thief's goals are intelligible to an honest man. The issue is less obvious, however, when one considers more complex intellectual and emotional experiences: can a scholar completely devoid of religious or aesthetic feelings hope to achieve any full understanding of religious or art history? Can someone who has never been in love understand a lover? Clearly, the range of one's own experience and sensibility may be an invaluable aid in such cases. Yet I think one's final position must be that adumbrations of even the "higher" experiences—religion, art, love—are present in the ordinary experience of all socialized men, who possess therefore at least the potentiality of imaginatively understanding experience in its more rarefied forms. This, surely, is what Weber meant by his dictum about Julius Caesar. (Actually, Weber, although one of the greatest students of comparative religion, described himself as "religiously amusical," a claim that has, however, been questioned by some of his biographers.)

But how can we *know* that our interpretation of another's goals and calculations is the correct one? The argument that we cannot, that we can only observe that a given external situation evokes a given human response, is the core of the behaviorist position. When combined with the conviction that science-building should be the primary aim of the disciplines studying human behavior, it leads to the view that the empirical validation of universal propositions asserting the conjunction of recurrent situations (or stimuli) with recurrent responses is the only worthy task for the social sciences to pursue and that physics provides us with the model of a science that has achieved a logically integrated corpus of such propositions.

Yet there is nothing in the postulate of *Verstehen* that precludes the empirical testing of our "imputations of meaning" to an action. We may, to begin with, ask the actor what he thinks he is doing. His answer, to be sure, may perhaps amount to no more than a rationalization of his real motives, in which case we may conclude that "actions speak louder than words" and construct an alternative meaningful interpretation of his conduct. Whether the actor's motivation is conscious or unconscious makes no difference: psychoanalysis is a method for uncovering meanings in conduct that may be hidden from the actor's own consciousness. The point is that we are constantly testing our imputations by checking them against both the actor's own account, his developing conduct, and the situation in which he is acting. This hardly reduces *Verstehen* to no more than a method of arriving at hypotheses, because at each stage in the process we are developing and testing *some* conception of the rationale for the actor's conduct instead of resting content with either its subjective plausibility or a mere correlation of stimulus and response. That we can thus test our imputations seems to me to be what Weber meant in arguing that interpretations which are "meaningfully adequate" (*Sinnzusammenhangen*) must always be complemented by consideration of their "causal adequacy." But Weber's analysis of causal adequacy led him into certain methodological problems of historical research and he never fully discussed the question of how one attempts to validate an imputation derived from *Verstehen*, thus leaving himself open to the charge of intuitionism.

Weber's contrast between "meaningful adequacy" and "causal adequacy" is sometimes interpreted as implying that the desire to uncover the meaning of human actions is merely a subjective need of the human mind. Meaning is regarded as no more than a penumbra hovering over events that increases our inner sense of certainty with regard to propositions the validity of which is independently established. Science, it is held, need concern itself only with objective causality. If I am correct in regarding *Verstehen* as a directive to seek for certain substantive aspects of human action, this conclusion is unacceptable. The goals, judgments, and motives of the actor which we seek to understand are true causal determinants of his action, not mere epiphenomena. To put it somewhat differently, goals and motives are "intervening variables" which we cannot ignore in trying to establish the causal series leading to a given action.

To recognize this, however, is in no way to suggest that the actor's ends and motives are the sole movers or ultimate determinants of his action. The accusation that the search for motives entails "psychological reductionism" mistakenly draws this inference.[36] To say that people decide to have more children because they like babies, while ignoring the specific social and economic considerations which serve as sufficient conditions for the conversion of their philoprogenitive feelings into actual decisions, is like saying that a man who has been shot died because his heart stopped beating. But to say that social and economic factors alone explain childbearing behavior is like saying that the fact that someone fired a gun at a man is a complete explanation of his death. The actor's goals and assessments, in short, are *part* of a causal series. An explanation that fails to refer to them is an incomplete one, but this does not mean that they are unmoved movers or "independent variables" and are not themselves dependent on the other items in a causal series. "Men make their own history; but they do not make it just as they please. . . ."

[36] Philip Hauser and Otis Dudley Duncan, eds., *The Study of Population: An Inventory and Appraisal* (Chicago: University of Chicago Press, 1959), pp. 96–102. Geoffrey Hawthorn discusses the general methodological issue as it applies to explanations of human fertility in "Explaining Human Fertility," *Sociology: The Journal of the British Sociological Association*, II (January, 1968), 65–78.

The concept of *Verstehen* is the link between Weber's methodological reflections on the social sciences and his general sociological concepts. It is at the root of what has been variously called Weber's "sociological nominalism," "methodological individualism," or "social behaviorism." If all adequate explanations of social action must include reference to the ends and motives of the individual actors, then all collective entities—institutions, customs, cultural values—must ultimately be defined in terms of the conduct of individual actors. To Weber, as to Simmel, the essence of social reality is individuals in interaction with others.

Thus Weber defined all sociological concepts "reductively" by treating the behavior of individuals as the ultimate referent of the concepts. He recognized that individuals often believe naively in the "reality" of collective entities, such as "states," "armies," or "corporations," and guide their conduct accordingly. "Actors thus in part orient their action to them [collective entities], and in this role such ideas have a powerful, often a decisive, causal influence on the course of action of real individuals." [37] But for the empirical sociologist it is precisely as *ideas* influencing the actions of individuals that collective entities function as causal determinants of behavior. To see them as possessing a supraindividual reality of their own is to reify them. "Society exists only in the minds of individuals," as Durkheim concluded, notwithstanding his own apparent earlier commitment to "methodological collectivism."

Weber insisted that this "individualistic method" in no way implied or validated an individualistic system of values. "Even a socialistic economy," he remarked, "would have to be understood sociologically in exactly the same kind of 'individualistic' terms; that is, in terms of the action of individuals, the types of 'officials' found in it, as would be the case with a system of free exchange analyzed in terms of the theory of marginal utility." [38] Nor does the method imply any brand of "psychologism." As a matter of fact, Karl Popper, the most vigorous proponent of "methodological individualism" among contemporary philosophers of the social sciences, is also a severe critic of psychologism in social theory.[39] The method does imply, however, as I have previously suggested, that the actor's goals and judgments—his "subjectively

---

[37] *E. and S.*, I, 14.
[38] Ibid., p. 18.
[39] Karl Popper, *The Open Society and Its Enemies* (London: Routledge & Kegan Paul, Ltd., 1949), II, 84–90. For a critique of Popper's position, see Richard Lichtman, "Karl Popper's Defense of the Autonomy of Sociology," *Social Research*, *XXXII* (Spring, 1965), 1–25.

intended meaning," as Weber put it—are causal determinants, or "efficient causes," of his behavior. But there is no suggestion that his goals and judgments have been shaped by "instincts," early conditioning, infantile traumas, a "self-system," or any other wholly or partly autonomous psychological force antedating the situation in which the actor acts. Weber was intellectually a pre-Freudian and, like his predecessors and contemporaries in classical sociological theory, he lacked an adequate psychology of motivation and tended to regard existing psychologies with suspicion as biologically reductionist. Weber's own substantive work in its concentration on historical detail and its comparative focus on large-scale institutions could scarcely be more removed from psychological concerns or lacking in any tendency to make explanatory use of presumed constants of human nature.

There is, it is true, a tendency in Weber's thought to see a system of cultural values or an institutional structure as embodied in a concrete human type. Thus Weber stresses the Calvinist rather than Calvinism: ascetic Protestantism is carried by a type of man who fears God, drives himself at work, and denies himself all material and sensual pleasures. In *The Protestant Ethic,* Weber selected Benjamin Franklin as the very prototype of the secularized Protestant impelled by inner-worldly asceticism to devote himself heart and soul to commerce. But, as Gabriel Kolko contends, there was nothing ascetic about Franklin's personal life: he was in many respects a representative late eighteenth-century *bon vivant* who enjoyed his wine and his leisure and had several mistresses.[40]

Similarly, Weber often tends to identify bureaucracy as a form of social organization with the bureaucrat as a human type. This raises difficulties because clearly only a small proportion of the individuals whose interactions constitute a bureaucracy have the classic traits of the bureaucrat: punctiliousness, a sense of vocation, secretiveness concerning the affairs of the organization, and the rest. Armies, factories, and hospitals are bureaucracies in Weber's sense, but combat soldiers, manual workers, and nurses and interns are certainly not bureaucrats. Only the administrative staff of large organizations is the habitat of bureaucrats. The tendency to link bureaucracy too closely to the bureaucrat as its essential embodiment has led contemporary sociologists increasingly to abondon the term, substituting for it "formal" or "large-scale" organization.

If Weber had possessed an adequate theory of personality, he might have avoided this tendency to overconcretize cultural values and social

[40] Gabriel Kolko, "Max Weber on America: Theory and Evidence," *History and Theory,* I, no. 3 (1961), 256.

roles. He might have recognized explicitly that values and roles do not completely shape their carriers even though they exist only in the subjective attitudes of living men.

In defining the recurrent forms of social action, those we give such labels as "social relationship," "convention," or "law," Weber treated them as *probabilities* that individuals will behave in a certain way. Our general sociological concepts merely express such probabilities. Not only do they not refer to supraindividual realities, but they make no assumptions whatever concerning the grounds of probability. Thus "An order will be called *law* if it is externally guaranteed by the probability that coercion (physical or psychological), to bring about conformity or avenge violation, will be applied by a *staff* of people holding themselves specially ready for that purpose." [41] " 'Power' is the probability that one actor within a social relationship will be in a position to carry out his own will despite resistance, regardless of the basis on which this probability rests." [42]

The statistical overtones of the term "probability" as used in Weber's characteristic procedure of definition have appealed to some quantitatively-minded social scientists. And the apparent emphasis on the predictability of behavior as the criterion for useful concepts has occasionally met with approval from behaviorists. Both views, however, are based on a misunderstanding. Weber's notion of probability certainly suggests a statistical estimate of the likelihood of a certain response that is entertained by a scientific observer generalizing from observed uniformities and recurrences in human behavior. However, Weber does not in his formal definitions abandon his view that the actor's "subjectively intended meaning" is a causal component of his action. In fact his definitions frequently include reference to the actor's "orientation" towards others as a central feature. Thus "A social relationship will be referred to as 'conflict' in so far as action within it is oriented intentionally to carrying out the actor's own will against the resistance of the other party or parties." [43] In Weber's classic and widely-accepted definition of the social itself, or of "social action," the state of mind of the actor is crucial: "Action is social in so far as, by virtue of the subjective meaning attached to it by the acting individual (or individuals), it takes account of the behavior of others and is thereby oriented in its course." [44] Weber goes on to distinguish between social action thus defined and mere physical contact, such as the collision of two

[41] Max Weber, *On Law in Economy and Society*, ed. and trans. Max Rheinstein and Edward A. Shils (Cambridge: Harvard University Press, 1954), p. 5.
[42] *E. and S.*, I, 53.
[43] Ibid., p. 38.
[44] Ibid., p. 4.

cyclists, unthinking habitual responses to others, the allegedly automatic imitation of others stressed by such writers as Tarde, and the identical responses of a number of people to the same nonsocial stimulus, such as a crowd of people on the street raising their umbrellas in a rain shower.[45] (Katz and Schank have named the latter kind of uniform behavior a "coenetrope." [46])

Although Weber does not make this explicit, one is, I think, justified in concluding that he regards the probability of a certain kind of action occurring as an estimate made not only in the mind of the scientific observer, *but also in the minds of the acting individuals who are being observed.*[47] The recurrent social interactions we conceptualize as "norms," "roles," or "groups" derive from estimates of the probable responses of others made by the actors themselves and are not merely quasi-statistical generalizations advanced by the sociologist in the same way that a natural scientist reports a correlation between two events, or estimates the probability that a given structure, say a bridge, will collapse or withstand a given physical impact. Sociological concepts and propositions are, in a sense, "meta" concepts: concepts and propositions *about* the concepts and propositions of the people whom sociologists observe—predictions based on the predictions made by the social actors themselves.[48] *A society is essentially a set of broadly warranted predictions made by its members about one another's behavior.* In this sense, it exists only in people's minds, or "subjectively intended meanings," but is at the same time the product of publicly observable social interaction.

RATIONALIZATION AND THE SOCIOLOGY OF RELIGION

The idea of the progressive rationalization of life as the main directional trend of Western civilization is the unifying theme of Weber's sociology. Just as Tocqueville saw the spread of equality as a master social process with ramifications in almost every sphere of life, Weber saw rationalization as a similarly far-reaching and accelerating trend. Both thinkers were preoccupied with the dissolution of traditional European culture and society under the impact of science, technology, industrialism, expanding capitalism, bureaucratization, and political cen-

---

[45] Ibid., pp. 23–24.

[46] Daniel Katz and Richard L. Schank, *Social Psychology* (New York: John Wiley & Sons, Inc., 1938), p. 14.

[47] Of Weber's interpreters, Julius Freund seems to me to come closest to taking this view of Weber's probabilistic propositions and definitions. See Freund, *The Sociology of Max Weber* (New York: Pantheon Books, Inc., 1968), pp. 117–18.

[48] This formulation is adapted from Alfred Schutz, *The Problem of Social Reality,* Collected Papers. vol. I (The Hague: Martinus Nijhoff, 1962), pp. 38–43.

tralization. Moreover, both men were ambivalent in their attitude towards the major trends they discerned, believing them to be irresistible and opposition to them therefore futile, yet full of foreboding about their eventual outcome. Weber, writing at the end of the nineteenth century, was more deeply pessimistic: "Not summer's bloom lies ahead of us, but rather a polar night of icy darkness and hardness." [49] Less attached to the old, premodern order than the skeptical French aristocrat, Weber had lived through the failures and disillusionments of the new: "The rosy blush of . . . the Enlightenment seems . . . to be irretrievably fading." [50]

By "rationalization" Weber meant the process by which explicit, abstract, intellectually calculable rules and procedures are increasingly substituted for sentiment, tradition, and rule of thumb in all spheres of activity. Rationalization leads to the displacement of religion by specialized science as the major source of intellectual authority; the substitution of the trained expert for the cultivated man of letters; the ousting of the skilled handworker by machine technology; the replacement of traditional judicial wisdom by abstract, systematic statutory codes. Rationalization demystifies and instrumentalizes life. "It means that . . . there are no mysterious incalculable forces that come into play, but rather that one can, in principle, master all things by calculation. This means that the world is disenchanted." [51] Rationalization creates a utilitarian world dominated by what Paul Tillich called "the dance of ends and means." Even in such nonutilitarian areas of culture as music and painting, Weber found evidence of progressive rationalization.

Rationalization does not "indicate an increased and general knowledge of the conditions under which one lives." [52] Weber is far from sharing the optimistic faith of the eighteenth-century *philosophes* that the diffusion of scientific knowledge and the discrediting of religious and magical beliefs will result in general public enlightenment. For while formal sets of rules, systematic technologies, and rationally planned enterprises clearly embody rationality, their very efficiency and reliability eliminate the need for wide knowledge and rational understanding on the part of the men who apply and operate them. There is a kinship between Weber's conception and the Marxist notion of alienation, as Karl Loewith has pointed out (in the selection translated for this volume). In the Marxist formulation, the capitalist exploits the worker's productive capacities by subjecting him to the process of

---

[49] *Essays.* p. 128.
[50] *Protestant Ethic,* p. 182.
[51] *Essays,* p. 139.
[52] Ibid.

commodity production for the market in which his own creations, embodying his crystallized labor power, stand out against him as an alien, external force. To Weber, the techniques and social structures created by and originally expressing man's rationality and mastery of his environment become self-maintaining processes no longer dependent on the rationality that created them but actually stunting and constricting the rational capacities of the men they dominate. As Karl Mannheim later put it, the "functional rationality" of the system expropriates the "substantive rationality" of the individual. Weber generalizes the worker's alienation under the factory system to all of the institutions and cultural activities of modern society, which at his most pessimistic moments seemed to him to represent the dialectical inversion of the Enlightenment's vision of a world mastered by Reason.

If the idea of rationalization as the major force in modern Western history is related to historical materialism, it also has an affinity with the tendency of German Idealism to interpret all cultures and epochs as expressions of a distinctive *Geist,* or ethos, that gradually penetrates institutions, technologies, and belief systems until its various forms are exhausted and a new *Geist* replaces it. Weber's approach, however, differs in crucial respects from that of the post-Kantian and post-Hegelian philosophers of history. He does not envisage rationalization simply as an immanentist process of change in which the rational ethos achieves ultimate self-realization in the social and cultural world. Rather, he sees it as altering its character as it evolves, entering into a dialectic with partially autonomous material interests, becoming an ineluctable response to the objective circumstances of vastly increased populations and expanded territorial administrations, and at the same time evoking counter forces—charismatic revolutionary upheavals—to challenge its supremacy. Far from manifesting a constant "inner logic" that gradually unfolds from its beginnings to its final self-objectification, rationalization in Western history reveals the "paradox of unintended consequences." [53] The Protestant reformers, attacking the materialism of the Church in the name of a purified dedication to a transcendent God, contributed to the creation of a secular world "of purely mundane passions . . . in which material goods have gained an increasing and finally an inexorable power over the lives of men as at no previous period in history";[54] the men of the Enlightenment, inspired by a vision of the rational ordering of existence, helped create a world of banal technicians and self-satisfied consumers in which man increasingly loses understanding of the forces shaping his life and his will to control them. "History has many cunning passages, contrived

[53] Gerth and Mills in "Introduction" to *Essays,* p. 54.
[54] *Protestant Ethic,* p. 181.

corridors/and issues, deceives with whispering ambitions,/guides us by vanities" (T. S. Eliot).

Nor does Weber conceive of rationalization as the most recent culture-shaping Idea to emerge on the scene, destined to grow and decay in conformity with the cyclical movements so many idealist philosophers have seen as the key to history. To begin with, whatever autonomous spiritual rhythms may govern history, the modern economic order created by rationalization rests on precarious material foundations and may possibly survive only "until the last ton of fossilized coal is burnt." [55] But even if this should not happen, the future of the "iron cage" of industrial society is indeterminate: perhaps charismatic leaders with a new prophecy will arise and reshape its values and institutions, old ideals may undergo a "great rebirth," or society may rigidify into "mechanized petrifaction." That rationalization does not represent unilinear progress towards a social order which is ethically and intellectually, rather than merely technically, superior, is evident from Weber's observation that "For of the last stage of this cultural development, it might well be truly said: 'Specialists without vision, sensualists without heart; this nullity imagines that it has attained a level of civilization never before achieved.' " [56]

Weber's conviction that in the modern world "precisely the most ultimate and most sublime values have retreated from public life either into the transcendental realm of mystic life or into the brotherliness of direct and personal human relations," [57] anticipates those themes of contemporary sociology and social criticism that characterize modern society as a "mass society" in which "loss of values," "alienation," and "identity confusion" are seen as the individual person's inescapable fate. Many other nineteenth-century thinkers were, of course, sensitive to the spiritual costs of scientific and economic progress; Weber's achievement was the specifically sociological one of locating complaints about the spiritual emptiness and materialism of modern life, already common by the end of the nineteenth century and which have since swelled into a deafening chorus of clichés, in the context of the expansion in scale of modern social organization and the consequent depersonalization of its functioning. Aware of the deeply-rooted, ineluctable nature of the trends towards bureaucratization and ever more

---

[55] Ibid.

[56] Ibid., p. 182. I am aware that I have previously, on page 5 below, quoted this devastating indictment of modern industrial civilization. I can only plead that so rich and varied is the texture of Weber's thought that it is hard to avoid reproducing the same quotations again and again viewed from a somewhat different vantage point.

[57] *Essays*, p. 155.

specialized knowledge, he was scornful of facile proposals for both the restoration and revitalization of old faiths and the utopian transcendence of alienation. Skeptical of the socialist critique of capitalism, he never indulged in the reactionary "politics of cultural despair" [58] that in Germany prepared the ground for the Nazi disaster.

Rationalization may not prove to be an irreversible trend in Western history, but it is clearly an unprecedented one that originated independently of outside influences only in the modern West. Since so many diverse cultures and civilizations have flourished since man appeared on the earth, one is led to ask: What peculiarity of the premodern West enabled it to become the seedbed of a trend now enveloping the world? Weber's famous essay *The Protestant Ethic and the Spirit of Capitalism* and his later comparative survey of world religions are essentially efforts to answer this question, although, of course, these studies uncovered much of significance independently of their bearing on the problem of the genesis in the West of the institutions of rational capitalism.

All religious world views are irrational, or, more properly, nonrational, conduct influenced by them corresponding to the form of social action that Weber called *Wertrationalität* (action oriented to the realization of a value). The values and norms they affirm were created out of the passion, vision, and inspiration of prophets and priests, seers and sages. This is no less true of Calvinistic Protestantism than of Catholicism, Judaism, Hinduism, Buddhism, or Islam. How, then, could a nonrational world view, inspired by a transcendental vision of the nature of things, give rise to the impulse to rationalization with its emphasis on the continual perfecting of means to achieve ends —ends that are, therefore, "empirical" in the sense that the degree of their attainment can be precisely measured and tested? [59]

The Reformation, and Calvinism in particular, was a revival of the Old Testament prophetic tradition in a world that was already breaking through long-established geographical, institutional, and intellectual barriers. The hunger and thirst after righteousness and justice in this life of the Hebrew prophets, revived by Luther, Zwingli, and Calvin, directed the attention of Protestants to reshaping the world around them rather than to the adoption of such alternative forms of religious conduct as mystical withdrawal, ritualism, scholarly systematization, magical divination, or the performance of good works in a social order

---

[58] Fritz Stern, *The Politics of Cultural Despair* (Berkeley and Los Angeles: University of California Press, 1961).

[59] Weber gives one meaning of "rationalism" as "the methodical attainment of a definitely given and practical end by means of an increasingly precise calculation of adequate means." *Essays*, p. 293.

perceived as fixed. The Reformation was a religious revolution (or counterrevolution?) that initially involved a redefinition of man's relation to God and to himself, but which was frequently broadened to include a redefinition of his relation to political authority and society, thus becoming a national and even a social revolution as well.

Weber concentrated on the effects of Calvinist teachings on economic behavior, seeing the injunction to work hard and seek success at one's vocation as the impetus to rational commercial and productive enterprise among bourgeois Calvinists. Herbert Luethy correctly argues (in chapter 5 of this book) that the effects of Calvinism were by no means confined to business activity, to the genesis of the "spirit of capitalism" in the narrow sense, but that they played a part in promoting all the nascent tendencies that have formed the modern world as we know it. In a word, the Reformation made a crucial contribution to what contemporary scholars call the "modernization process." To be sure, the thesis that Calvinism was a sufficient condition for the development of capitalist enterprise remains not proven in the sense that we cannot and probably never will be able to say, as Luethy puts it, "that's the way it is" rather than merely "there's something in it." Given the erosion of feudalism, the growth of the towns, and the expansion of geographical horizons that had already taken place since the High Middle Ages, it cannot be positively asserted that some "functional equivalent" of Calvinism might not have directed the energies of men towards capital accumulation and the methodical rationalization of economic activity.

Yet the uniqueness of Judaeo-Christianity among world religions emerges fully from Weber's comparative sociology of religion: Christianity contained within itself the latent dynamism of the prophetic tradition, a dynamism that was lacking in the Eastern religions. The values of Buddhism, Hinduism, and Confucianism were so closely interwoven with daily life and the traditional social organization of the Asian civilizations that, unlike Christianity, they scarcely gave rise to specialized religious institutions differentiated from the total social structure. Religious values became intellectually stratified in many diverse esoteric and exoteric forms in the absence of a central body to interpret them authoritatively to the populace. Their impact, therefore, tended to be traditionalist and conservative. Their dedicated adepts and interpreters turned away from the magical and ritualistic externalizations of religion in everyday life to look inwards into the spiritual depths of the self, to scholarly exegesis of sacred texts, or to otherworldly forms of communion with the holy. These forms of religious experience were not, of course, lacking in Christianity as well, but there was also the prophetic tradition striving to overcome the

tension between the sacred and the profane through the militant transformation of the world. In addition, Christianity established highly
organized ecclesiastical and monastic institutions which in their separation from the rest of the social order were capable of exercising an
independent influence on it.

If the Eastern religions were so embedded in the social structure
that they lacked the potentiality of initiating changes in secular behavior, or even of reinforcing ongoing changes, recent work in social
history suggests that it was not until the time of the Reformation and
the Counter-Reformation that the moral teachings of Christianity fundamentally penetrated and altered patterns of daily life in the premodern West.[60] Weber's examination of the connection between religious values and economic behavior was designed to correct a one-
sided emphasis (both Marxist and non-Marxist) on technology and conflicts of material interest as the sole decisive factors in the Great Transformation. However, in the oft-quoted concluding paragraph of *The
Protestant Ethic*, he insisted that "it is, of course, not my aim to substitute for a one-sided materialistic an equally one-sided spiritualistic
causal interpretation of culture and history." [61] Some contemporary
scholars have, at least implicitly, ignored this caveat and have invoked
the authority of Weber to justify the elevation of "changing values" to
a dominant role in the interpretation of social change. But the very
separation of religion from daily life in the premodern West that
allowed it ultimately to play so dynamic a role also suggests that other
features of social organization, partially independent both of religious
influence and of the class struggle or technology narrowly conceived,
were permissive of rational economic development to a degree un-
matched in the East. Recent economic, social, and demographic historians have directed increasing attention towards marriage and family
customs, patterns of population growth, the politics of feudalism, and
the relations between town and country life in seeking to specify the
uniqueness of premodern Western civilization; Weber's own studies of
the medieval city point the way to this line of inquiry.[62]

Even scholars who are critical of the overemphasis of much post-
Durkheimian sociological theory on the autonomy and centrality of

[60] For example, Philippe Ariès, *Centuries of Childhood* (New York: Alfred A.
Knopf, Inc., 1962), esp. pt. III.

[61] *Protestant Ethic*, p. 183. See also pp. 90–92.

[62] See, for example, Ariès, op. cit.; Barrington Moore, Jr., *Social Origins of Dicta-
torship and Democracy* (Boston: Beacon Press, 1966); Karl Helleiner, "The Vital
Revolution Reconsidered," *Canadian Journal of Economics and Political Science*,
XXIII (February, 1957). For Weber's analysis of the distinctiveness of the Occidental
City, see *E. and S.*, Vol. III, chap. 16; also Weber, *General Economic History* (Glen-
coe, Ill.: The Free Press, 1950), chap. 28.

values, concede the potential energizing role of a new ideology introduced into a society, either endogenously or from the outside, at the
appropriate historical moment.[63] That the consequences of efforts to
"realize" such an ideology are likely to transcend, distort, and often
negate its manifest aims is also generally recognized. Awareness of these
commonplaces among social scientists today owes much to Weber, however successfully later scholars have challenged details of his thesis on
Calvinism and capitalism.

BUREAUCRACY

Weber saw that rationalization by creating new elite groups set limits
to the spread of equality and democracy regarded by Tocqueville and
others as so central a feature of modernity. Not only were individual
freedom and rational self-determination reduced by the objectification
of rationality in rules of systematic procedure and centrally planned
coordination of activity, but new controlling groups of specialized
experts, administrators, capitalist organizers, and party politicians
emerged to replace the hereditary ruling classes and authorities of the
past. The spread of hierarchical bureaucratic forms of social organization exemplifies the process of rationalization in the sphere of social
structure, standing in the same relation to social life as science, technology, secularism, and legal formalism stand to their respective
spheres of culture. Bureaucracy is the distinctively sociological manifestation of the process of rationalization.

What is bureaucracy? The term has become popularly encrusted
with a good many ambiguous and misleading connotations. Bureaucracies are organizations purposefully adapted to attaining a single functional goal rather than multiple goals; they are organized hierarchi-
cally with a strict chain of command from top to bottom; they create
an elaborate division of labor, assigning specialized roles to their personnel to an extent that often seems to reduce the individual to the
status of a small cog in the vast machinery of the whole; detailed
general rules and regulations govern all conduct in the pursuit of
official duties; personnel are selected primarily on the basis of competence and specialized training rather than according to prerogatives
of birth and privilege; office-holding in a bureaucracy tends to be a
lifelong vocation.

Any activity that requires tight coordination of the actions of large
numbers of men and that necessitates the utilization of specialized

[63] See Moore, *Social Origins of Dictatorship and Democracy*, pp. 485–87; Peter L.
Berger and Thomas Luckmann, *The Social Construction of Reality* (Garden City,
N.Y.: Doubleday & Company, Inc., Anchor Books, 1967), pp. 116–28.

skills is likely to give rise to bureaucratic organization. "The decisive reason for the advance of bureaucratic organization," Weber wrote, "has always been its purely technical superiority over any other form of organization. The fully bureaucratic mechanism compares with other organizations exactly as does the machine with nonmechanical modes of production." [64]

Population growth and the development of the centralized and territorially extensive nation-state encouraged the rise of governmental bureaucracy as early as the age of absolute monarchy in Europe. Later, the large production units demanded by machine technology promoted the bureaucratization of economic life. Today the need for centralized administrations serving large populations has led to the adoption of bureaucratic forms in finance, religion, philanthropy, education, medicine, and even entertainment. A government department is a bureaucracy, but so are General Motors, the United Automobile Workers union, a modern hospital, the administration of a large university, and a radio or television studio.

Bureaucracies have, of course, also existed in the civilizations of the past. Weber mentions armies as one of the earliest forms of bureaucratic organization, notably the Roman legions with their integration of specialized infantry and cavalry units into a single fighting force. A contemporary scholar, Karl Wittfogel, pursuing certain leads suggested by both Marx and Weber, has argued that the great Oriental civilizations developed highly centralized and despotic forms of bureaucratic administration out of the necessity of regulating river levels for irrigation and flood control purposes. [65] Yet in past civilizations only a few areas of life were subject to bureaucratic control; family and kinship groupings, feudal institutions, and groups held together by traditional loyalties and obligations usually played a much larger role. Thus bureaucracy must be seen as a distinctively modern and, in its origins, Western phenomenon.

Weber is quite frequently accused of overestimating the rationality and efficiency of bureaucracy and of ignoring the clogging effects of "red tape," the petty conservatism of officials, and the operation of such processes as "Parkinson's Law" that "work expands so as to fill the time available for its completion." [66] These objections are irrelevant to Weber's analysis. Of course individual bureaucracies are often top-heavy, inefficient, and slow-moving. The point remains that most of the activities of bureaucracies could not under modern conditions

[64] *E. and S.*, III, 973.
[65] Karl Wittfogel, *Oriental Despotism* (New Haven: Yale University Press, 1957).
[66] C. Northcote Parkinson, *Parkinson's Law* (Boston: Houghton Mifflin Company, 1957), p. 2.

even be carried out badly by nonbureaucratic organizations. Without a bureaucratic organization it would be impossible to collect taxes from tens of millions of people according to a graduated scale prescribed in advance. Nor could a variety of highly complicated machines and specialized human skills be coordinated to manufacture large quantities of a standardized product. These tasks may be carried out with varying degrees of efficiency by different bureaucratic organizations, but they could not be essayed at all except by an organization possessing the main structural features of bureaucracy: job specialization, a hierarchy of authority, detailed rules and regulations, and impersonal relations among co-workers.

Whether such goals *should* be pursued is, of course, another matter altogether. There is nothing in Weber's outlook that precludes a preference for a world of small, decentralized local communities in which nonbureaucratic structures can adequately attain collective goals.[67] Weber is not, as he is sometimes depicted, an advocate of bureaucracy nor even an apologist for it: he argues merely that *if* you wish to achieve certain administrative or productive goals in a large and territorially extensive society, *then* you must have a bureaucratic organization to do so. True, Weber tended to regard bureaucratization as an irreversible historical trend; as in the related cases of science and specialized education, he was often impatient with romantic and antiquarian resistance to its spread. Yet he loathed and feared many of the consequences of bureaucratization, as is evident in the quotation on page 5 where he deplores the "parcelling out of the soul" under a bureaucratic way of life.

Another major feature of bureaucracy that is independent of whether or not particular bureaucracies actually operate rationally and efficiently is that bureaucracy *must* justify its existence solely by standards of functional efficiency, even though in practice it may fail to meet these standards. If someone accuses a government department of gross inefficiency, its employees do not defend their way of doing things by appealing to hallowed traditions or by claiming a moral right to act as they do. The charge of inefficiency immediately puts them on the defensive. Note, however, the different response if Congress or the family farm, both nonbureaucratic organizations, are similarly attacked. Both will be vigorously defended—properly in the case of

---

[67] This seems to me to amount to at least a partial rejoinder to Paul Goodman who, in a letter to the *Columbia University Forum*, V (Fall, 1962), 3, accused Weber, C. Wright Mills, and myself of assuming the inevitability of bureaucratization and minimizing its inefficiencies. He was responding to an article of mine, "Max Weber: The Scholar as Hero," *Columbia University Forum*, V (Summer, 1962), 31–37.

Congress, more dubiously so in the case of the family farm—as incarnating priceless values which cannot be measured by narrow criteria of efficient performance. The principle of legitimacy governing bureaucracy, in other words, contrasts sharply with that of nonbureaucratic organizations. At least in the modern West, bureaucracy exemplifies the type of legitimate authority that Weber called "rational-legal."

Contemporary sociologists have criticized Weber's concept of bureaucracy from a somewhat different standpoint. They have treated it as if it were intended to serve as a guide to the study of particular bureaucratic organizations. Students of such organizations have argued that Weber fails to take into account alternative ways of solving the problems of an organization which may have different effects on its efficiency. As Blau points out in the selection reprinted in this volume, Weber does not consider the relative advantages and disadvantages of seniority or merit systems for promoting personnel; nor, in his stress on hierarchical authority as a major feature of bureaucracy, does he compare the effects of exacting rigid obedience from subordinates with those of a possible rival policy of encouraging initiative and independence on their part. On discovering that organizations vary greatly in the extent to which their prescribed formal rules actually control behavior as opposed to an "informal structure" of social relations that develops spontaneously, other analysts of bureaucracy have criticized the Weberian concept for overstressing the rationality, impersonality, and hierarchical character of bureaucratic social relations. Weber's enumeration of the main features of bureaucracy has been viewed as a "set of hypotheses" to be tested in empirical research on different types and examples of bureaucratic organization (see Blau), or as an "ideal type" to guide investigation rather than as a concrete description.

Weber's definition of bureaucracy is indeed one of his "ideal type" concepts which abstracts and accentuates selected interrelated aspects of a social phenomenon rather than aiming at a full description of it. But in formulating it, Weber was chiefly concerned with drawing a sharp contrast between bureaucratic and *nonbureaucratic* forms of organization rather than with developing a model to employ in the comparative study of particular, concrete bureaucratic organizations. To regard Weber as essentially the creator of a pioneering, if crude, conceptual scheme for the empirical study of what are nowadays called large-scale or formal organizations, is to "de-historicize" his conception of bureaucracy by dissociating it from his theory of rationalization as the dominant tendency of Western history. It is a distortion of his purpose and vision to demand of his conception of bureaucracy that

it should help us to specify the differences between this industrial enterprise, government department, or hospital, and that one, valuable as
the comparative study of large-scale organizations may be in its own
terms. Weber's unparalleled achievement is his description of the
generic features of bureaucracy as a form of organization, no matter
how modifiable and overridden by other influences these features may
be in particular cases. However just the strictures of his critics on the
utility of his conception for the detailed examination of variations
among bureaucratic organizations, they have misconstrued his central
purpose, which was to contrast bureaucracy with the feudal and patrimonial administrative structures that preceded it in Western history.

POLITICAL SOCIOLOGY

The State and Political Power

Weber's political sociology centers on the counterconcepts (or "paired
concepts" [68]) of *force* and *legitimacy*. Just as his double vision of bureaucracy as both an indispensable rational instrumentality in the
modern world, and a huge, impersonal organizational machine
robbing men of their spontaneity and creativity, has led to one-sided
interpretations that have pictured him as either an apologist for bureaucracy or as its unrelenting critic and opponent; so have some
interpreters of his political sociology seen him as a hard-boiled neo-
Machiavellian insisting on the primacy of force and violence in history,
while others, notably Talcott Parsons and his followers, have invoked
Weber in support of the view that effective power is always legitimate
and ultimately derived from the consent of the governed.

An analysis of Weber's famous definition of the state brings out the
two-sided nature of his conception of power. Weber defined the state
as "a human community that successfully claims the monopoly of the
legitimate use of violence within a given territory." [69] Note that this
definition includes reference both to force—or rather to physical force
or violence, the most extreme form of force—*and* to legitimacy. Weber
is plainly not asserting that the state exacts obedience from its subjects only by threatening them with the exercise of force or that, as

---

[68] Bendix and Berger, op. cit., pp. 92–112.

[69] *Essays*, p. 78. I have changed Gerth and Mills' "physical force" to "violence"
in this definition. E. V. Walter has argued that even Gerth and Mills, who unlike
Parsons are not committed to a "consensual" view of society that underplays
coercion, have weakened Weber's stress on violence in their translation of a number
of his terms. See Walter, "Power and Violence," *American Political Science Review*,
LVIII (June, 1964), 359–60.

Machiavelli put it, the ruler relies primarily on fear rather than love to impose his will. For, if this is what he meant, why the reference to legitimacy? *Who* confers legitimacy on the state's use of violence? Obviously the answer must be *some* of the state's subjects who regard the state as justified in using coercion against *other* subjects who fail to comply with its laws and directives. In principle, of course, a subject who is coerced as a result of his noncompliance may himself acknowledge the right and even the obligation of the state to use force against him—for example, the criminal who when apprehended feels that the sentence he receives is justly deserved. But clearly those who confer legitimacy on the state's use of violence are first of all citizens who do *not* violate the law and who approve of the coercion of their fellows who do. The implication is inescapable that they themselves obey the directives of the state on grounds other than fear of the negative sanctions of violence that they would incur by noncompliance.

Thus it is not an adequate criticism of Weber's definition to point out, as some writers have, that modern governments do not rely primarily on the threat of force to assure the compliance of their subjects but employ more extensively persuasion, appeals to duty or self-interest, and the promise of rewards—all forms of influence or power that are distinguishable from force. Weber's very definition, when explicated, recognizes this indeed to be the case.[70] The definition takes for granted that among the many subjects of the state there will be some who will not acknowledge the legitimacy of its laws, or, what is more to the point, will fail to abide by those laws in their conduct. Therefore the state must use force to compel their compliance, or at least to make it impossible for them to persist in their noncompliance. But such coercion of criminals, rebels, or revolutionaries is seen as legitimate by other subjects who themselves obey the law because they regard it as their duty to do so, or consider its content to be substantively right, or find obedience to be in their self-interest. Like Durkheim, Weber recognized that the very existence of legal norms implies and even creates the possibility and the actuality of their violation. Also, like Durkheim, he is concerned not merely with the relation between the state and the lawbreaker but with a triadic relationship between state, lawbreaker, and the community. Durkheim argued that punishment of the criminal was necessary to reaffirm and dramatize the sanctity of the law in the eyes of the law-abiding public. Weber saw that it is those subjects who uphold the law who confer legitimacy on the use of violence against lawbreakers. Thus political power is

[70] Moreover, Weber immediately adds: "of course, force is not the normal or the only means of the state. . . ." *Essays*, p. 78. See also his discussion in *E. and S.*, I, 54–55; II, 901–4.

both coercive and legitimate, and the very coercion of some subjects is regarded as legitimate by others.

In concrete cases, of course, motives for conforming to the commands of the state—or of any powerholder—are likely to be mixed, as Weber fully recognized.[71] They may be so mixed, so "over-determined" in the psychoanalytic sense, that the power-subject is unable himself to specify clearly his reasons and motives for compliance.[72] Even the most upright and law-abiding citizen, convinced of the majesty and justice of the law, may be tempted on occasion to violate it and is not unaware of the risk he runs of being caught and punished should he succumb to the temptation. By monopolizing the ultimate means of power—violence—the state is able to utilize more effectively such noncoercive means as persuasion, appeals to duty, and inducements. Thus its subjects, especially in the antiauthoritarian moral climate of contemporary democratic societies, may prefer to think of themselves as having been persuaded rather than ordered to take certain actions, although they are not blind to the fact that the power of the police and the army is at the disposal of the ruler who flatters and cajoles them over the mass media.

I have analyzed Weber's definition of the state in some detail in order to bring out the interdependence of force and legitimacy in his political sociology. It remains to consider whether he has adequately defined the state. Political sociology originated in the middle of the nineteenth century when a number of thinkers arrived at a clear perception of the separateness of state and society.[73] Indeed, sociology itself could only emerge as a disciplined intellectual perspective when social relations were seen as distinct from political and economic relations—that is, when the relation between individual and society was no longer collapsed into or confused with the relation between the state and its subjects or between traders in a market economy. The hallmark of classical nineteenth- and early twentieth-century sociological thought was the assertion of the historical, causal, and moral priority of society over the state, a perspective common to the radical Karl Marx, viewing the economic substructure as shaping the political, legal, and ideological superstructure, and to the conservative William Graham Sumner, insisting that "stateways cannot change folkways."

Yet if we regard as the fathers and founders of sociology those

[71] Ibid., I, 34–36.
[72] See the lucid argument and the examples of Peter Bachrach and Morton S. Baratz, "Decisions and Nondecisions: An Analytical Framework," *American Political Science Review*, LVII (September, 1963), 637.
[73] W. G. Runciman, *Social Science and Political Theory* (Cambridge: Cambridge University Press), 1963, pp. 22–42.

thinkers who first grasped and conceptualized the autonomy of the social order, Weber almost alone among them avoided treating the state and politics as mere epiphenomena or "dependent variables" of the social structure. Tocqueville, today belatedly accorded recognition as a sociologist, is the only other exception, and he was far less concerned than Weber with systematic conceptualization. Weber's insistence on the independence of the political, his refusal to regard it as no more than a manifestation or expression of the underlying class and group structure of society, is what makes him today seem more of a contemporary than any of the other classical sociologists, even than Marx, in a world of combined social and national revolutions, of totalitarian regimes restructuring ancient social orders, and of welfare and warfare bureaucracies penetrating the daily affairs of more and more citizens.

How adequate, then, is Weber's definition of the state with its joint stress on territoriality and monopoly over the legitimate use of violence? His emphasis on territoriality has been justly criticized in light of the existence of nomadic peoples with specialized political roles and institutions, but his definition can easily be modified to accommodate this objection.[74] Some writers have preferred the term "polity" or "political system" to "state" on the grounds that differentiated political institutions do not exist in many precivilized and some civilized societies although such societies nevertheless successfully mobilize their members to pursue collective goals, punish non-conformists, adjudicate disputes, and perform other functions assumed by the state in modern societies. Clearly, such societies are neither anarchic nor anomic, though they may properly be characterized as "stateless."[75] But the emergence of a single institutional structure permanently monopolizing the legitimate use of force has been a comparatively recent historical development. Weber noted that in the past kinship groups, medieval guilds, and manorial households headed by feudal lords have controlled and legitimately employed the means of violence in large-scale civilized societies. A single center of political authority effectively exercising power over an entire population has often had only an insecure, temporary existence.[76] Far from ignoring such considerations, Weber regarded the emergence of a permanent and effective state as a specifically modern phenomenon, a

[74] Ibid., p. 30; Scott Greer and Peter Orleans, "Political Sociology," in *Handbook of Modern Sociology*, ed. R. E. L. Faris (Chicago: Rand McNally & Co., 1964), p. 810.

[75] Runciman, op. cit.

[76] See Rushton Coulborn's discussion of "ghost empires" in *Feudalism in History* (Princeton: Princeton University Press, 1956), pp. 236–53.

result of the process of rationalization. A major theme of his historical researches was to trace the development of a single center of political power, controlling material resources and an administrative staff sharply separated from the personal property and the relatives and retainers of the head of state, from feudal decentralization of power as well as from forms of patrimonial rule in which no clear distinction existed between governmental functions and personal services to the rulers.[77]

Weber's territorial criterion is intended to indicate the unique extensiveness of political authority.[78] To incorporate this feature more directly into a definition of the state requires, as Runciman has suggested, reference to the binding nature of political authority over a much larger and more inclusive constituency than the constituencies subject to the social controls of families, local communities, churches, and the many other groups composing the social order.[79] The Aristotelian identification of politics with the realm of "public" concerns in contrast to the "private" affairs of the household is the earliest formulation of this attribute of political authority.[80] The state's distinctive concern with "what is general to a society" [81] is also implied by those contemporary social scientists who variously define the "state" or the "political system" as concerned with the "authoritative allocation of values," [82] as the agency for the attainment of "systemic goals" on behalf of an entire society,[83] or as the source of decisions binding on and influencing, at least potentially, all members of a society.[84] The state is the only society-wide decision-making body whose functionaries,

[77] Lenski calls the premodern view of the state "the proprietary theory of the state," according to which "the state is a piece of property which its owner may use, within broad and somewhat ill-defined limits, for his personal advantage." See Gerhard Lenski, *Power and Privilege* (New York: McGraw-Hill Book Company, 1966), p. 214.

[78] By "extensiveness" I mean simply the relative number of people subject to a particular authority, as Bertrand de Jouvenel uses the term. See de Jouvenel, "Authority: The Efficient Imperative," in *Authority*, ed. Carl J. Friedrich, Nomos I (Cambridge, Mass.: Harvard University Press, 1958), p. 160.

[79] Runciman, op. cit., pp. 37–38.

[80] Ibid. See also Hannah Arendt, *The Human Condition* (Chicago: University of Chicago Press, 1958), chap. 2; and Sheldon Wolin, *Politics and Vision* (Boston: Little, Brown and Company, 1960), chap. 10.

[81] Wolin, op. cit., p. 492.

[82] David Easton, "The Perception of Authority and Political Change," in Friedrich, ed., op. cit., p. 172.

[83] Talcott Parsons, "An Outline of the Social System," in *Theories of Society*, eds. Parsons, Edward A. Shils, Kaspar D. Naegele, and Jesse R. Pitts (New York: The Free Press of Glencoe, 1961), I, 49–53.

[84] William A. Gamson, *Power and Discontent* (Homewood, Ill.: The Dorsey Press, 1968), chap. 2.

unlike those of any other group or organization, act in a representative capacity in the name of the entire collectivity. The modern state possesses, therefore, what one writer has called *integral power,* whereas all other groups and organizations are part of a system of *intercursive power* that is limited both by the checks they impose upon one another in competition, conflict, and bargaining, and by the powers of the state itself.[85]

The Types of Legitimacy

A distinctive feature of the modern state is its *rational-legal* basis of legitimacy, which Weber contrasted with two other bases of legitimacy, *traditionalism* and *charisma,* to arrive at his famous threefold typology of legitimate authority, or domination, as the German term *Herrschaft* has been variously and controversially translated.[86] Considerable confusion and ambiguity exists in the ways this typology has been interpreted and utilized. Do the three types refer to different motives for obeying political authorities? Or do they represent different structures of political power? Or are they different types of normative justification for obeying the commands of a powerholder? The latter view is the correct one: the types of legitimacy are essentially normative principles that are regularly and publicly invoked to justify compliance with the commands of an authority rather than specifications of "real" motives for obedience. They are ideological rather than psychological constructions, instances of what Gaetano Mosca called "political formulas." Weber maintained, however, that "for a domination, [the] kind of justification of its legitimacy is much more than a matter of theoretical or philosophical speculation; it rather constitutes the basis of very real differences in the empirical structure of domination." [87] He proceeded to relate in a far-ranging comparative historical analysis the types of legitimacy to the types of administrative structure and the distribution of resources usually associated with them.

Obedience to a traditional authority, whatever the variable motives underlying it in individual cases, is publicly justified by such arguments as "what was good enough for my father is good enough for me," or "that's the way things have always been done." The authority of "eternal yesterday," as Weber put it, is invoked to uphold compli-

---

[85] This distinction was developed by Theodore Geiger and is elaborated by J. A. A. Van Doorn, "Sociology and the Problem of Power," *Sociologica Nederlandica,* I (Winter, 1962–63), 16–18. See also Dennis H. Wrong, "Some Problems in Defining Social Power," *American Journal of Sociology,* LXXIII (May, 1968), 674–76.
[86] For a discussion of this controversy, see below pp. 55–56.
[87] *E. and S.,* III, 953.

ance with established norms and rulers in the present. Traditional
authority embodies the fundamental conservative conviction that
"what is, is right," which contains the unspoken premise that it is
right *because it is*, that is, because it preserves continuity with the past
and with the values of our dead forefathers. Conservative thinkers
and ideologues elaborate this unspoken premise into a Burkean view
of history in which the enormous complexity of the "providential
forces" shaping human institutions are seen as beyond the comprehension of mortal men with their inevitably time-bound outlooks. The
authority of existing forms of society must therefore be upheld and
preserved, an authority seen as deriving, in Burke's famous words, from
"a partnership between those who are living, those who are dead, and
those who are to be born." As Karl Mannheim noted, conservatism as
an ideology is essentially traditionalism become conscious of itself, and
it is, therefore, always a counterideology articulated only in response
to liberal and radical challenges to the existing order.[88]

Rational-legal legitimacy affirms the obligation to obey by invoking
an existing statute in enacted law that empowers ("authorizes") a particular authority to issue commands. Whereas under traditionalism
"obedience is owed not to enacted rules but to the person who occupies a position of authority by tradition or who has been chosen for
it by the traditional master," [89] under rational-legal authority the
superior is obeyed only by virtue of his incumbency in an office the
rights and duties of which are specified in an abstract and impersonal
body of regulations or laws. Similarly, "the person who obeys authority
does so . . . only in his capacity as a 'member' of the organization and
what he obeys is only 'the law' " [90] whether the organization in question is a nation-state, an association, or a church. The legal system is
seen as having "usually been intentionally established" [91] to achieve
particular administrative or regulatory goals whatever ultimate affinity
may be believed to exist between positive law and "natural law," the
will of God, or other supramundane values.

Defiance of a legally appointed authority is often justified in the
name of higher ideals than legality itself, but proposals to change a
legally ratified hierarchy of authority usually challenge the efficacy of
the existing structure in achieving the goals it is organized to pursue.
Thus, as noted above in connection with bureaucracy, the officials of
a government agency under attack for inefficiency or wasteful use of

---

[88] Karl Mannheim, *Essays on Sociology and Social Psychology* (New York: Oxford
University Press, Inc., 1953), p. 99.
[89] *E. and S.*, I, 227.
[90] Ibid., pp. 217–18.
[91] Ibid., p. 217.

resources are not apt to defend themselves by appealing to a traditional prescriptive right to act as they do, nor by claiming personal qualities entitling them to the loyalty and support of the public. Such appeals to tradition or personal worth are also unlikely to be publicly made in cases where charges of abuse of authority or dereliction of official duty are leveled. Rational-legal authority is associated with bureaucratic forms of organization where efficient and impersonal performance in the service of functional goals is the major standard legitimizing a particular structure and indeed the very existence of an organization.

Rational-legal authority is the basis of the claim to legitimacy of modern states. The development of a rationalized governmental administration and system of law has been, along with the growth of capitalist economic enterprise, the major locus of bureaucratization, which is the manifestation of the trend towards rationalization in the sphere of social organization. The expansion of state services under the welfare state has, as Michael Walzer has cogently argued, demystified and instrumentalized the very idea of the state itself, just as in the sphere of culture the ascendancy of scientific knowledge has led to the "disenchantment of the world." As Walzer observes, "The state still does depend on ideology and mystery, but to a far lesser degree than ever before. . . . It is judged, as it ought to be, by the amounts of welfare it produces and by the justice and efficiency of its distributive system." [92]

Weber's third type of legitimacy, charisma, has recently achieved the dubious fame of becoming a popular journalistic cliché. In contrast to traditional and legal-rational authority, Weber regarded charismatic authority as an innovating and revolutionary force, challenging and disrupting the established normative and political order. Charismatic authority is like traditional authority in that it is based on obedience to a *person* rather than, as in rational-legal authority, to an impersonal system of law empowering the incumbent of a position to exercise authority solely in his official capacity. The charismatic leader asks for obedience from his followers on the grounds of his distinctively personal gifts—his divinely inspired mission, his heroic deeds, his extraordinary endowments setting him apart from and above other men. Moreover, his followers share with him his belief in his charisma, which literally means "gift of grace." For Weber, the prototype of charismatic authority is the leader who says, "It is written, but I say unto you," an appeal that openly challenges the authority of the existing normative order.

Charismatic legitimacy is inherently unstable because it depends

[92] Michael Walzer, "Politics in the Welfare State," *Dissent,* XV (January–February, 1968), 27.

on a single individual who may through failure or defeat destroy his followers' belief in his mission and who is destined eventually to die. Hence a "problem of succession" is faced by all movements created by charismatic leaders. The possible rival solutions to this problem were the subject of Weber's well-known discussion of the "routinization of charisma." The attempt to transmit the charisma of a leader to a successor, or to vest it in a position or office with some provision for regular recruitment in the future, implies that charisma has a more comprehensive reference than to the magnetism of an individual personality. Weber's initial identification of charisma as an attribute of personality (though, to be sure, a *relational* attribute since its presence depends on the beliefs of others) has been criticized by some sociologists concerned with drawing a sharp distinction between personal or psychological qualities and institutional or role-dependent qualities.[93]

Edward Shils, on the other hand, has argued that Weber defined charisma too narrowly and that implicit in his own broadening of the concept when discussing its routinization is the idea of it as a quality that may inhere in offices, norms, beliefs, and institutions as well as in personalities.[94] Both Shils and Robert Nisbet, following the lead of Talcott Parsons, equate charisma with Durkheim's concept of the "sacred." [95] Weber's contrast between the "charismatic" and the "everyday" (or the "routine" as most translators have rendered the German *alltäglich*) thus becomes identical with Durkheim's dichotomy of the "sacred" and the "profane." Moreover, "charisma" and the "sacred" are first employed by both Weber and Durkheim as strictly religious concepts and are then extended to secular objects, roles, and symbols as well. Shils and Nisbet argue accordingly that Weber's emphasis on the revolutionary, innovating character of charisma represents only a special case of the phenomenon. Both insist that charisma, when dissociated from the limited notion of it as an individual personality trait, also maintains and conserves an existing normative order by investing it with "miracle, mystery and authority," in the words of Dostoevski's Grand Inquisitor.

This broadened conception of charisma, however, is scarcely distinguishable from the reverential attitude towards the past that character-

[93] Robert Bierstedt, "The Problem of Authority," *Freedom and Control in Modern Society*, ed. Morroe Berger, Theodore Abel, and Charles Page (New York: D. Van Nostrand Co., Inc., 1954), pp. 70–71.

[94] Edward A. Shils, "Charisma, Order and Status," *American Sociological Review*, XXX (April, 1965), 199–213.

[95] Ibid.; Robert Nisbet, *The Sociological Tradition* (New York: Basic Books, Inc., Publishers, 1966), pp. 251–57; Talcott Parsons, *The Structure of Social Action* (New York: McGraw-Hill Book Company, 1937), pp. 658–72.

izes traditionalism. Weber, in fact, speaks of a "sacredness of tradition" and the "sanctity of age-old rules and powers,"[96] and "sacredness" and "sanctity" are here obviously synonymous with the idea of charisma as a generic attribute of an institutional order stressed by Parsons, Shils, and Nisbet. Furthermore, if charisma is not necessarily revolutionary, it is also the case that not all revolutions are led by charismatic leaders.[97] Unfortunately, Weber never wrote the chapter on revolutions intended for *Economy and Society* and the lack of any theory of revolution is perhaps the most notable deficiency of his political sociology.

As in the case of Weber's ideal-typical definition of bureaucracy, which was designed to draw a contrast with nonbureaucratic organizations rather than to aid in the comparison of different bureaucracies, the notion of charismatic leadership was intended to contrast sharply with the other two types of legitimation. Yet charisma, first treated by Weber at length in its original religious meaning in his comparative sociology of religion, was indeed something more to him than one mode of the legitimation of authority. Weber employed the term "charisma" to characterize the way the world is perceived by men sustaining an emotional relationship to it that stands in polar contrast to the schematizing matter-of-factness of the rationalizing ethos. When ultimate values and transcendental meanings are experienced as inhering in and emanating from the world rather than as "arbitrary" human creations projected upon it by man, the world possesses charisma—the capacity to inspire awe, reverence, and the felt conviction that human life is part of a larger order of things in which it serves a definite purpose. Religions express in different ways this charismatic experience of the world, although they are not the only expressions of it; secular world-views, in particular the various forms of *Lebensphilosophie* produced by German idealism and romanticism, also endow the world with charisma. Rationalization promotes the "disenchantment of the world" by divesting it of its charismatic qualities.

Weber sees the process of rationalization as draining the world of charisma in a manner analogous to the reduction of physical energy to dead level postulated by the second law of thermodynamics. Shils correctly observes that "Weber's intent was to characterize the modern social and political order as one in which belief in transcendent values and their embodiment in individuals and institutions was being driven into a more and more restricted domain, as a result of the process of rationalization and bureaucratization."[98] Charisma in its most "con-

---

[96] *E. and S.*, I, 37, 226.
[97] Freund, op. cit., p. 243.
[98] Shils, op. cit., pp. 202–3.

centrated and intense" form is a quality of individual persons.[99] Weber regarded prophets, revolutionaries, and inspirational innovators of all kinds as the purest types of charismatic leaders; in established organizations charisma tends to be "concentrated at the peak" in the person and office of their heads—monarchs, presidents, party chairmen, or commanding generals.[100] In its depersonalized form, charisma is ascribed to the ultimate, often transcendental values that sanctify an organization and legitimate its goals, indeed its very existence. Shils argues, however, that an "attenuated and dispersed charisma" also permeates an entire structure of authority; even under a rational-legal order *some* charisma is attributed to such lowly functionaries as policemen and minor civil servants.[101]

Significantly, Shils has been one of the most vigorous critics of the theory of mass society, charging its proponents with an unbalanced hatred of modern life stemming from frustrated elitist aspirations, romantic pessimism, and disenchanted Marxism.[102] So, not surprisingly, we find him arguing that Weber's view of modern society "hindered his perception of the deeper and more permanent features of all societies" and is therefore "too disjunctive in its conception of the uniqueness of modern societies . . . too historicist." [103] Maybe so: Weber is not Durkheim (nor Parsons) and "a way of seeing is also a way of not seeing." Undeniably, much prevailing social criticism, whether expressing a "romantic protest" against life in society as such or a disappointed rationalism, projects a nightmarish view of modern society that is little more than caricature. Fed by a number of cultural, intellectual, and political currents that are at odds with major trends in modern life, our language of social criticism and protest frequently degenerates into no more than, if I may quote myself, "a general hum of lamentation about the fate of man in modern society, in which each individual word loses its conceptual clarity in contributing to an overall tonal effect." [104] The irrationalism and nihilistic anti-institutionalism often found among supporters of the New Left represent the most recent and extreme manifestation of this tendency.

[99] Ibid., p. 202.
[100] Ibid., p. 207.
[101] Ibid., p. 206.
[102] See Edward A. Shils, "Daydreams and Nightmares: Reflections on the Criticism of Mass Culture," *The Sewanee Review*, LXV (October–December, 1957); and "The Theory of Mass Society," in *America as a Mass Society*, ed. Philip Olson (New York: The Free Press of Glencoe, 1963), pp. 30–47.
[103] Shils, "Charisma, Order and Status," p. 203.
[104] Dennis H. Wrong, "Identity: Problem and Catchword," *Dissent*, XV (September–October, 1968), 428.

But diagnoses of the alienating and dehumanizing tendencies of modern society could hardly have acquired the resonance and evocative power they so clearly possess if they did not correctly sense something about the quality of modern life that is discontinuous with the past. That many critics of modern life hold a false and idealized image of the past, exaggerate the novelty of the present, and cling to an excessively visionary and apocalyptic view of the future is, as Shils insists, certainly the case. But even if we choose to regard mass society theorists as simply the "pathologists of contemporary society," [105] compulsive explorers of the spiritual underside of modernity, they are the heirs to a tradition of cultural criticism that is now nearly 200 years old and that today is voiced just as stridently by men of the Left as by reactionaries and apolitical aesthetes.[106]

Weber was indeed primarily concerned with specifying what was different and distinctive about the dominant trends of modern Western society rather than with stressing its continuities with past social orders; this emphasis doubtless needs correction now that the traditional societies of Asia and Africa are undergoing the throes of political revolution and technical modernization. If, however, as I have previously suggested, our deepest sociological insights spring from the effort to discover an intimate connection between the inner doubts and conflicts of men and the major currents of historical change in which they are caught up, then Weber's stress on the waning of charisma in a rationalized world is a major achievement of the sociological imagination—a greater one, in my view, than Durkheim's perception of the sacred as an attribute of all societies viewed *sub specie aeternitas*.

If a generalized and depersonalized conception of charisma blurs Weber's distinction between traditional and charismatic legitimation, Shils' contention that charisma also pervades rational-legal systems of authority blurs the distinction between rational-legal and charismatic legitimation. This raises the question of the degree to which Weber's types are to be understood as analytical abstractions or as concrete historical entities. Raymond Aron is one of a number of critics who has complained that "Weber has not really distinguished between purely analytical concepts and semi-historical concepts." [107] Aron in-

---

[105] William Kornhauser, "Mass Society," *International Encyclopedia of the Social Sciences*, Vol. 10 (New York: The Macmillan Company and The Free Press, 1968), p. 64.

[106] For an excellent history of the concept of mass society, see E. V. Walter, " 'Mass Society': The Late Stages of an Idea," *Social Research*, XXXI (Winter, 1964), 391–410.

[107] Raymond Aron, *Main Currents in Sociological Thought* (New York: Basic Books, Inc., Publishers, 1967), II, 239.

sists that "the three modes of domination should be regarded purely and simply as analytic concepts; but Weber also terms them historical or semi-historical types." [108]

Aron notes the parallelism between the types of legitimacy and Weber's classification of types of social action. Since the latter classification is explicitly based on underlying motivations, one is easily led to conclude that the types of legitimacy also refer essentially to different concrete motives for obeying. But, as Aron indicates, Weber's discussion in *Economy and Society* of motives for complying with a legitimate order stresses the enormous variety and mixture of motives likely to be present in individual cases, a consideration casting doubt on the utility of the typology of legitimacy as a classification of the motivational grounds for obedience. The types of legitimacy, as I have already noted, refer to publicly acceptable *reasons* for obeying rather than to *motives*, or, as Parsons puts it, to "motives for attributing legitimacy to [an] order" rather than to "motives for maintaining a legitimate order in force." [109]

Aron points out that there are four types of social action and only three types of domination or legitimacy. There is an obvious correspondence between rational action (*Zweckrationalität*) and rational-legal legitimation, habitual action and traditionalism, and affectual action and charisma. But what of value-oriented action (*Wertrationalität*)? As a matter of fact, Weber does allude in section seven of the first chapter of *Economy and Society* to a possible fourth type of legitimation involving the affirmation of an absolute value, [110] but he makes no use of this type in his survey of historical examples of the types in Part Three, a survey that was actually written before the condensed and abstract array of definitions presented in Part One. As an illustration of value rational legitimation, Weber mentions belief in natural law from which binding norms of conduct are logically deduced as opposed to being derived from revelation, tradition, or enacted law. Perhaps the fact that natural law thinking has been of significance only in the West and even there only in a particular historical period accounts for Weber's failure to make any further use of value-rational legitimation as a distinctive type. But a deeper explanation suggests itself.

Tradition, faith, and legality are themselves values, or at least *forms*

---

[108] Ibid.

[109] See Parsons' editorial note in Max Weber, *The Theory of Social and Economic Organization*, trans. A. M. Henderson and Talcott Parsons, ed. Talcott Parsons (New York: Oxford University Press, Inc., 1947), pp. 126–27.

[110] *E. and S.*, I, 36–37.

of valuing.[111] Thus actions designed to maintain tradition, affirm the mission of a charismatic leader, or uphold the norms of enacted law, are instances of value-oriented action, or *Wertrationalität*. But by no means all of the actions of individuals that are, in Weber's words. "oriented to the existence of a legitimate order" are motivated by the aim of affirming or upholding such an order. Some such actions may be strictly expediential, following from the actor's knowledge that other people are guided by certain norms which may be expected to influence their conduct towards him, and are therefore instances of instrumentally rational actions, or *Zweckrationalität*. (Weber gives the obvious example of the thief acting surreptitiously.) Other actions taking into account the existence of an order may be habitual, while still others are affectual or expressive. "In a very large proportion of cases, the actors subject to the order are of course not even aware how far it is a matter of custom, of convenience, or of law." [112]

Whatever the motive, or mixture of motives, underlying an individual's compliance with a norm or the command of an authority, a legitimate order exists only where reasons are presented and accepted as to why men *should* comply. Tradition, legality, belief in the mission of a prophet or leader—Weber's three types of legitimacy—are different sorts of reasons typically put forward to justify different structures of authority. As Carl Friedrich has argued, legitimate authority exists only when orders possess the "potentiality of reasoned elaboration." [113] Weber's typology presupposes that at least *some* men who obey an authority do so out of a sense of obligation to obey that transcends self-interest, habit, or impulse and that, when verbalized in the imperative mode, provides a legitimizing rationale for conformity and obedience. But one who abjures personal advantage, blind habit, or emotional release in order to abide by tradition or the law, or to serve a revered leader, is clearly engaged in value-rational conduct. Thus there is not a separate value-rational mode of legitimization: *all* conduct that is based on a subjective affirmation of the legitimacy of an order is value-rational even though "the transitions between orientation to an order from motives of tradition [the fourth of Weber's four types of social action] or of expediency [Weber's first type] to the case

---

[111] See Peter Blau's discussion of values as forms "abstracted from substantive content" in "Objectives of Sociology," in *A Design for Sociology: Scope, Objectives, and Methods*, ed. Robert Bierstedt (Philadelphia: American Academy of Political and Social Science, 1969), pp. 56–58.

[112] *E. and S.*, I, 38.

[113] Carl J. Friedrich, "Authority, Reason, and Discretion," in Friedrich, ed., op. cit., p. 35.

where a belief in its legitimacy is involved are empirically gradual." [114]

The four types of social action are clearly universals found in all societies. The three modes of legitimation also represent, as Bendix puts it, "archetypes of human experience." [115] But they differ from the types of action in that one or the other of the modes is dominant in particular large-scale political systems or institutional orders. Thus rational-legal legitimation characterizes the modern state and bureaucratic organizations, reflecting the historical trend towards rationalization. Traditionalism predominates in virtually all past social orders from primitive societies to the various forms of patrimonialism, patriarchalism, and feudalism in premodern Europe that Weber analyzes in such historical detail in Part Three of *Economy and Society*. Charisma, unlike rational-legal and traditional legitimacy, is essentially an ahistorical phenomenon capable of erupting under any existing order —even in primitive societies[116]—although it is fated to become routinized over time into one of the other types of legitimacy.

This association of traditional and rational-legal legitimacy with different historical social orders leads Weber apparently to obscure the analytical status of the three types and to treat them as concrete historical concepts, as both Aron and Blau have argued. Hence also the arguments of such critics as Shils to the effect that he neglects the charismatic elements present even in a rational-legal order. Others have pointed out that examples of all three types of legitimation can be found in the political institutions of contemporary societies. There are, for example, rational-legal, traditional, and charismatic bases for the authority of an American president.[117] Established institutions are often sustained in practice by all three modes of legitimation just as they also are supported by expediential, emotional, and purely habitual motives. Even the characteristically modern rational-legal mode of legitimacy exists in nascent form in traditional social orders. Yet since the types represent prevailing rationales for obedience, one type may clearly predominate over the others. However, as Bendix has acutely shown, each type contains within itself the dialectical potentiality of evolving into one of the others "when its rulers fail to live up to the standards by which they justify their domination and thereby jeopardize the beliefs in those standards among the public at large." [118] Such a view is implicit in Weber's analysis but is obscured by his moving

---

[114] *E. and S.*, I, 31.

[115] Reinhard Bendix, *Max Weber: An Intellectual Portrait* (Garden City, N.Y.: Doubleday & Company, Inc., Anchor Books, 1962), p. 389.

[116] Peter Worsely, *The Trumpet Shall Sound* (New York: Schocken Books, 1968).

[117] Weber on a number of occasions used this example himself.

[118] Bendix, op. cit., pp. 296–97.

directly from a characterization of each type to a comparative historical analysis of political systems primarily exemplifying it. He himself, however, unmistakably regarded the types as analytical abstractions rather than as concrete entities, maintaining that "the forms of domination occurring in historical reality constitute combinations, mixtures, adaptations, or modifications of these 'pure' types [of legitimation]." [119] Indeed he devotes an entire section (section thirteen of chapter three, of Part One) of *Economy and Society* to a discussion of "combinations of the different types of authority," [120] in which he gives numerous examples of belief in legality becoming habitual and therefore traditional, and of charismatic elements in the authority of heads of both traditional and bureaucratic administrations.

Legitimacy and Coercion

Weber's stress on the importance of legitimacy in general, and on the types of legitimacy as crucial variables of political systems, have been enormously influential in American social science—disproportionately influential, in fact, in relation to the rest of his political sociology and his substantive historical analyses. In part this is a result of the fact that, until very recently, only parts of *Economy and Society* were available in English translation and these in several different translations.[121] In part it is because Weber's ideas were first introduced by scholars, most notably Talcott Parsons, whose primary theoretical concerns were with the conditions promoting consensus and stability in society rather than with conflict and change. Amitai Etzioni is correct in maintaining that:

> Studies conducted in the tradition of Weber . . . tend to focus on authority, or legitimate power, as this concept is defined. The significance of authority has been emphasized in modern sociology in the past in order to overcome earlier biases that overemphasized force and economic power as the sources of social order. This emphasis, in turn, has led to an overemphasis on legitimate power. . . . Since the significance of legitimate power has been fully recognized, it is time to lay the ghost of Marx and the old controversy, and to give full status to both legitimate and non-legitimate sources of control.[122]

Much of Weber's work, including his conception of legitimacy, was,

[119] *E. and S.*, III, 954.
[120] Ibid., I, 262–66.
[121] Roth refers to some of the misleading impressions created by the previous availability in English of only parts of *Economy and Society*. See "Introduction," ibid., I, lxxxii–lxxxiii, ciii.
[122] Amitai Etzioni, *A Comparative Analysis of Complex Organizations* (New York: The Free Press of Glencoe, 1961), pp. 14–15.

of course, an effort to correct and modify historical materialism, even if Albert Salomon's much-cited claim that his sociology is "a long and intense dialogue with the Ghost of Karl Marx" [123] is an exaggeration. Conventional versions of the three ideas of Weber's which, along with legitimacy, have had the greatest impact on American social science also reveal a bias that assigns greater weight to values than to material interests, and to consensus and social harmony over conflict and coercion. I have in mind his conception of bureaucracy, his thesis that the Protestant Reformation contributed to the rise of capitalism, and his stress on status honor as a factor promoting group solidarity independently of economic considerations.

In the case of bureaucracy, American sociologists have usually criticized Weber's characterization as too hierarchical and authoritarian. They have charged Weber with ignoring the informal networks of association that emerge spontaneously within bureaucratic organizations, modifying their formal structure of authority, allowing greater autonomy to the individual worker, and promoting a more democratic and egalitarian atmosphere than is allegedly possible under Weber's "Prussian" model.

Weber's thesis that the religious doctrines of Calvinism played a crucial part in the emergence of capitalism in Western Europe was certainly directed polemically against "a one-sided materialistic . . . causal interpretation of culture and history." [124] But Weber wrote *The Protestant Ethic* relatively early in his career, before his comparative survey of world religions, which indeed he undertook in order to test his theory of the influence of Calvinism on capitalism. Yet Carlo Antoni, in the selection in chapter six, is one of a number of critics, including Gerth and Mills, who have insisted that in the end Weber's studies suggest that "even the most profound difference between East and West is, below all the differences of faith, primarily a question of classes." Antoni concludes that "this sociology of religion would be differentiated from materialism only by its substitution of the concept of social class for that of economic class."

In the study of social stratification, Weber's conception of "status groups" as collectivities distinct from economic classes has had enormous influence. The stress on common values and shared styles of life as a basis of group cohesion is often seen as a corrective to Marxist insistence on the primacy of clashing economic interests and conse-

[123] Albert Salomon, "German Sociology," in *Twentieth Century Sociology*, ed. George Gurvitch and Wilbert E. Moore (New York: Philosophical Library, 1945), p. 596.
[124] *Protestant Ethic*, p. 183.

quent class conflict. Weber is the source of the prevailing tridimensional conception of social stratification that treats wealth, prestige, and power—or class, status, and power—as partially independent bases of stratification. Since distinctions of status imply a common set of values by which individuals and social positions are judged and differentially ranked, Weber is sometimes cited in support of the view that social inequality conforms to a "social status continuum" which both promotes and reflects the unity of society as a whole stemming from consensus on values.[125] Such a view stands in sharp contrast to the idea that inequality creates classes that enter into bitter conflict over the distribution of wealth and power. While it was certainly Weber's aim to go beyond the limits of a purely materialist theory of the differentiation of societies into hierarchical segments, he was concerned with describing different status *groups* rather than with identifying a continuous scale of status evaluations on which individuals or positions could be located.[126] Nor did he imply that the relations among status groups are necessarily harmonious, reflecting underlying common values. Status groups engage in political and economic conflict that is as intense as conflict between classes whose solidarity derives from common material interests rather than from common notions of honor and a shared style of life.

My point is not, of course, that Weber was "really" a Marxist, nor that "the whole of Max Weber's facts and arguments fits perfectly into Marx's system." [127] Still less that he belongs in the long Machiavellian tradition of political thought that starts with Thrasymachus in Plato's *Republic,* includes Machiavelli and Hobbes, such moderns as Pareto and Mosca, and, at least in parts of their work, such contemporaries as Lasswell, Mills, and Dahrendorf.[128] However, unlike many of the critics of Marxism and the Machiavellian tradition, Weber did not simply deny the centrality of economic coercion and violence in society and history and relegate them to the status of pathological exceptions.

[125] See Stanislaw Ossowski, *Class Structure in the Social Consciousness* (New York: The Free Press of Glencoe, 1963), chap. 6.

[126] Dennis H. Wrong, "Social Inequality Without Social Stratification," *Canadian Review of Sociology and Anthropology,* I (Spring, 1964), 7.

[127] Joseph A. Schumpeter, *Capitalism, Socialism, and Democracy,* 3rd ed. (New York: Harper & Brothers, 1950), p. 11.

[128] See Ralf Dahrendorf's stimulating essay, "In Praise of Thrasymachus," in Dahrendorf, *Essays on the Theory of Society* (Stanford, Calif.: Stanford University Press, 1968), pp. 129–50. Dahrendorf's conception of the "Thrasymachean Theory" is somewhat broader than what I have labeled the "Machiavellian tradition"; he includes under this rubric C. Wright Mills, Wilbert E. Moore, Irving Louis Horowitz, Raymond Aron, and myself among contemporary sociologists.

If one explores his notion of the relationship between values and material or power interests in the context of his work as a whole, it is evident that he holds a subtle and dialectical view which strives to give each its due in the manifold richness of historical reality.

True, Weber devoted far greater attention in *Economy and Society* to the conceptual elaboration of the types of legitimacy than to the coercive face of power. Nor did he, as Blau points out in the selection reprinted in chapter eight, concern himself with the process by which legitimate authority evolves out of coercive or utilitarian power relations. He tended to take the existence and importance of violence and economic power, so heavily stressed in late nineteenth-century social thought by Marxists and Social Darwinists alike, for granted. Yet, as we have seen, he makes a monopoly of violence the defining criterion of the state and politics—so much so that he has often been regarded as an exemplar of the Prussian spirit of *Realpolitik* and even as an ideological precursor of the Nazis. If Americans have for the most part seen Weber strictly as a scientific theorist and have selectively stressed those aspects of his thought that are congruent with the normative functionalism of American sociological theory and the democratic liberalism of most American academic men, Germans have in the wake of the Nazi catastrophe been considerably more sensitive to the nationalist passion, the conviction of the need for a charismatic chief of state, and the emphasis on the violence at the core of all politics evident in Weber's political writings. (See, for example, Mommsen in chapter ten of this volume.) These two distinct orientations were revealed at the 1964 Heidelberg conference commemorating the centenary of Weber's birth, as has been pointed out by Raymond Aron and by Guenther Roth (in chapter eleven of this book) in their summaries of that conference.[129]

Yet even if we ignore the remainder of Weber's work and confine ourselves to a formal analysis of the general definitions of power and domination in *Economy and Society*, it is plain that he had no disposition to minimize the importance of force and economic coercion. "Power" he defined as "the probability that one actor within a social relationship will be in a position to carry out his own will despite resistance, regardless of the basis on which this probability rests."[130] The reference to resistance clearly suggests a view of power as constraint rather than as voluntary submission, although in my opinion such a suggestion is both unnecessary and undesirable in an initial

[129] Aron, op. cit., pp. 246–51. See also Carl Cerny, "Storm over Max Weber," *Encounter*, XXIII (August, 1964), 57–59.
[130] *E. and S.*, I, 53.

general definition of power.[131] The final phrase in the definition points to the multiple and diverse bases on which someone may exercise power over another, bases that obviously include the threat of violence, economic coercion, prestige considerations, manipulation, habit, and personal magnetism. Weber goes on to remark that "all conceivable qualities of a person and all conceivable combinations of circumstances may put him in a position to impose his will in a given situation." [132] Therefore, a "more precise" concept is needed and Weber proposes the concept of "domination" as "a special case of power." [133] His most extensive definition of domination is offered in Part Three of *Economy and Society*:

> Domination will thus mean the situation in which the manifested will (*command*) of the *ruler* or rulers is meant to influence the conduct of one or more others (the *ruled*) and actually does influence it in such a way that their conduct to a socially relevant degree occurs as if the ruled had made the content of the command the maxim of their conduct for its very own sake. Looked upon from the other end, this situation will be called *obedience*.[134]

This definition does not exclude a relationship in which a subordinate obeys a superior solely out of fear that he will suffer physical punishment or economic deprivation should he resist. Weber's term *Herrschaft* therefore—translated in the above quotation as "domination"—cannot be identified with *legitimate* power, which is a special case of *Herrschaft*, just as *Herrschaft* is a special case of power in general. One may, like David Easton, use the term "authority" as the equivalent of Weber's concept and then distinguish between *legitimate* and *nonlegitimate* or *coercive* authority.[135] The trouble with this is that "coercive authority" sounds like a contradiction in terms in view of the widespread tendency both in ordinary speech and in sociological usage to identify authority with a relationship in which the subordinate obeys out of *consent* based on his acceptance of an obligation to obey, or in other words out of a belief in the legitimacy of the command-obedience relationship. Since such terms as "boss-ship" or even "rulership," which are more literal translations of *Herrschaft,* have a clumsy ring, the most acceptable alternative is probably "domination"

---

[131] I prefer an adaptation of Bertrand Russell's definition, "power is the production of intended effects by some men on other men," which can then be followed by a classification of the various forms of power. See Dennis H. Wrong, "Some Problems in Defining Social Power," op. cit., LXXIII, 676–77.

[132] *E. and S.,* I, 53.

[133] Ibid.; also III, 941–42.

[134] Ibid., p. 946 (italics in original).

[135] Easton, op. cit., p. 181.

both in English and in French, as has been argued by Bendix, Roth, Aron, and Freund among interpreters and translators of Weber.[136] Parsons alone has preferred "imperative control" and, later, "authority" because these terms suggest "the integration of the collectivity, in the interests of its effective functioning" rather than a unilateral leader-follower relation.[137] But whether Weber intended such an implication is precisely the point at issue: both a literal reading of his definition and the emphasis of so much of his substantive political analysis compel agreement with Bendix that "as a realist in the analysis of power he would have been critical of any translation that tended to obscure the 'threat of force' present in all relations between superiors and subordinates." [138]

Weber gives many illustrations of domination based on economic interests. In fact, he refers to "domination by virtue of a constellation of interests" as one major type of domination, the other polar type being domination based on "power to command and duty to obey." He notes marginal cases on the borderline between these two types, observes that the former often develop into the latter, and cites a variety of relevant economic examples including the relationship between a central bank and its debtors and between breweries and tavern owners. He then states that he will use the term in the narrower second sense in which "*domination* shall be identical with the authoritarian power of *command*." [139] He immediately offers the detailed definition already quoted.

In the more compressed treatment of domination in chapter three of Part One of *Economy and Society*—written at a later date than the discussion in Part Three reviewed in the preceding paragraph—Weber comments, after defining domination, that "every genuine form of domination implies a minimum of voluntary compliance, that is, an *interest* (based on ulterior motives or genuine acceptance) in obedience." [140] This statement could be interpreted as excluding a purely coercive power relationship from falling under the category of domination, especially since Weber in the next paragraph lists custom, affectual ties, material interests, and ideal or *wertrationale* motives, *but not fear* as possible motives binding an administrative staff "to obedience to their superior." He then observes that "in addition there is nor-

---

[136] Bendix, op. cit., note 31, pp. 481–82; Roth. *E. and S.*, I, ed. note 31, 61–62; Aron, op. cit., pp. 235–36; Freund, op. cit., pp. 221–23.
[137] Talcott Parsons, "Max Weber" (Review Article), *American Sociological Review*, XXV (October, 1960), 752.
[138] Bendix, op. cit., p. 482.
[139] *E. and S.*, III, 946 (italics in original).
[140] Ibid., I, 212.

mally a further element, the belief in legitimacy." He argues that "it is useful to classify the types of domination according to the kind of claim to legitimacy typically made by each," and mentions seven additional clarifying and qualifying considerations, each of them numbered, bearing on the nature of domination and legitimacy in general, before proceeding in a new section to present his threefold classification of types of legitimacy.[141]

It is easy to see how this presentation has led some readers virtually to equate domination with legitimate authority and to minimize its coercive aspects. However, when Weber makes "voluntary compliance" based on "interest" a criterion of domination, he clearly does not mean to exclude a power-subject's interest in avoiding the imposition of painful physical sanctions when confronted with a credible "threat of force" from a powerholder. The actual application of force to the body of the power-subject is all that the criterion excludes. The distinction between the threat of force and the exercise of force is a crucial one, for the former does not negate the reciprocal interaction and communication that characterize and indeed *define* a social relationship, whereas the latter is no longer a social relationship at all since it "reduces" the victim of violence to no more than a physical object, or at most a biological organism capable of pain. Like many other theorists of power and authority, Weber fails to differentiate explicitly between force and the threat of force,[142] although elsewhere in *Economy and Society* he recognizes the relevance of the distinction: in a discussion of the relation between law and economic behavior, he cites the Latin maxim *coactus tamen voluit* ("Although coerced, it was still his will") and observes "this is true, without exception, of all coercion which does not treat the person to be coerced simply as an inanimate object." Our experience of totalitarian regimes, which have been described as "rule by ideology and terror," makes this apparently abstract and formal distinction seem far more important than it did in Weber's day.

In general, much of the difficulty with Weber's elaboration of his definitions arises from his constant tendency to move very rapidly, often from one sentence to the next, between at least three different levels of abstraction. Many of his initial distinctions and illustrations are analytical universals, referring to motives for obedience that are present in some men at all times and in all men at some times, and that correspond to his four basic types of social action. But he goes on

---

[141] Ibid., I, 213.
[142] David Easton is one of the few contemporary theorists who has developed such a distinction and realized its full significance, op. cit., pp. 180–83.
[143] *E. and S.,* I, 334.

to recognize that all durable collective structures of domination mobilize all of these motives—material interests, affectual ties, duty based on legitimizing beliefs—in their support, some of them predominating in some of their subjects while others underlie the obedience of other subjects. Moreover, even a single subject may obey out of plural motives and remain uncertain as to which is his ruling motive. Weber then focuses on belief in legitimacy as a powerful and universal prop to the maintenance of a system of domination and contends that different types of belief are associated with different actual structures. He next moves on to his detailed and extensive analysis of such particular historical structures as Occidental feudalism, sultanism, modern state bureaucracy, *et al.*

Undeniably, Weber devotes far more attention to conceptually elaborating and stressing the significance of the types of legitimacy. And he undoubtedly did so because he felt that economic power and coercion had already been overemphasized by his post-Marxist and post-Darwinian contemporaries. Yet, as I have tried to show, his definitions are formulated so carefully and his grasp of concrete reality was so firm, that he does not in fact eliminate, even at an abstract, theoretical level, economic domination and violence from his purview. Thus he bears only a partial responsibility for the overemphasis on legitimate power by contemporary social scientists to which Etzioni alludes in the citation at the beginning of this section. Moreover, several recent scholars, including Etzioni himself, who acknowledge large intellectual debts to Weber, have devoted themselves to redressing the one-sided stress on legitimacy of some of their predecessors without swinging all the way back to a narrowly Thrasymachian view of power in society.[144]

Politics and Ethics

Weber's types of legitimacy refer to publicly proclaimed and accepted arguments enjoining obedience to an established order. The political man, the man with a true calling for politics, however, does not accept the present order in its entirety: he espouses ideal values or identifies himself with collective goals that he strives to promote and serve, which are not fully embodied or realized in existing institutions. What general principles guide him in attempting to advance his cause in a refractory world in which other men are committed to rival causes?

Weber discerned two polar moralities that provide answers to this question: an ethic of responsibility (*Verantwortungsethik*) and an ethic

---

[144] Etzioni, op. cit.; Walter, "Power and Violence"; Gamson, op. cit.; Edward W. Lehman, "Toward a Macrosociology of Power," *American Sociological Review,* XXXIV (August, 1969), 453–63.

of absolute ends (*Gesinnungsethik*). Although he discussed these two ethics chiefly in relation to politics, they represent general attitudes towards the world, just as the three types of legitimacy also apply to institutions other than the political. Essentially they are religious in origin and represent different responses to "the age-old problem of theodicy . . . the experience of the irrationality of the world which has been the driving force of all religious evolution." [145]

Weber, in fact, argues that the ethic of absolute ends is specifically inappropriate to politics. Because "politics operates with very special means, namely power backed up by *violence*," there is an irreducible tension between the requirements of political action and absolute ethical values. "He who seeks the salvation of the soul, of his own and of others, should not seek it along the avenue of politics, for the quite different task of politics can only be solved by violence. . . . Everything that is striven for through political action operating with violent means and following an ethic of responsibility endangers the 'salvation of the soul.' " [146]

The proponent of an ethic of absolute ends strives in his conduct to live by principles and values, whether religiously inspired or secular, that are for him the *summum bonum*. He does not take into account the possible or probable consequences of strictly abiding by his principles in an imperfect world in which other men do not honor or live by them; it is enough that he has acted in conformity with a moral standard that is for him an absolute. Weber quotes in illustration the maxim "the Christian does rightly and leaves the results with the Lord." In effect, the believer in an ethic of absolute ends acts as if he were already living in the Kingdom of Heaven, the Good Society, or in a Utopia beyond the terror of history. Although he knows that evil has not yet been vanquished, he "feels 'responsible' only for seeing to it that the flame of pure intentions is not quelched." He avoids the moral dilemma posed by "the fact that in numerous instances the attainment of 'good' ends is bound to the fact that one must be willing to pay the price of using morally dubious means or at least dangerous ones—and facing the possibility or even the probability of evil ramifications." [147] The believer in an ethic of absolute ends chooses, as it were, to "live his end"; he thus denies any possible tension between means and ends by refusing to distinguish between them, merging or collapsing his means into his ends. Since politics makes use of the "morally dubious means" of violence, he must either renounce the world of politics altogether or confine himself to recommending exemplary action.

[145] *Essays*, p. 122, also pp. 274–86.
[146] Ibid., p. 126.
[147] Ibid., p. 121.

Whereas all or most men engage on occasion in value-rational—*wertrationale*—actions, the believer in an ethic of absolute ends elevates this mode of conduct into a principle or standard for all conduct. The follower of an ethic of responsibility, on the other hand, is concerned with the ultimate historical fate of his cause and recognizes the necessity of acting instrumentally, or in a *zweckrationale* manner, in order to promote it. Thus he cannot escape confronting the antinomies of means and ends. He holds himself responsible for the actual consequences of his decisions and actions rather than feeling responsible only to God, to an ideal, or to the inner dictates of his conscience. He does not hesitate to dirty his hands by engaging in politics: "he lets himself in for the diabolic forces lurking in all violence." Weber's insistence on the violence of politics follows, of course, from his definition of the state and of politics as the "striving to share power or striving to influence the distribution of power, either among states or among groups within a state." [148] Apart from implicating himself in the violence that is the ultimate means, the court of last resort, in all politics, the responsible participant in even the peaceful, routine politics of democracy cannot avoid compromising other values he may cherish as ideals or in personal relations: he indulges in "campaign oratory," making promises he knows he cannot completely fulfill; he conceals unpleasant truths from his supporters; pretends to a moral superiority over his opponents that he may not truly feel; and, in general, resorts to a demagoguery that is both potentially corrupting and unavoidable if he is to win and to hold the support of the masses.[149]

The two ethics are ideal types. Few men—at least today with the waning of religious faith—have the courage, or, if you like, the fanaticism, to hold genuinely and consistently to an ethic of absolute ends. Most men are not even failed saints, for, as George Orwell pointed out in his essay on Gandhi, the average human being does not truly aspire to sainthood. Weber recognized that many men affected to follow an ethic of absolute ends, but he dismissed most of them as "windbags who do not fully realize what they take upon themselves but who intoxicate themselves with romantic sensations." This is surely no less true today. One recalls those professed apostles of Gandhi, Albert Camus, and Martin Luther King who within the space of a few short years renounced the nonviolence to which they had previously been committed and began to advocate guerrilla warfare in the urban

---

[148] Ibid., p. 78.

[149] That "demagoguery" is an inevitable consequence of democratic politics was recognized by Weber in his article, "Parliament and Government in a Reconstructed Germany," which is included as Appendix II in *E. and S.*, III, 1381–1469.

ghettoes and on the campuses, now hailing Che Guevara, Frantz Fanon, and Ho Chi Minh as their heroes.

Saints, "the great *virtuosi* of acosmic love of humanity and goodness," are the most complete exemplars of the ethic of absolute ends. Here Weber has sometimes been misinterpreted. Daniel Bell, for example, regards the political extremist for whom "all sacrifices, all means are acceptable for the achievement of one's beliefs" as a follower of the ethic of absolute ends, whereas "for those who take on responsibility . . . one's role can be only to reject all absolutes and accept pragmatic compromise." [150] Bell reserves rational, expedient, "responsible" conduct for the politics of compromise and moderation he favors, so he assigns the extremist, the revolutionary, the totalitarian to Weber's other type, the believer in an ethic of absolute ends. But the political fanatic who believes that his end justifies *any* means stands at the opposite pole from the man of boundless faith who refuses to separate means from ends at all. The former is in truth an extreme or ultimate proponent of Weber's ethic of responsibility, justifying whatever course of action promises to be successful in advancing his cause. Arthur Koestler's polarity of the Yogi and the Commissar refers to the extreme versions of each ethic.[151] True, in a psychological sense it is often the case that *les extrèmes se touchent,* as Weber acutely perceived in noting that: "In the world of realities, as a rule, we encounter the ever-renewed experience that the adherent of an ethic of ultimate ends suddenly turns into a chiliastic prophet. Those, for example, who have just preached 'love against violence' now call for the use of force for the *last* violent deed, which would then lead to a state of affairs in which *all* violence is annihilated." [152] Thus peacemaking statesmen become ardent leaders of a "war to end all wars," anarchist-pacifists suddenly turn into bomb-throwing terrorists, and the "flower child" preaching love and peace becomes a mini-revolutionary adopting "up against the wall!" as his slogan.

But if few men are courageous or otherworldly enough to be true practitioners of the ethic of absolute ends, it is also the case that few men are ruthless enough to act *only* with regard to the immediate consequences of their acts which bear on the fortunes of their cause. The extreme adherent to an ethic of responsibility is also an ideal type infrequently encountered in reality. If all politics—indeed all life among men—involves acting in accordance with the maxim "the end

---

[150] Daniel Bell, *The End of Ideology* (New York: The Free Press of Glencoe, 1960), pp. 288–89.

[151] Arthur Koestler, *The Yogi and the Commissar* (New York: The Macmillan Company, 1945), pp. 3–14.

[152] *Essays*, p. 122.

justifies the means," this does not mean that any and all efficacious means are equally acceptable. Actually the phrase "the end justifies the means," far from expressing an amoral Machiavellianism, is a simple tautology, for "means" *are* nothing but acts that are chosen because it is believed they will achieve given ends. Only the ends they are thought to serve *can* justify particular means. The Machiavellian in the popular sense, or the follower of Koestler's "Commissar Ethics," is not he who justifies his means by the ends they serve, but he who is prepared to act without restraint and with total opportunism to advance his ends. He is no less a follower of the ethic of responsibility than a moderate, compromising politician: "responsibility" was not to Weber a "halo word," whatever it may be to Daniel Bell, but a purely descriptive term connoting the taking into account of the consequences of one's actions rather than merely the intentions motivating them.

Since most politicians are neither saints nor ruthless Machiavellians, they combine at some level the two ethics. They act responsibly up to a point where they find themselves inwardly compelled to announce in Luther's words "here I stand; I can do no other." At some point they take their stand on a principle that is absolute for them even though the consequences of complying with it may be temporarily or permanently unfavorable. They will fight an election campaign fiercely but acquiesce in a negative verdict of the voters even if they could stay in office by force; they will wage a war but refrain from the wanton killing of civilian populations (unhappily, this century has seen few such national leaders!); they will strive to persuade their constituents to support a policy they approve, but if unsuccessful will vote their principles rather than their interest in re-election. Some of these examples suggest rare political courage. For men who display it, Weber observed, "an ethic of ultimate ends and an ethic of responsibility are not absolute contrasts but rather supplements, which only in unison constitute a genuine man—a man who *can* have the 'calling for politics.' " [153] Men who live *off* rather than *for* politics, making a living from political office as other men do from the pursuit of other occupations, are, Weber thought, far more common. And many of those who "profess the *ethos* of politics as a cause" are romantics or braggarts who lack "the trained relentlessness in viewing the realities of life and the ability to face such realities and to measure up to them inwardly" that a true calling for politics requires. Weber's admiration for the exceptional man, the hero, the charismatic leader of his people, is evident in these passages. But the average politician is neither a hero, a scoun-

[153] Ibid., p. 127.

drel, nor a totally self-interested timeserver: he too at some level combines an ethic of responsibility with an ethic of absolute ends.

Weber died in 1920 before the disorder, violence, and horrors of twentieth-century politics had reached their zenith—before Stalin and Hitler, the interwar triumphs of fascism, nuclear weapons, and the rise of revolutionary nationalism in the third world. It is illuminating to extend his analysis of the two political ethics by examining the strains they have undergone and the new forms and combinations they have assumed in the experience of recent ideological movements.

Weber regarded anarcho-syndicalism as a contemporary, secularized example of adherence to an ethic of absolute ends. But, as we have seen, he remarked on the tendency of believers in universal love and altruism to become by dialectical reversal "chiliastic prophets," advocating a last great explosion of violence that would for once and for all destroy the gap between the Kingdom of Necessity and the Kingdom of Freedom and achieve the leap from history to Utopia. Karl Mannheim has provided a fuller analysis of the chiliastic mentality from the Anabaptists to modern anarchism. "Chiliasm," he maintained, "sees the revolution as a value in itself, not as an unavoidable means to a rationally set end." [154] He cites in support Bakunin's famous statement, "the will to destroy is a creative will," and his avowal, "I do not believe in constitutions or laws. . . . We need something different. Storm and vitality and a new lawless and consequently free world." Collective solidarity and the ecstasy of brotherly communion forged by revolutionary struggle are the ultimate values affirmed by this outlook rather than destruction and revolution as such. The chiliastic revolutionary sees the purifying, ennobling experience of collective revolt as redeeming men, transvaluing all values, and burning away the husks of their old corrupt selves—this is what moves him to action rather than a coherent vision of a new, more just social order which can only be attained after the painful but necessary surgery of the violent overthrow of existing institutions. Fanon's Sorelian belief in the psychologically liberating role of violence in achieving manhood for the victims of colonial exploitation is a contemporary version of this outlook.[155] Some observers have detected such thoroughly un-Marxist chiliastic aspirations in Mao's effort to revive a revolutionary *élan* in China nearly two decades after his successful conquest of power.

But chiliastic movements have not succeeded in transforming the

---

[154] Karl Mannheim, *Ideology and Utopia* (New York: Harcourt, Brace & Company, Inc., 1946), p. 196.
[155] Frantz Fanon, *The Wretched of the Earth* (New York: Grove Press, Inc., 1963).

world by storming its gates. Sometimes their failure has been followed by a reversal of the transition from saint to revolutionary that Weber described, in which the movement turns inward and "no longer dares to venture forth into the world, and loses its contact with worldly happenings." [156] Chiliasts, however, have also taken the alternative direction of a nihilism that regards violence and banditry to be of exemplary value in constantly "rekindling the flame of protest against the injustice of the social order." [157] That wing of anarchism represented by Nechayev and the Black International with its extolling of the "propaganda of the deed" and the total commitment of the revolutionary to acts of terrorism embodies a nihilism in which violence and heroic conflict are seen as their own justification apart from consequences.

Mannheim noted the similarity between the "absolute presentness" of chiliastic faith and the ahistorical "apotheosis of the deed" he saw as characteristic of fascism. The writings of Georges Sorel were an ideological link between fascism and the revolutionism of the Left in the early part of this century. Today many observers have discerned similarities to nihilism and fascism in the crude *soi-disant* guerrilla Marxism of New Left student movements. The German sociologist, Jürgen Habermas, an erstwhile sympathizer, has described the German student movement as a species of "left fascism." Lewis Coser has noted the resemblances between Nechayevism, Mannheim's characterization of the fascist outlook, and the ideology of guerrilla warfare in the influential writings of the young French philosopher-revolutionary, Régis Debray.[158] Many others have commented on the extent to which the tactics of confrontation, disruption, and the presentation of "nonnegotiable demands" have seemed to become ends-in-themselves for student radicals lacking any systematic ideology but full of militant determination to make a "revolution for the hell of it," as one of them has only half-facetiously put it.

Mannheim's analysis of fascism drew largely on the somewhat more structured ideology of Italian fascism rather than on Nazism. But, as all of Hitler's biographers have noted, the experience of front-line combat in the First World War fundamentally shaped his outlook and that of most of the other early Nazis, who were aptly described by Konrad Heiden as "armed bohemians to whom war is home and civil war fatherland." At its crudest level, Nazism worshipped war, violence,

---

[156] Mannheim. *Ideology and Utopia*, p. 213.

[157] *Essays*, p. 121.

[158] Lewis A. Coser, "Nechayev in the Andes," *Dissent*, XV (January–February, 1968), 41–44.

physical brutality, and marching men as absolute values, rationalizing these sentiments with clichés and vulgarizations drawn from Neitzschean, Darwinian, and racist theories. To Weber, the Christian who truly lives by the teachings of the Sermon on the Mount, turning the other cheek and eschewing all violence, was the true apostle of the ethic of absolute ends. He failed to see that the total inversion of these teachings can also lead to a kind of ethic—or antiethic—of absolute ends, exalting violence, war, and the slaughter of one's enemies rather than peace, love, and the service of others.[159] But then he died before Hitler.

Nihilism and violence worship still represent individualized attitudes or credos, attracting Heiden's "armed bohemians," Arendt's "leaders of the mob," and Stern's "apostles of cultural despair" in a world that seems hostile or indifferent to their aspirations. The leaders of a totalitarian party in power, however, are compelled to develop at least exoteric legitimations to win the allegiance of their ordinary, conservative subjects. Weber did not foresee the peculiar blend of charismatic and bureaucratic elements in totalitarian appeals for legitimacy. The totalitarian rulers' personal resolution of the ends-means dilemmas posed by political action—the elite's esoteric legitimation of its role, as it were—suggests another route away from an ethic of responsibility towards an ethic of absolute ends.

Its nature is best revealed in the famous speech of Orwell's Prosecutor, O'Brien, in *1984*:

> The Party seeks power entirely for its own sake. We are not interested in the good of others; we are interested solely in power. Not wealth or luxury or long life or happiness; only power, pure power. . . . We are different from all the oligarchies of the past in that we know what we are doing. All the others, even those who resembled ourselves, were cowards and hypocrites. The German Nazis and the Russian Communists came very close to us in their methods, but they never had the courage to recognize their own motives. They pretended, perhaps they even believed, that they had seized power unwillingly and for a limited time, and that just around the corner there lay a paradise where human beings would be free and equal. We are not like that. We know that no one ever seizes power with the intention of relinquishing it. Power is not a means; it is an end. One does not establish a dictatorship in order to

---

[159] "The point . . . is not the use of violence *per se*, not even on an unprecedented scale, but that 'totalitarian indifference' to moral considerations is actually based upon a reversal of all our legal and moral concepts, which ultimately rest on the commandment, 'Thou shalt not kill.' Against this totalitarian 'morals' preaches almost openly the precept: Thou shalt kill!" Hannah Arendt, "Discussion," in Carl J. Friedrich, ed., *Totalitarianism* (New York: Grosset & Dunlap, Inc., 1964), p. 78.

safeguard a revolution; one makes the revolution in order to establish the dictatorship. The object of persecution is persecution. The object of torture is torture. The object of power is power.[160]

Orwell, as Philip Rahv has noted, intended this speech both to recall and to refute the ideas of Dostoevski's Grand Inquisitor, whose famous argument for the despotism of a "dedicated sect doing evil that good may come" deeply influenced Weber's formulation of the inevitable tension between ethics and politics. Orwell meant in O'Brien's speech to lay bare the fundamental praxis of totalitarian movements according to which the exalted utopian goals they profess to serve become mere ritual incantations imposing no limits on their freedom to maneuver with a maximum of opportunism and flexibility, to reverse the "party line" overnight, if necessary. Totalitarian movements are, as Raymond Aron has brilliantly put it, "orthodoxies without doctrines." Their real aims are those expressed by O'Brien and their ultimate object of worship is the "organizational weapon" of the party cadres. As Irving Howe and Lewis Coser, writing of the Stalinists, observe, it was not "ideology as such which bound the members . . . in reality it was *the organization as the faith made visible* which was the primary object of loyalty." [161] The totalitarian activist collapses his professed ends into his means, reversing the procedure by which the saintly adherent to an ethic of absolute ends abolishes the ends-means distinction and the painful choices it involves. In Weberian terms, the organizational instrument for attaining power, the party, becomes itself a charismatic object even as it continues to be a disciplined, purposeful, rationally organized association. Thus bureaucracy is invested with charisma to a degree seldom achieved by most bureaucratic structures, which in their functional rationality spread disenchantment and alienation rather than passionate dedication.[162] Or, in another Weberian dichotomy, the totalitarian party commands the total allegiance of its members that is characteristic of the religious sect while retaining at the same time the hierarchical and differentiated structure of an established church.

The power worship of the totalitarian *apparatchik* is not accounted for by the familiar argument that ruthless means corrupt those who

[160] George Orwell, *1984* (New York: Harcourt, Brace & Company, Inc., 1949), pp. 266–67.

[161] Irving Howe and Lewis A. Coser, *The American Communist Party: A Critical History* (Boston: Beacon Press, 1957), p. 521 (italics in original). The best analysis of the totalitarian belief in "organizational omnipotence" is Hannah Arendt, *The Origins of Totalitarianism* (New York: Harcourt, Brace & Company, Inc., 1951), pp. 396–98.

[162] Helen Constas, "Max Weber's Two Conceptions of Bureaucracy," *American Journal of Sociology*, LIII (January, 1958), 400–409.

use them and thus defeat noble ends, although this occurs often enough in reality. The follower's loyalty to the movement is a form of belief with *sui generis* psychological sources rather than the eventual outcome of a process of socialization, or rather desocialization. It is a belief differing markedly from that of the committed revolutionary who is convinced that "Alas, we who wished to lay the foundations of kindness could not ourselves be kind" (Brecht), or who, like Sartre's Hoederer in *Les Mains Sales*, argues that humanity can only be saved by those who are prepared to "plunge their hands up to the elbows in blood and shit." Such men are extreme representatives of an ethic of responsibility, acutely aware of the tragic tension between means and ends; they are usually the founders and earliest followers of revolutionary movements long before the conquest of power. After the movement has triumphed, they are likely to be the victims of purges carried out by new men who are thralls to the fetishism of the organization.

But the totalitarian conversion of an organizational instrument into a finalistic value is only an extreme instance of a more general process that has been noted by many students of bureaucracy. Michels' "iron law of oligarchy," for example, involves the substitution by the leaders of a mass organization of organizational survival and their own continued incumbency in office for the ideological goals and the interests of the rank-and-file members which are the organization's ostensible *raison d'être*. Eduard Bernstein, who was neither a totalitarian nor even a revolutionary but a convinced democrat, said "the goal is nothing, the movement is all," a slogan that appealed to Sorel, who influenced both anarcho-syndicalist and fascist ideology.[163] Merton's "bureaucratic personality type" and Whyte's "organization man" also attribute intrinsic value to functional, special-purpose organizations and their operating rules, and are pictured as flourishing today in all such organizations.

What Merton refers to as the "process of sanctification" of bureaucratic methods and structures, however, does not imply that those subject to it are fully conscious of and able to articulate the values that are revealed in their behavior. Merton and other analysts of the pathologies of bureaucracy are describing rather an objective tendency implicit in the daily routines of the bureaucratic functionary. The junior business executive is likely to be somewhat shamefaced if he becomes aware of the degree to which he has permitted the corporation to dominate his mind and spirit—at least the alleged success of Whyte's book among executives suggests as much. Even in the case of the totalitarian partisan, Orwell's O'Brien maintains that the Nazis and Com-

---

[163] E. H. Carr, *Studies in Revolution* (London: Macmillan & Co., 1950), p. 158.

munists, unlike himself, were unable to face up to what they were really doing and deceived themselves with rationalizations. Since O'Brien is a fictional character, one may readily agree with Philip Rahv that:

> Orwell fails to distinguish, in the behavior of O'Brien, between psychological and objective truth. Undoubtedly it is O'Brien, rather than Dostoievski's Grand Inquisitor, who reveals the real nature of total power; yet that does not settle the question of O'Brien's personal psychology, the question, that is, of his ability to live with this naked truth as his sole support; nor is it conceivable that the party-elite to which he belongs could live with this truth for very long. Evil, far more than good, is in need of the pseudo-religious justifications so readily provided by the ideologies of world happiness and compulsory salvation, ideologies generated by both the Left and the Right.[164]

I have moved some distance from Weber's discussion of different orientations towards politics, for he was primarily concerned with manifest judgments and values and the degree of "inner poise" with which they were held. Yet, as his account of the evolution of ascetic Calvinism into a shallow, worldly acquisitiveness indicates, he was highly sensitive to the tortuous dialectic of ideas in history that so often produces caricatures and travesties of what their original adherents intended. Weber anticipated the obsolescence of the leading political ideologies of his time and was to that extent a herald of what later came to be called with considerable overstatement the "end of ideology." Yet he died before the grip of ideologies on men, including the nationalism to which he himself was commited, helped bring about a European civil war that reduced not only Germany but Europe itself to the status of a second-rate power in world politics.

Weber's political sociology remained incomplete. He developed an exhaustive typology of religious attitudes and beliefs in his sociology of religion and the starting-point of his analysis of different political outlooks was the recognition of inescapable conflict between religious ethics and the "demon of politics." He was aware of the continuing dependence of political ideals on religious world views. One has the impression that today political ideologies have become more autonomous, that religious ideas have become parasitic upon secular belief systems rather than the reverse. Divorced from their religious origins, political ideologies become more menacing in their remorseless worldliness, their failure to provide experiences of transcendence while unavoidably frustrating the millenarian hopes and expectations they

---

[164] Philip Rahv, "The Unfuture of Utopia," *Partisan Review*, XVI (July, 1949), 743–49.

arouse. We need urgently to understand the modalities of political faith and apostasy; Weber and Mannheim provide a valuable beginning.

That Weber himself possessed charismatic gifts is incontestable. Julius Freund remarks skeptically that the number of German university teachers who claim to be former students of Weber is surprising in view of the two very short periods, separated by nineteen years, in which Weber engaged in active teaching. Yet when he returned to teaching at Vienna and Munich at the end of the First World War, so many flocked to hear him that it was difficult to find a lecture hall large enough to hold them all. Anyone who has spoken with Weber's former students and colleagues—and I have encountered them in quite out-of-the-way corners of the United States—will have been struck by their apparently total recall of their contacts with him. I met one who produced a booming imitation of a classroom witticism of Weber's; another who described in detail Weber's dignified and stately appearance as he marched in an academic procession at the University of Munich where he held a chair for the last year of his life; still another recalled the color of the dress and the demeanor of Weber's wife at his funeral; a memorialist has given a detailed account of a visit to Weber on his deathbed. Perhaps there is a good deal of German hero-worship in all this, as well as the nostalgia of elderly exiles who "want to say that we're at the dwarf end of all times and mere children whose only share in grandeur is like a boy's share in fairytale kings, beings of a different kind from times better and stronger than ours." [165]

Perhaps. Yet the combination of soaring eloquence and biting realism Weber's prose sometimes achieves is capable of enthralling readers —even in translation—across the years and conveys a sense of the moral and intellectual intensity of the man behind it. As Ernest Topitsch recalls: "In the midst of this twilight atmosphere of insidious intellectual dishonesty, the work of Max Weber shed a flood of cold hard light. Anyone who has once been thunderstruck by contact with him can never see the world in the same light again." [166] The "twilight atmosphere" to which Topitsch alludes is that of Vienna at the end of the Second World War, but which of us in this troubled, apocalyptic century has escaped an atmosphere of "insidious intellectual dishonesty"? One cannot read "Politics as a Vocation" and "Science as a Vocation"

[165] Saul Bellow, *The Adventures of Augie March* (New York: The Viking Press, Inc., 1953), p. 60.
[166] Quoted by Carl Cerny, op. cit., p. 57.

today without contemporary parallels to the attitudes Weber describes and decries springing to mind—these essays possess in full the "relevance" students are now demanding so insistently from their teachers, though not perhaps precisely in the way the students have in mind. And they spoke just as directly to me when I first read them in 1946 in the Gerth-Mills translation in New York rather than in Topitsch's Vienna.

I am therefore at a loss to understand how Gary Runciman in an otherwise excellent discussion of Weber's political sociology could have written: "Nobody can ever have said of Weber what Bernard Shaw is supposed to have said after reading *Capital*: 'Karl Marx made a man of me.' " [167] Perhaps English *sang-froid,* or insularity, or distrust of intellectual difficulty and complexity explain it, although Runciman's own valuable sociological writings would seem to disprove the latter. But the comparison with Marx is inevitable. Marx converts people— or at least did so at the time when Bernard Shaw read him and for some time afterwards—to a new and complex but essentially affirmative view of things. Weber is more likely to disillusion them, to suggest that stoicism is the only honest and noble attitude towards life and history. Marx has truly been called the last great thinker of the Enlightenment. For Weber "the rosy blush of the Enlightenment has irretrievably faded," and worthwhile action is only possible for "he who can say 'in spite of all.' "

Max Weber, Sigmund Freud, and George Orwell have been my intellectual heroes for many years, since the period immediately after the Second World War when my outlook was formed. Not very original choices for one coming of intellectual age at that time, for all three exemplify what Philip Rieff has called the "post-liberal imagination," all three are stoics, fanatical believers in intellectual integrity who rejected both cynical and Dionysian antinomianism while refusing to offer consolation of any sort. Such a choice of heroes dates me in a period when enthusiasms, angers, and utopian hopes have, to the surprise of us all, once again powerfully gripped the more sensitive and thoughtful of the younger generation. Are we in the presence of a genuine new prophecy or is this a revival of the "sterile excitation" and the "ubiquitous chase after 'experience' " that Weber detected in German youth fifty years ago? We must withhold final judgment. But one's intellectual heroes seem to possess an enduring relevance transcending both their own historical period and the period in which one first responded to them—that indeed is what makes them one's heroes. One's heroes of action, on the other hand, are inevitably far more time-

---

[167] Runciman, op. cit., p. 52.

bound: my own list begins and ends with such names as Father Bernhard Lichtenberg, Franz Jägerstätter, Kurt Gerstein—the saints and martyrs of the Nazi resistance.

Weber's reputation has steadily grown in the last twenty years to the point where probably only Marx and Freud are more widely known and respected as social thinkers by the general intellectual public in Western countries. Superficial acquaintance with Weber's leading ideas has become *de rigueur* for the knowledgeable intellectual, as the increasing frequency of reference to them in both high-brow and even middle-brow journals of opinion in England and America indicates. Undoubtedly, the protest against rigid centralized bureaucracy in the advanced industrial countries, of which the New Left is the most salient manifestation, has contributed to wider familiarity with at least a few catchwords culled from Weber. For Weber rather than Marx often appears to be the prophet of the past who has most fully drawn the face of the contemporary enemy, even though he was no revolutionary, described himself as a "class-conscious bourgeois," and to a degree accepted, though in a fatalistic spirit, the spread of bureaucracy as an irreversible social process.

Within academic sociology, Durkheim has, of course, been a figure of comparable influence. I confess that I find many aspects of Durkheim's thought repellent and have always had, like Raymond Aron, "to force myself to recognize the merits, however splendid, of Durkheim, whereas Max Weber never irritates me even when I feel most remote from him." [168] Conceding this bias, there seem to me to be two respects in which the treatment of Weber by sociologists differs from that accorded Durkheim. First, they are less inclined unconsciously to patronize him as a kind of icon of their profession by referring respectfully to him but paraphrasing or translating his ideas into a more contemporary idiom. Weber simply does not lend himself to this—he *is* too much our contemporary, grappling with intellectual problems we still confront in a conceptual language that, far from striking us as outdated, we have yet to master fully ourselves. Secondly, at the point where social science blends with social criticism and moral vision, American social scientists of widely different ideological persuasions have found sustenance for their views in Weber: C. Wright Mills, a founding father of the New Left; H. Stuart Hughes, a liberal socialist; Robert Nisbet, an articulate Tocquevillian conservative; Benjamin Nelson, a tireless critic of utopian thinking; and such sympathetic defenders and interpreters of modern industrial society as Talcott Parsons and Edward Shils, all owe something not merely to Weber's ideas

---

[168] Aron, op. cit., p. viii.

but to his spirit and his vision. Important as we may find Durkheim as a sociological theorist, "we are not," as Aron observes, "really interested either in Durkheim's political ideas or in the moral theories which he hoped to disseminate in teachers' colleges." [169]

But the situation is rather different in Germany where Weber's political views remain controversial, as the 1964 Heidelberg conference and the debate over Wolfgang Mommsen's book attest. Weber was a nationalist who wished Germany to be a great power; he favored democracy not as an ultimate value but because he thought it the system of government most likely to produce great mass leaders, and, as has recently been thoroughly documented,[170] his ideals of heroic individualism owed much to Nietzsche. Understandably, German intellectuals cannot be expected to overlook the possible affinities between these beliefs and the words and deeds of the Nazis. But Weber was a peculiar kind of nationalist who attacked the Kaiser, the Junkers, the bourgeoisie, and the military leaders far more bitterly than he assailed the Social Democrats and the working class, who rejoiced when he took frequent trips outside Germany before 1914, who shared Nietzsche's contempt for racism and anti-Semitism, and whose views, even in the period when he was most aggressively a nationalist, were so offensive to the nationalist Right that his classes were often disrupted by right-wing students. Certainly there was much of the *furor teutonicus* in him,[171] but we have for a long time sensed a connection between what is greatest and most sublime in German thought and the brooding passion, the black romanticism, that the Nazis embodied in their crudest and most demonic form. As Nietzsche wrote: "Furthermore, it is quite possible that the very value of those good and honored things consists, in fact, in their insidious relatedness to these wicked, seemingly opposite things—it could be that they are inextricably bound up, entwined, perhaps even similar in their very nature." [172]

The value of objectivity, stressed so heavily by Weber in his methodological essays, obviously meant more to him than simply the specification of a prerequisite for sound scholarship or conformity to scientific method. Objectivity is also a moral demand reflecting a vision of the world, a way of doing full justice to the "irreconcilable conflict" between the values of "the various life-spheres in which we are placed,

---

[169] Ibid., p. 245.

[170] Eugene Fleischman, "De Weber à Nietzsche," *Archives Européenes de Sociologie,* II (1964), 190–238.

[171] For a balanced appraisal, see Guenther Roth and Bennett Berger, "Max Weber and the Organized Society," *New York Times Book Review,* April 3, 1966, pp. 6 ff. and 44 ff.

[172] Friedrich Nietzsche, *Beyond Good and Evil* (Chicago: Henry Regnery Co., 1955), p. 3.

each of which is governed by different laws." As Weber insisted in "Science as a Vocation":

> The primary task of a useful teacher is to teach his students to recognize "inconvenient" facts—I mean facts that are inconvenient for their party opinions. And for every party opinion there are facts that are extremely inconvenient, for my own opinion no less than for others. I believe the teacher accomplishes more than a mere intellectual task if he compels his audience to accustom itself to the existence of such facts. I would be so immodest as even to apply the expression "moral achievement," though perhaps this may sound too grandiose for something that should go without saying.[173]

By "moral achievement" Weber did not have in mind the value of objectivity to the service of science or the accumulation of knowledge for its own sake, as too many contemporary academic men are inclined to assume in their self-satisfied professionalism. To Weber, objectivity is to be valued for the contribution it makes to "self-clarification and a sense of responsibility," to helping the individual "to give himself an account of the ultimate meaning of his own conduct." There is no rational criterion for choosing between the demands the different lifespheres make upon us, demands which none of us can entirely escape, but a wise teacher can at least confront us with the necessity of making a choice and with some of the probable consequences of whatever choice we make.

Weber himself was for most of his life torn between the demons of politics and of scholarship as vocations. Thus "Politics as a Vocation" and "Science as a Vocation" in combination amount to a kind of *apologia pro vita sua* in addition to summarizing in superbly condensed form the major themes of his scholarship. His political views were profoundly shaped by his Nietzschean conviction of the need for exceptional men, charismatic heroes who could rise above both tradition and bureaucratic mechanism to cope with the turbulence of the no longer voiceless masses and the dangerous tensions within the European system of competing nation-states. Yet characteristically he also defined the charismatic leader in an ethically neutral fashion, insisting that such a leader might serve good or evil ends, that he might be either a saint and a heroic prophet or a charlatan and a demagogic man of war. There can be no doubt that he was aware of his own charismatic gifts. His political aspirations were never realized, for much of his life he was no more than a private scholar suffering from a paralyzing neurosis, his massive work remained highly incomplete, he died before

---

[173] *Essays*, p. 147. See also the more extensive discussion, first published fourteen years earlier, in *Methodology*, pp. 52–57.

he was sixty. Yet he carries an unmistakable aura of personal heroism that even his bitterest critics have been unable entirely to resist.

A NOTE ON THE SELECTIONS

Since Max Weber has been one of the three or four most influential social theorists of this century, there is no shortage of published discussions of his work. In addition to seeking excellent summaries and interpretations of broad rather than narrowly specialized areas of his scholarship, I have employed two main criteria in choosing contributions to this book.

First, I have looked for writings that are not already well-known and easily available in anthologies or paperback editions to students of sociology and social science in the United States; and secondly, I have tried to include treatments of Weber's work that are to some degree representative of the thinking of contemporary scholars. The first rule explains why I have omitted selections from such valuable essays as the Gerth and Mills introduction to the first—and still the best—book-length collection in English of Weber's writings, Leo Strauss' critique, and such famous contributions to the debate over the Protestant ethic thesis as those of R. H. Tawney and others. But perhaps my two criteria tend to cancel each other out—the reader will have to be the judge of that. For the effort to achieve representativeness necessitates the inclusion of Weber's most prominent and prolific interpreters: an anthology of commentaries on Weber that left out Raymond Aron, Reinhard Bendix, or Talcott Parsons would be like *Hamlet* without the Prince of Denmark. I have, however, tried to find early or less accessible contributions from these men.

On the other hand, the desire to avoid the familiar has, in light of inevitable space limitations, led me to omit any discussion of Weber's views on social stratification and to include only one short contribution on bureaucracy, although his ideas have undoubtedly influenced more sociological research in these two fields than in any others. But Robert Nisbet's observation that "no one has yet added to Weber's theory . . . of bureaucracy any theoretical element that is not at least implicit in his own statements on the subject" [174] seems to me to apply with even greater cogency to the subject of social stratification.

Part One, on Weber's methodological views, opens with two differing judgments of Weber's conception of social science and its relation to natural science: Raymond Aron is sympathetic to Weber's historicism, while Talcott Parsons regards it as an obstacle to the search for

[174] Nisbet, op. cit., p. 142.

general propositions that he sees as the goal of all science. This section ends with a brief reminder by Benjamin Nelson, a sociologist-historian, of the scope and depth of Weber's historical scholarship.

Karl Loewith's long two-part article, "Max Weber und Karl Marx," was originally published in 1932 in one of the last issues of *Archiv für Sozialwissenschaft und Sozialpolitik,* the famous social science journal of which Max Weber himself became co-editor in 1904 and which was suppressed after Hitler came to power. The section of this essay dealing with Weber here appears in English translation for the first time. The extent to which later interpreters of Weber are indebted to Loewith's frequently cited article for their understanding of the concept of rationalization as the key to Weber's thought should now become evident to a wider reading public. Loewith's argument that Weber's individualistic values are reflected in his very methodological categories is also worthy of attention in that it suggests the need for modification of Weber's sharp distinction between "value-relevance" as the basis for the choice of a problem and "value-free" methods as the means of investigating it, now that a new generation of sociologists has become increasingly dissatisfied with the positivist dichotomy of fact and value.

Herbert Luethy is a Swiss historian who has also contributed a number of brilliant essays on contemporary politics and culture to such English-language journals as *Commentary* and *Encounter.* In the selection reprinted here, Luethy does more than merely review the controversy over the relation between Calvinism and capitalism initiated by Weber but makes an original contribution to it. The brief selection from Carlo Antoni, Italian philosopher and pupil of Benedetto Croce, suggests that in the context of Weber's sociology of religion as a whole his outlook was less antithetical to historical materialism than conventional summaries of the Protestant ethic thesis usually assume.

Peter Blau's brief discussion of Weber's theory of bureaucracy, adapted for a symposium on the major fields of American sociology from what was originally a textbook presentation,[175] has been included as a fairly typical expression of the viewpoint of American students of formal organization. Originality rather than typicality, however, dictated my choice of Blau's longer article on Weber's theory of authority, in which the author not only subjects Weber's concepts to a detailed critical analysis but advances a new definition of authority that impresses me as being superior to all previous ones.

The promiscuous abuse of Weber's notion of charisma as an attribute of some political leaders is the starting-point of Reinhard Bendix's

[175] Peter M. Blau and W. R. Scott, *Formal Organizations* (San Francisco: Chandler Publishing Co., 1962), pp. 32–36.

essay, which ably suggests the complexity of leadership as a phenomenon in reviewing the biographies of four Asian heads of state.

The last two selections indicate the political and ideological ambi-
ence of Weber's political sociology and the controversies to which it
continues to give rise. Wolfgang Mommsen, a German historian, re-
states his thesis that Weber was primarily a nationalist and an elitist
rather than the liberal democrat pictured by some of his admirers, a
thesis which was first advanced in Mommsen's 1959 book *Max Weber
und die deutsche Politik, 1890–1920*. Guenther Roth, a young American sociologist of German origin, defends Weber from his critics on
both the Left and the Right as a realist who cast a cold eye on all
salvationist ideologies.

PART ONE

METHODOLOGICAL VIEWS

ONE

THE LOGIC
OF THE SOCIAL SCIENCES

RAYMOND ARON

Max Weber always declared himself, so far as the logic of science is concerned, a disciple of Rickert. I shall try to show what Weber acquired from Rickert and what he did with it. Rickert's fundamental ideas are well known. The sensible world is infinite and no knowledge can be complete. Science deals with this infinity either, as in the case of physics, by confining its attention to the general and repeatable, or, as in the case of history, by selecting from the phenomena only those which interest us, which are related to human values. Thus a distinction is made between the natural sciences which seek to establish general laws, and the cultural sciences which isolate individual phenomena in order to trace their unique development.

Weber preserves the intention behind this attempt, namely that of establishing the special character and the objectivity of history. One of the strongest prejudices of positivism is to regard as scientific only those disciplines which establish laws. Durkheim's sociology is dominated by the idea that history, dealing with a mass of isolated facts, can never be a science. Weber's sociology, on the contrary, has as its

"The Logic of the Social Sciences." From Raymond Aron, *German Sociology* (Glencoe, Ill.: The Free Press, 1957), pp. 68–82. Reprinted by permission of Heinemann Educational Books Ltd. and The Macmillan Company. Footnotes have been omitted for reasons of space.

77

starting point a recognition of history as an objective science of development. This does not mean that, in the field of social phenomena, only
the study of unique events or sequences is legitimate or useful. It will
be seen later how Weber's sociology gradually becomes distinguished
from history. But it is not distinguished as a discipline which establishes laws, or as a genuine science as popularly conceived; it is a com-
plementary discipline, defined by another direction of man's desire
for knowledge.

Weber also retains the idea of the infinitude of the sensible world,
and of selection by values; but these ideas take on a different aspect
in his writings. They are effective weapons against naturalistic prejudices, they contribute to the definition of a method, and they establish
within the realm of science the liberty of the individual. Weber's
theories always have, in fact, this triple significance, polemical, methodological and philosophical.

Reality is not reducible to a system of laws. The plenitude of the
sensible world makes impossible any complete explanation. These
observations are equally valid for the reality studied by the natural
sciences. Prediction is only successful within closed or simplified systems. We could not calculate in advance the ways in which a shattered
stone or an exploding grenade would splinter. This inability does
not greatly disturb us, since in this case we are only concerned with the
general laws of such events. But in cultural matters, we are interested
also in the specific characteristics of qualitative phenomena. No body
of laws (economic laws, evolutionary laws) exhausts the task or constitutes the aim of the science of culture.

Weber also regards the "relation to values" as a fundamental procedure in order to apprehend scientifically the singular or unique. In
Rickert's work, this procedure is intended to transcend the sensible
world, to create a meaningful reality and to establish the objectivity
of historical science. It is the case that, in a particular society, all the
members accept, not the same value judgments, but the same formal
scheme of values. Not everyone considers the problems of the state in
the same way, but everyone agrees that these problems raise questions
of values, and this is enough to make the selection of the objects of
historical science, within a particular group, objectively valid. Moreover, there is at least one value which must be admitted by any science,
namely truth. This is sufficient to justify theoretically the idea of a
universal system of values, and therefore the possibility of a universal
history.

What does Weber make of this notion of selection by values? The
first two functions are conserved, namely that of transcending the

infinity of the sensible world, and that of distinguishing the field of culture. But it is no longer held that the same objects attract the interest of all historians or of all members of a particular society. It is quite natural that different historians should interest themselves in different aspects, and that they should select their object from the abundance of things in accordance with their particular values. Weber never seems to conceive the objectivity of history as founded upon a universal system of values. On the contrary, such a system (supposing it to be possible, which Weber questions) would be a matter for philosophy and not for science. Further, while Rickert emphasised the need to relate facts to the values of the period studied, Weber refers principally to their relation to *our* values. The past is brought into relation with the present. Or rather, *we* ask questions of the past, and without such questions there would be no historical science.

It follows, that *there is no objective science of the entire past or of society as a whole*. Any science of culture is partial (even if it establishes laws) because its point of departure is *legitimately arbitrary*. It can only be a positive science if it is conscious of this unavoidable limitation. It establishes objectively the causal relations which explain the development of one sector of reality. Consequently, it leaves intact the freedom of the politician, while showing him the means by which to attain his end (in this way the scientist chooses his object). The relations are still closer; the choice of the historical object is determined by the value strivings of the politician. Finally the methodological theme becomes a philosophical conception; the historical flux moves towards an unknown end, always presenting new meanings and new spiritual constructions. In the face of a world which is always new, man does not and will not cease from renewing his curiosity and his knowledge so long as "an ossification of our minds, in the Chinese style, has not made us unaccustomed to posing continually new questions to the inexhaustible wealth of life."

I have shown briefly the place which Rickert's ideas occupy in Weber's thought, in order to emphasise the unity of the man and his work. But it is clear that his methodological principle does not lose any of its rigour for being infused with philosophical intentions. The choice of an object means an enlargement, not a narrowing, of the historical vision. Durkheim invokes *the* unique and definitive sociology of the future which is to supply *the* system of social laws, and believes that he already possesses *the* classification of societies. Weber opposes to this dogmatism the legitimate multiplicity of approaches and researches, corresponding to the diversity of the spiritual worlds which human societies create. It is the whole man who is the central concern of history and sociology, and the historian who asks questions of the past has the right to become completely involved in the questions which he poses.

But this liberty is not anarchy, for once the choice has been made the historian must submit entirely to reality. Once the historical object is determined, we are no longer free either in the choice of material (which is fixed by the values involved) or in the establishment of causal connections. In other words, the relation to values is a means of subjecting a cultural reality, made up of human desires, to objective study.

The special character of the cultural sciences results, in Rickert's system, mainly from the uniqueness of historical phenomena and from the selection by values. These ideas form only the introduction to Max Weber's work, the two essential aspects of which are a theory of scientific concepts, and a definition of historical knowledge as a synthesis of *understanding* and *causality*.

The "ideal type" should be regarded less as a distinct variety of concept than as a generic name for all the concepts used by the cultural sciences. The ideal type is related to two other features in Weber's thought: first, a thoroughgoing nominalism, and secondly, a conviction that the concepts applied to cultural phenomena cannot be reduced to the framework of traditional logic.

Idea and reality, the general and the particular, "ought" and "is," are always distinct. What "is" cannot be deduced from any law. Concepts are simply indispensable instruments for apprehending the world, and they are always being transcended by a knowledge which only progresses by transcending them. Thus it is necessary to define rigorously the terms employed, not in order to turn science into a closed system, but in order to compare our ideas with reality and then, having realised their inadequacy, to attempt to make our thinking more profound. The function of the ideal type is to make such comparison possible and fruitful.

Furthermore, Weber opposed the ideal type to the concepts of traditional logic and to average types. How could capitalism, liberalism, socialism, or the State, be defined by the rule of *per genus proximum et differentiam?* It is equally impossible to define the "romantic" or the "Greek" or the "entrepreneur" in terms of characteristics common to all romantics, Greeks, or entrepreneurs, or even in terms of an average of the qualities of individuals belonging to these groups. In practice, we carry out a "stylisation," and retain only what seems characteristic; we construct a type. Thus the ideal type is defined as a mental construct obtained not by a generalisation of the features common to every indi-

vidual but by a Utopian rationalization. We bring together characteristics which are more or less evident in different instances, we emphasize, eliminate, exaggerate, and finally substitute a coherent, rational
whole for the confusion and incoherence of reality.

It is obvious that these two features are not sufficient to define
the ideal type. But it would be difficult to advance any further along
this path, since here, as in all the problems of logic and philosophy,
Weber is an *oppositional* thinker. He only suggests indirectly the more
detailed characteristics and the varieties of the ideal type, in his critical
discussions of the scientific and metaphysical theories which he rejects
or refutes.

The ideal type is, in the first place, a concept which is opposed to
the *concepts of essence,* and represents, so to speak, a positive substitute for them. There are no essences except in relation to, and by
means of, a value judgment. "Authentic Christianity" or "true socialism" are the product of the preferences of the historian or the theologian. Such notions have no place in positive science.

Weber, in harmony with the Kantian tradition, renounces all but
empirical knowledge; modern science does not go beyond the ordering
of experience and the establishment of causal relations. We have
abandoned the illusion that knowledge can attain to the essence of
things, the true being behind appearance, the laws of God and of
Nature. In the same way, in the field of culture, essences such as *Volks-
geist* (the spirit of a people), and holistic concepts applied to phenomena such as the State or the Church, to which we are inclined to attribute a unity and a transcendental existence, have to be abandoned. They
go beyond the scope of scientific knowledge and obstruct attempts at
explanation. Once these metaphysical substances have been rejected,
man becomes a free agent in the world of immanent experience. Similarly, science, freed from essentialist prejudices, is able to construct,
out of any historical phenomenon, a multiplicity of ideal concepts, according to the direction of our interest and the needs of research. We
are doubtless ignorant of the spirit of capitalism. But we can freely
create ideal types of capitalism: e.g., an economic system motivated by
the pursuit of private profit, or a rationalized economic system in
which enterprises, separated from the family and organised in accordance with definite rules, produce for the market and use free labour.
There are no true or false definitions, but only definition which are
more or less fruitful.

The ideal types emancipate us from naturalistic prejudices as well
as from metaphysical illusions. The positivist is tempted to regard as
essential those characteristics which are universal; he would define
religion *essentially* by those characteristics which are present in all

religions. He then strives to establish *the* valid definition; at the beginning of his enquiry he chooses the characteristic which is most obvious or most frequent, and hopes to arrive in due course at a complete definition (assuming that he does not, by degrees, come to regard his initial definition as adequate). On the contrary, in Weber's work, still more than in his theory, the ideal type is employed to discover the *unique features* of each historical phenomenon. His definition of capitalism is obtained by distinguishing those facts peculiar to Western civilisation, or at least especially developed in this civilisation. In its application to historical entities the ideal type, as distinct from the general concept in traditional logic and in positivism, is intended to reveal individual and unique characteristics rather than similarities or general features. The ideal type can be used equally well in formulating a problem (how did capitalism, regarded as the achievement of a particular kind of organization of labour which is only found in the West, originate?), or in expounding the results, or in research (to what extent does reality conform to the ideal type?).

The ideal type, which expresses the scientist's liberty to determine the object of his enquiry and which is an instrument of a science of the particular, becomes clearer by this twofold contrast with essence and universality. It is further defined by the elimination of any confusion between itself and reality. Such confusion is particularly easy since ideas and ideals are also real phenomena (of a psychological order). If, for example, we construct an ideal type of liberalism, we are concerned with liberalism as a political system or as a human attitude. But liberals themselves had a certain conception and a certain ideal of liberalism. We can, therefore, also construct an ideal type of the liberal ideal. It is important to be always aware of this distinction between the ideal conceptions held by individuals in past ages, and the ideal types of which we are speaking. A particular legal rule has an influence upon conduct through the conceptions which it produces in the consciousness of individuals. The philosophy of law and jurisprudence also have an effect through the conceptions which they produce. It may appear, therefore, that in this case we can identify the ideal meaning of a law, or of a body of legislation, with reality. But Weber insisted upon a careful distinction between law as a norm and law as fact. For the sociologist, a law signifies only a certain degree of probability that specific actions will be followed by other actions on the part of other persons. The ideal type of a law, or of a body of laws, and the constructs of science or of jurisprudence, are used as instruments for research, for circumscribing the object of enquiry, and for formulating a problem.

In other words, the ideal type can be deduced from ideal or normative realities without changing its character. It is only necessary to distinguish between the sense which *we* give to a rule in our ideal construct and the sense which it had for the men who conformed to it or the jurists who interpreted it. Sociology is concerned with the experienced meaning.

Finally, the ideal type is defined (and this no doubt is the essential point) by contrast with a too ambitious interpretation of economic theory. The so-called classical laws are only a body of ideal-typical constructs; they are instruments of knowledge and not final results. The marginal utility theory, for instance, is not based upon psychology. It indicates what would happen if the behaviour of individuals were similar to the decisions of a merchant continually engaged in the calculation of his liabilities, assets and requirements. It has to be verified empirically; or at least we should try to determine the gap between this ideal type and reality.

The theory of ideal types is, no doubt, incomplete. Perhaps we should distinguish between historical types (modern capitalism), general types (bureaucratic power), and types of rational behaviour (economic theory). Nevertheless, in this case as in others, Weber has grasped what is essential. What needs to be done, in addition to making the distinctions we have just mentioned, is to examine more closely and to make more precise the idea of methodological rationalisation, so as to give full significance to the twofold requirement of causal adequacy and adequacy of meaning.

The uniqueness of the cultural sciences is above all due to the particular satisfaction which human curiosity obtains in this field as a result of "understanding." In the domain of culture positive science apprehends a meaning which, in the study of nature, is only accessible to metaphysics. It is difficult to define "understanding" strictly and Weber himself does not so much define it as suggest its characteristics. He refers to the special kind of evidence associated with the apprehension of meaningful relations, such as those between motive and act, or between end and means. We have an impression of being able to reproduce in ourselves the process of consciousness which we identify in other people.

This transcendence of sense data was, in Weber's view, a characteristic of the cultural sciences, since it allows us to explain an event in its uniqueness, rather than in terms of a general law. Moreover, it leads us beyond a simple ordering of experience such as that of the natural sciences, and provides a means of taking into account the specifically human character of the phenomena we are studying. In other words, we can say that interpretative sociology, in contrast with Durkheim's philosophy, treats the historical world not as a collection of objects, but as a process of development of human lives.

Weber's theory of understanding is extremely difficult to study because its basis is ambiguous, and because, once again, it is used only in controversy. The concept of meaning, which is associated with that of understanding, is likewise obscure; does meaning, as with Rickert, occupy a third sphere between the physical and the mental, or does it denote an aspect of mental phenomena? On the whole, Weber is inclined to accept the latter view, probably under the influence of Jaspers. Further, Weber criticises at length those theories which distinguish the sciences in terms of the objects studied rather than in terms of the directions of human curiosity. The peculiar features of cultural phenomena have an influence upon method, since they permit the supplement of "understanding," but they do not impose the basic principles of individualisation and reference to values. Above all, Weber denies that intuition has a different role in the cultural sciences from that which it has in the natural sciences. The cultural sciences arrive at valid judgments and make use of rigorously defined concepts. The starting point of history is lived experience, but in order to establish a science, this confused experience has to be analysed with reference to values.

Further, relationships, no matter how obvious, are never anything more than hypotheses as long as the motivation to which they point has not been analysed. In other words, Weber wished to establish two principles: first, that there is no immediate apprehension of the object in the cultural sciences, and secondly that science requires an analysis of the given fact and a series of researches in order to establish causal connections.

In order to make more precise the notion of "understanding" it is necessary to refer to Jaspers' conception from which it is derived. Jaspers opposes interpretative relations and causal relations. Understanding is an ultimate datum; the person who has been deceived takes his revenge, the angry man wants to attack his adversary, and so forth. We understand such relations directly; no science can make them clearer to us than they were at first. A causal relation, on the contrary, such as that between the destruction of cortical tissue and aphasia, cannot be understood; the regularity of succession allows us to formulate a rule which we then try to subsume under a more general law. For the psychologist, therefore, there is an absolute distinction between an interpretative relation and a causal relation. The interpretation of behaviour in terms of resentment is incommensurable with its explanation in terms of a condition of the nervous system. Weber's central notion is perhaps best apprehended if one thinks of the need to establish a connection between understanding and determinism. The psychologist is satisfied with the intelligible relation between resentment and a certain type of behaviour, but the sociologist and the historian wish to account for a particular action in terms of resentment. How in fact, is it possible to validate an interpretation which, however obvious it appears, remains a hypothesis in the particular instance being considered?

The rational character of the conceptual schemes employed further reinforces, if it may be so expressed, the hypothetical character of the relation. A rationalising method does not imply any particular conception of human psychology, and still less a metaphysic. No doubt we are tempted to explain human beings in too rational a way because this type of explanation is the nearest to hand and the most convenient, but in every case it is necessary to find out whether our interpretation corresponds to the facts.

Every intelligible relation is by nature hypothetical; that is a fundamental ambiguity. Different individuals react differently to the same external situation. The motives which the individual attributes to himself may be pretexts or justifications; within the consciousness of each individual there is again an ambiguity. Finally, in an identical situation, individuals are struggling with contradictory desires. The interpretative relation is possible as long as it has been demonstrated to be a causal connection. In the case of a particular action we have recourse to explanations which are more or less verifiable (which take account of the knowledge we possess of the person concerned). If it is a question of formulating a rule, repetition (and occasionally statistics) allow us to transform the possible into the actual.

Psychology can contribute to understanding but has no decisive rule. Following Rickert, Weber refused to regard psychology as the basic discipline of the cultural sciences. So-called scientific psychology seemed to him of little value to the historian, since it had a different aim, namely the establishment of laws. The general propositions to which the historian has recourse are, in Weber's view, those of the "wisdom of nations" or of common sense, which it would be pedantic to formulate. The sociologist can and should make use of a more refined psychology, an interpretative psychology such as that of Nietzsche or Freud. Such a psychology does not, however, enable us to choose between the various interpretations which it suggests. For this, whether we are concerned with a single action, or with a type of action, it remains necessary to show that one of the possible relations is the real one, and this is a task for the historian or the sociologist since it requires the introduction of causal explanations. Moreover, it is almost always necessary for us to understand the reaction of an individual to a particular situation, and no psychological factor can account for this. What we have to grasp is, above all, the intention, the combination of means in order to attain an end which is suggested or imposed by the circumstances.

Thus we are always led back to the central problem of single causal connections. In order to be valid, the science of development, of which the point of departure is subjective, must attempt to establish objective relationships. The ideal types are only constructs which are useful in understanding or explaining phenomena, while the interpretative relation is valid only so far as it is also causal. What theory meets these requirements?

To seek the causes of an event is not to reduce succession to a law; this procedure of the natural sciences would eliminate history. The latter attains its end by integrating the particular event which we wish to explain in a unique complex of events. For this, it is indispensable to make a selection among the consequences and to limit the antecedents which are taken into account. The primary condition for establishing historical causality is this selection. It is impossible to give an account of the whole of reality, and a historical cause can only be defined with reference to particular aspects of a given phenomenon. Thus, if one studies the origins of capitalism it is essential to state those aspects of capitalism which are to be taken into consideration. A causal relation cannot be established between one total situation and another, or between one historical moment and another; it is never more than one strand in the whole, and is only established by a conceptual transformation of the crude reality.

The selection of antecedents is carried out in the following way: In order to determine the importance to be attached to a particular antecedent we have to conceive it as changed or nonexistent. We then attempt to visualise, on the basis of our general knowledge, what would have happened in these hypothetical circumstances. If the phenomenon whose cause we are studying would have been different in these circumstances, in respects which come within our field of interest, we can attribute these aspects of the phenomenon to this particular antecedent (without implying that it was the *only* cause). This approach, which may appear difficult in the abstract, expresses a very simple idea. If we are studying the causal significance of the battle of Marathon we shall ask ourselves: What would have happened if the Greeks had not been victorious?—and we shall try, not to imagine the detail of events (for this would be an impossible task), but to determine whether the evolution of Greece would have been different in one important aspect or another. The battle of Marathon will then be regarded as *one* cause of these aspects. Can we, in fact, reconstruct the evolution which the victory of the Greeks prevented? Such a reconstruction is possible, since a study of analogous cases, such as the conduct of the Persians in those countries which they conquered, enables us to visualize the theocratic regime which might have been established. The difference between this hypothetical evolution of Greece under Persian rule and the evolution of Greece as an independent nation, indicates the importance of this battle which, from a material point of view, was insignificant.

This conceptual scheme, which in Weber's view only made explicit the practice of all historians, can be applied equally well to a limited event as to large scale phenomena. Using Weber's own examples, it is just as essential for analysing the motives which have led a mother to slap her child, as for determining the causes of capitalism. For to say that if the mother had not been exasperated by her cook she would not have slapped the child, is to suppose an antecedent eliminated and to infer that the event would then have been different.

It will be objected, no doubt, that this scheme is useless as long as we do not have the knowledge which would allow us to reconstruct in a valid manner the hypothetical evolution. But we have no need to describe in detail what would have happened; it is enough for us to know that things would have been different. Further, the comparative method is intended to facilitate these hypothetical reconstructions. And finally, we are not seeking necessary relations, but trying to establish adequate or possible relations.

The evolution of Greece under Persian rule, as we imagine it, cannot be described as necessary. Without even taking into account the subjective probabilities, associated with the imperfections of our knowledge, the facts which appear to us to determine certain consequences create in reality only an objective possibility. Fortuitous events would have been added to these basic conditions and might have changed the course of development. Consequently we can only say that a development towards theocracy would have been an adequate effect of a Persian victory, in the sense that the circumstances would have produced this result in the majority of cases. Similarly, if we assert that a revolution was inevitable in 1848, we simply mean that the basic circumstances, combined with a large number of antecedents, would have produced this revolution (or rather, would have combined with a number of antecedents which is very large in comparison with the number of those which would not have produced the revolution). In the same sense, one might say that a circumstance renders a certain effect more likely if it increases the number of favourable accidents.

On the contrary, if it is held that the firing on the boulevards was the real and fortuitous cause of the revolution, this implies that the revolution is not adequately explained as the result of a particular set of antecedents (the number of accidents which, added to these antecedents, would have produced the revolution was small). It is admitted that it was fortuitous in relation to these antecedents. Thus the two notions of adequate and accidental causality, of law and accident, are reciprocal, both being based upon arguments of probability.

This theory of historical causality poses a number of problems. How are the antecedents to be selected? Does not the determination of rules and of accidents involve circular reasoning? Further, though an event is an accident in relation to one group of antecedents, is it not at the same time a necessary effect in relation to another group, so that these two notions are, as it were, completely relative? Do we possess experiential rules which confer a sufficient degree of probability upon our reconstructions? At what level, and at what stage, can we and should we raise the question of probability?

Despite its incompleteness this causal theory proved adequate for Weber's work. . . . It forms the framework of his studies of the origins of capitalism. One of its chief features is that it entails a continuous collaboration between history and sociology. Causal imputation requires, in fact, the establishment of rules, not in the form of laws, but of frequent succession between two types of event (the influence of specific circumstances upon other specific circumstances); certain conditions facilitate, or in the most favourable case have as adequate effects, a certain type of behaviour, or again, certain economic phenomena are associated with certain legal institutions or religious attitudes. We have before us, therefore, a history which does not ignore irregularities and a sociology which does not eliminate either accidents, or ideas, or human strivings. The historical world as a whole, with its dramatic character, can find a place within these categories.

By means of this causal reasoning we are able to transport ourselves to a vanished actuality, and to give life to potentialities which were never realised, in order to become aware of the events which determined what appears to us as destiny. By an appropriate selection of antecedents we can distinguish human decisions from the external circumstances and thus discover those acts by which man has made his history.

This conception of causality seemed to Weber not only reconcilable with an interpretative explanation in terms of motives, but also indispensible to the objectivity of science. In his view, only causality assures the universal validity of a scientific proposition, and he came to regard all the non-causal forms of understanding as nothing more than an introduction to research. The understanding of a work of art, of a spiritual creation, or of a human mind, was, in his view, only an analysis of values. Genuine science is causal explanation.

TWO

NATURAL AND SOCIAL SCIENCE

TALCOTT PARSONS

THE FIRST IMPORTANT QUESTION is that of the standards Weber would lay down for the selection out of the total flux of raw experience of elements which are significant for the concepts of the social sciences, since such selection is the necessary logical prerequisite of *knowledge* as distinguished from raw experience. The starting point is Weber's statement that these standards are to be found in the subjective "direction of interest" of the scientist. In interpreting what are in turn the determinants of this direction of interest in the two groups of sciences, Weber's position is not altogether clear and consistent, and hence it is here that the first serious methodological difficulty of his position arises.

He holds that our interest in natural phenomena so far as it is a scientific interest is centered in their aspects of abstract generality, not of concrete individuality. Hence the aim of the natural sciences is the formulation of a system of universally applicable general laws. For the natural sciences general concepts constitute an end in themselves. With the social sciences, on the other hand, this is not so. Our interest in human beings and their cultural achievements is not that of abstract generality but of individual uniqueness. They are not to us "cases" of general laws. A man does not love "woman" but a particular woman; he is not fond of "pictures" but of particular paintings. Since in the social field interest is in the aspect of concrete individuality, general concepts cannot stand in the same relation to this interest; their formulation and verification cannot be an end in itself for the scientist's labor; they are

"Natural and Social Science." From Talcott Parsons, *The Structure of Social Action* (Glencoe, Ill.: The Free Press, 1949), pp. 591–601. Copyright 1949 by The Free Press of Glencoe. Reprinted by permission of The Macmillan Company and George Allen & Unwin Ltd. Some footnotes have been omitted for reasons of space.

only means to the elucidation and understanding of the particular, unique and individual phenomena. This is the formula Weber advances to cover the basic methodological distinction of the two groups of sciences. Can its grounds of justification be analyzed still farther?

In Weber's view, as far as it seems clear on this point, there is a common human basis for the interest in natural phenomena, that is, control. It is through the aspects formulable in terms of abstract general concepts that this is possible; in the application of science to technology, the forces of nature are subjected to the service of human ends. Hence the interest in them is in the general aspect, and is a uniform interest which can have, for all times and places, a common aim. Apart from this interest in control, natural phenomena are, as an object of science, indifferent to human values.

But this is just where the difference lies between natural phenomena and the social case. Human beings, their actions and cultural achievements are the embodiments of value toward which we must, in some degree, take a value attitude. Hence our interest in them is directly determined by their relevance to the values which either the scientist himself shares or which are significant to him by agreement with his own values or conflict with them. It is this "relevance to value" (*Wertbeziehung*) which constitutes the selective organizing principle for the empirical material of the social sciences.

Even in this case, it is important to note, the concrete individuality in which our interest is centered is not that of "raw experience." There is no reason to deny such individuality to our experience of natural phenomena. It is rather a constructed, selected individuality. From the elements given in experience are selected a limited number which are important from the point of view of relevance to value. This process results in a constructed concrete phenomenon, what Weber calls the historical individual.

Now, unlike the natural science case, the important elements of the direction of interest are not here common to all humanity. For it is one of Weber's basic theorems that value systems are diverse; there is a plurality of different possible systems. In so far then, as the selection of material is determined by relevance to such systems the same concrete materials will give rise not to one historical individual but to as many as there are, in this sense, points of view from which to study it. It is, in turn, in the process of analysis of the historical individual and comparison of it with others that general concepts are built up. It follows, then, that the process will not issue in one ultimately uniform system of general concepts but in as many systems as there are value points of view or others significant to knowledge. There can be no one universally valid system of general theory in the social sciences. This is one of the main routes by which Weber arrives at his view of the "fictional" nature of social science concepts, so important to his doctrine of the ideal type.

Before discussing this, however, it is necessary to prepare the ground by clarifying a number of related issues. In the first place, the principle of value relevance combined with that of the relativity of value systems introduces an element of relativity into the social sciences which raises in an acute form the question of their claim to objectivity. Does it not reduce their structures of so-called knowledge to mere "manifestations of sentiments"?

In the first place, Weber distinguishes carefully between determination of scientific interest, through value relevance (and thus of the immediate objects of scientific study, the historical individuals) and the exercise of value judgments. Value judgments (*Wertungen*) cannot claim the objective validity of science, and science must, as a methodological ideal, be kept free from them. Even though a value element enters into the selection of the material of science, once this material is given it is possible to come to objectively valid conclusions about the causes and consequences of given phenomena free of value judgments and hence binding on anyone who wishes to attain truth, regardless of what other subjective values he may hold.

This is possible first because even though in describing a concrete phenomenon what is made the subject of scientific analysis is not the full totality of experienceable fact about it, but a selection, the facts included in the historical individual as it is constructed are objective, verifiable facts. The question whether a statement of fact is true is clearly distinguishable from that of its significance to value. The relativity of *Wertbeziehung* touches only the latter, not the former, question. Secondly, once a phenomenon is descriptively given, the establishment of causal relations between it and either its antecedents or its consequences is possible only through the application, explicitly or implicitly, of a formal schema of proof that is independent of any value system, except the value of scientific truth. This formal schema is basic to all empirical science, and only in so far as they conform with it can scientific judgments that pretend to assert causal relationships be valid. It may be remarked in passing that this scheme involves the use of general concepts transcending the historical individual.[1] Thus in spite of the relativity introduced by the concept of *Wertbeziehung* Weber maintains both that it is possible to keep value judgments logically distinct from those claiming objective scientific validity, and

[1] Weber's historical individual is clearly simply a unit or combination adequately described for theoretical purposes within a frame of reference.

that the latter judgments can be made with confidence, escaping the subjectivity inherent in all value judgments.

So far Weber's position is acceptable. It is not, however, possible to accept his view of the methodological relations of the natural and the social sciences. It has been pointed out that his critique of the objectivist and intuitionist methodologies has gone a long way to bridge the gap between the two groups of disciplines created by the Kantian dualism. There are two main criticisms of this methodological position. The first is that he did not go far enough, but that in following Rickert in this distinction he attempted to stop at an unstable halfway point. He should have gone all the way to the view that in a purely *logical* aspect there is no difference whatever. The differences all lie on a substantive level.

The first source of difficulty seems to lie in Weber's attempt to draw too rigid a distinction between the subjective directions of interest of the scientist in each of the two groups of sciences. There seems to be no reason to doubt the importance of the motive of control with reference to the phenomena of nature. But it is possible to doubt both the extent to which that is the exclusive or even dominant motive of interest in the natural science field and that it is as unimportant as Weber maintains by implication in the sociocultural field. Indeed in the latter case it is curious that Weber took the position that he did, for one of his major theses throughout his work was that of the importance of scientifically verifiable knowledge of human affairs as a guide to rational action. Moreover in just this connection he strongly emphasized the need for general, theoretical knowledge. In so far as this is the context in which social studies are considered it would seem that, on the cognitive level, the ultimate aim of research was the building up of one or more systems of valid general theory, which would be equally applicable to any concrete situations that might arise.

Indeed, with reference both to nature and to action and culture two main types of nonscientific motives of cognitive interest may be differentiated. One is the "instrumental" interest. This is manifested whenever the question arises of using elements of the situation of action as means, or adapting action to them as conditions. But surely in rational action generally the social environment looms at least as large as does the natural. Particularly in the field Weber had primarily in mind, that of political action, this seems to be the case. The other main type of nonscientific motive of cognitive interest is what may be called a "disinterested" value attitude. This is not a matter of using things, but of defining one's attitude toward them in themselves. It is here that the element of concrete individuality becomes most prominent and that the principle of value relevance as formulated by Weber is applicable. There is no reason to deny that this element is quantitatively much more important in the social situation. But even if this is true it is not sufficient ground to justify its being made the basis of a radical methodological distinction between the two groups of sciences.

There is indeed no reason to exclude radically a value interest in this sense from the field of the natural sciences. In so far as value relevance is made the basis for an element of relativism in the theoretical systems of science, it may well be suspected that this relativism enters into the natural science field to a much greater extent than Weber intimated. Indeed a comprehensive comparative study of the interpretations of nature to be found in different civilizations with widely differing value systems would almost certainly reveal that this relativity existed to a surprising extent.

Moreover, there is no reason to believe that a value interest as distinguished from a control interest is always necessarily one which concentrates on the aspect of concrete individuality. Indeed Weber himself, in the *Protestant Ethic,* gives several hints of the existence of religious motivation in the promotion of natural science in the Puritan era, a view which has been substantiated by later studies. This urge, to know God through his works, was directed to the element of order in the physical world, and thus to those aspects of it that could be formulated in abstract and general terms. Indeed it may be suspected that Weber's distinction, in the rigid form in which he advanced it, is itself the manifestation of a particular value attitude of its author. It has been held to be a protest against the bureaucratic tendency to fit human beings as cogs into a machine, in which their place is defined by impersonal capabilities and functions rather than by their unique personality. In addition it is probable that Weber was misled into an exaggerated view of the unity of all natural science by lingering vestiges in his thought of Kantian empiricism, which blinded him to the elements of relativism to be found there.

A further element seems not to have received sufficient consideration on Weber's part. It is that, whatever the motives of original interest may be, there is an inherent tendency for the theoretical structures of all science in whatever field to become logically closed systems. Then, in so far as there is an instrumental interest in the social field, the general conceptual products of this interest will tend to become integrated in the same systems as those issuing from the value aspect. Once this has happened to an appreciable degree there will exist, as has been emphasized throughout this study, a secondary basis of interest in concrete phenomena—that derived from the structure of the theoretical system itself. The interest to this extent will be directed to those aspects of concrete phenomena which are important to the theoretical system.

Indeed, throughout, Weber seems not to have laid sufficient emphasis on the fact that scientific knowledge involves not only the fact that a selection is made from the possible data of "raw experience," but that what is experienced is itself determined, in part, by what scientific knowledge we have and, above all, by the general conceptual schemes that have been developed. Observation is always in terms of a conceptual scheme.

In all these respects, then, there seems to be no basis for a radical distinction in principle between the natural and the social sciences with regard to the roles of individuality and generality. Quantitative differences of degree there may be, but these are not sufficient to justify such a distinction.

The principle of value relevance helps to explain the element of relativism, in scientific methodology, but it is applicable to both groups of sciences, not to one alone.

For the classification of the sciences the methodological arguments Weber has developed seem to indicate a basic division into two groups, substantially on the lines he has suggested, with a dominant direction of interest, on the one hand, toward the concrete individuality of one or a class of historical individuals and, on the other hand, toward a system of abstract general principles and laws. But this division does not coincide with that between the natural and the sociocultural sciences. There are, rather, examples of both in each field. The first group may be called the historical sciences, which concentrate their attention on particular concrete phenomena, attempting as full an understanding of their causes and consequences as is possible. In doing this they seek conceptual aid wherever it may be found. Examples in the natural science field are geology and meteorology; in the social field, history, above all, but also anthropology as it has generally been conceived. The other group, the "analytical," sciences, is concerned primarily with building up systems of general theory verifiable in terms of and applicable to a wide range of concrete phenomena. To them the individual phenomenon is a "case." In the natural science field theoretical physics is the leading example, but chemistry and general biology may also be included; in the social sciences theoretical economics is by far the most highly developed, but it is to be hoped that theoretical sociology and certain others will find a place by its side.[2]

[2] Then for the historical sciences theoretical concepts are means to understanding the concrete historical individual. For the analytical sciences, on the other hand,

These two types of sciences cut across each other in their application to fields of concrete phenomena. The same historical science will necessarily draw theoretical aid from a number of different analytical sciences, for example geology from physics, from chemistry and, in explaining the origin of organic deposits like coal, from biology. Similarly history should draw on biology, psychology, economics, sociology and other sciences. On the other hand, the theoretical system developed by an analytical science will normally be applicable to a number of different classes of concrete phenomena, for example physics to celestial bodies and the behavior of terrestrial objects; economics to human actions in the market place and, in a less crucial role, to the church and the state. A distinction between the natural and the social sciences is possible on both levels. Historically considered the latter group is confined to the concrete phenomena of human life in social groups, analytically to those conceptual elements which are applicable only to this concrete subject matter.

But the basic distinction between historical and analytical is not to be identified with that between the natural and the social sciences. Indeed on no account is it possible to identify the distinction with any classification of concrete phenomena, for the analytical sciences of necessity cut across all such classifications. From this point of view it may be said that to make this identification is the basic fallacy of all of what has here been called empiricism, common to all three of the varieties discussed above. The result is invariably a dilemma. On one hand, the class of concrete phenomena in question may be treated by the method of an analytical science. Then the result is "reification," the fallacy of misplaced concreteness, with all its consequences. Or, on the other hand it may be treated by the method of a historical science alone, in which case the result is, theoretically considered, irrationalism, the denial of the validity of general conceptualization at all. On an empiricist basis there is no escape from this dilemma. Weber made his way out of it to a great extent, failing only to take the final step.

---

the reverse is true; concrete historical individuals are means, "cases" in terms of which the validity of the theoretical system may be tested by "verification."

From this it follows that there are two different possible meanings of the term "theory" which are often confused. On the one hand, we speak of the total explanation of a given concrete phenomenon, a historical individual or class of them, as a "theory," thus a "theory of eclipses" or Weber's own "theory of modern capitalism." On the other hand, we may apply the term to systems of general concepts as such, thus the "Newtonian physics" or the "classical economics." Weber points out quite correctly that a theory in the second sense cannot *by itself* explain a *single* empirical fact. It requires *data* which are always empirically unique, are part of a concrete historical individual, for any concrete explanation or prediction. See *Wissenschaftslehre*, pp. 171–72.

Before concluding this phase of the discussion it should be remarked that Weber's methodological work has succeeded to a notable degree in synthesizing, on the methodological plane, elements which are central to science and to action, indeed in establishing a very close solidarity between the two. The traditional methodology of science has tended to think of it in complete abstraction from action. Hence, whenever the close factual interdependence of the two has been brought to attention it has tended to result in a wave of scientific skepticism. Weber has succeeded in bringing a much needed element of relativity into his methodology thus relieving it of the necessity of making claims to an empiricist absolutism which would place it in a vulnerable position. At the same time he has vindicated its claims, properly qualified, to objectivity. Above all he has established the logical independence of the standards of objectivity, the schema of proof, from the relativistic elements.

Finally, among the principal elements of relativity in science prove to be elements that are of central importance to the analysis of action —the value elements. Scientific investigation, then, takes its place as a mode of action to be analyzed in the same terms as any other, rather than as a class of actions set apart. At the same time not only is it possible to place the development of science in the context of action without destroying its claim to objectivity but also verifiable knowledge itself is seen, with great clarity, to be an indispensable element of action itself. For the norm of intrinsic rationality in relation to the means-end relationship is devoid of meaning unless there is valid knowledge as a guide to action. Thus the two are elements of the same fundamental complex; a knowledge of action and its elements is indispensable to ground the methodology of science and, vice versa, scientific knowledge itself constitutes an element indispensable to the analysis of action. This insight is basic to the analytical system that has been emerging in the course of the present study.

It is well to emphasize again just what the element of relativism introduced by Weber means for the objectivity of scientific knowledge. In the first place, it means that scientific interest in any given action setting is not in the full totality of knowable facts, even about the concrete phenomena studied, but in certain selected elements of the latter. Hence at any given time even the total body of knowledge is not a complete reflection of humanly knowable reality. But to counterbalance this relativism, once the direction of interest is given and the relevant historical individuals constructed and correctly described, the system of propositions is, so far as it meets the requirements of the logical schema of proof, verifiable and objective. It follows that even though values change and with them the direction of scientific interest, in so far as past investigation has yielded valid knowledge, it remains valid, a permanently valid precipitate of the process. And however different from each other the conceptual schemes are, in terms of which such knowledge has been formulated, they must if valid be "translatable" into terms of each other or of a wider scheme. This implication is necessary to avoid a completely relativistic consequence that would overthrow the whole position.

Furthermore, it is one of Weber's basic theorems that while there is a plurality of possible ultimate value systems, their number is, in fact, limited. From this it follows that on Weber's own principles there is a limited number of possible constructions of historical individuals from the same concrete objects of experience, on the one hand, and of systems of theoretical concepts, on the other. From this it follows further that there is in principle a finite totality of humanly possible scientific knowledge. Even this totality would not by any means be a complete reflection of the totality of conceivable objective reality but would stand, like all objective knowledge, as Weber often puts it, in a functional relation to it. That is, the development of scientific knowledge is to be regarded as a process of asymptotic approach to a limit. The concrete impossibility of actual attainment at any given time or at any predictable future time does not affect the principle. Thus Weber's principle of value relevance, while it does introduce an element of relativity into scientific methodology (and a much-needed one by comparison with all empiricist views), does not involve the skepticism that is the inevitable consequence of any really radical relativity.

THREE

WEBER'S LEGACY

BENJAMIN NELSON

. . . PARSONS REMARKS THAT Weber cannot truly serve us as a model today. Many sociologists will be quick to take refuge behind this comforting verdict, explaining that they have no wish to become either sociological historians or historical sociologists of ideas and institutions. They want to be free to fulfill the distinctive tasks of sociology and social psychology—by procedures many have come to regard as the only reliable methods of social research: e.g., surveys describing the attitudes and activities of clergy and religiously-oriented laymen, cross-correlated for class, income, ethnic origin, and so forth. Weber does, indeed, set us an impossible example. As extravagant as this sounds, he takes the whole of recorded history as his area and then struggles to identify homologous structures for which he then develops hypotheses. To be a sociologist of Weber's sort, one must advance in areas left uncovered in his graduate training. Of course, the outcome of restorative efforts of this sort is not assured, for those who begin with little Latin, less Greek, and no historical training at all cannot expect readily to match the performance of the pioneer to whom Mommsen himself was prepared to cede his place.

But it would be a blunder of first magnitude to tell oneself that Weber's explorations are only of anecdotal historical interest. His method is comparative and sociological through and through. His structural intentions are constantly in evidence as he interlaces homologies. His comparative analysis embraces every aspect of the structure and workings of the major historic civilizations—China, India, the ancient Hebrews, Islam, Greece, Rome, Apostolic Christianity, European Christendom—with particular emphasis . . . on the Middle Ages.

"Weber's Legacy." From Benjamin Nelson, "Review Article," *American Sociological Review*, XXX (August, 1965), 598–99. Reprinted by permission of the author and the publisher.

Sociologists need to be warned that if they do not earn Weber's legacy, they will end by canonizing a few imperfectly understood "ideal types," originally designed to serve as props, as the established, irreversible, historical record. Criticism of these tendencies among sociologists by historians and literary critics has been increasingly sharp in recent years. Indeed, Kurt Samuelsson's shaky polemics against Weber would never have been so widely hailed by sociologists had he not seemed to strike a needed blow against ill-founded historical-sociological constructions.

Weber's *Sociology of Religion* and *Sociology of Law* should spur sociologists to take up the comparative historical and systematic study of the cultures of complex societies where he left off. If despairing sociologists renounce this task, the way is clear for anthropologists, who have already gone far along the road, to pre-empt the field entirely. The "moment of truth" in respect to the central problems I have broached can only be deferred for a few more years. Even now, my colleague at Stony Brook, Guenther Roth, is completing the first full and thoroughly collated variorum translation of *Wirtschaft und Gesellschaft*, based on a critically revised edition of the text. Thanks to Roth, several hundred of Weber's thorniest pages, roughly one-third of the original, will soon become available in English for the first time. Once this task is completed and the whole of *Wirtschaft und Gesellschaft* is in our hands, there will be no escape from the evidence that our horizons and resources simply do not match Weber's.

Weber sought to secure us against two serious risks we now run. The first risk is that of promoting and propounding a *surface sociology of the specious present*. Many sociologists, especially those who suppose that our available fund of "ideal types" suffices for any necessary or desirable "historical" reconstruction, take less seriously the second risk, that we shall promote and propound a *specious sociology of the surface or imaginary past*.

Only one remedy exists for this condition. A reasonable number of us (sociologists and their colleagues in related areas) must labor to keep Weber's "synthesis" alive, safe from the incessant risks of petrification. We must aim, as he did, to promote and propound a *sociology of the social and cultural depths*. (One should not confuse this undertaking —surely Weber never did—with "depth psychology" or the psychoanalytic study of the individual or "collective" unconscious.) In the spirit of Weber, Burckhardt, and others, including Parsons, we must strive to deepen our analysis of social experience, sensibility, action, communication, control, and organization—recurrent as well as current, Oriental as well as Western, "primitive" as well as contemporary.

PART TWO

RATIONALIZATION
AND FREEDOM

WEBER'S INTERPRETATION
OF THE BOURGEOIS-
CAPITALISTIC WORLD IN TERMS
OF THE GUIDING PRINCIPLE
OF "RATIONALIZATION"

KARL LOEWITH

THE FUNDAMENTAL THEME OF
MAX WEBER'S RESEARCH

THE FIELD SPECIFICALLY "worthy of being known" in which Weber's investigations move is basically a single one. The scholarly investigation of this single field was his chief concern in the midst of all his methodological discussions and variously divided inquiries; it was not this or that particularity, nor merely the phenomenon of capitalism "in its general cultural meaning." According to Weber himself:[1]

"Weber's Interpretation of the Bourgeois-Capitalist World in Terms of the Guiding Principle of 'Rationalization.'" From "Max Weber und Karl Marx," in Karl Loewith, *Gesammelte Abhandlungen* (Stuttgart: Verlag W. Kohlhammer GMBH, 1960). Reprinted by permission of Harper & Row, Publishers, Inc. and Verlag W. Kohlhammer GMBH. Translated by Salvator Attanasio.

[1] [Most of the quotations in this essay are taken from Weber's *Gesammelte*

The type of social science in which we are interested is an empirical
science of concrete reality. Our aim is the understanding of the characteristic uniqueness of the reality in which we move. We wish to understand on the one hand the relationship and the cultural significance of
individual events in their contemporary manifestations, and on the other
the causes of their being historically so and not otherwise.[2]

Thus historical inquiry does not have the significance of understanding how things have been (Ranke) or how they were foredestined
to be because of historical necessity (Marx). Rather, its purpose is to
make intelligible how we have become as we are today. Capitalism,
among other things—and preeminently so—belongs to this contemporary history (itself only a "segment of the course of human destinies"). This knowledge of the meaning of the reality which surrounds
and determines us, this sociohistorical self-knowledge is explicitly set
off by Weber against a search for ultimate "factors" and general "laws."
"The significance of a configuration of cultural phenomena and the
basis of this significance cannot however be derived and rendered intelligible by a system of analytical laws. . . . Since the significance of
cultural events presupposes a value-orientation towards these events.
. . . Empirical reality becomes a culture to us because and insofar as
we relate it to value ideas. It includes those segments of reality and
only those segments of reality which have become significant to us
because of this value-relevance." [3] Thus our human reality can never
be known "without presuppositions." "A chaos of 'existential judgments' about countless individual events would be the only result of a
serious attempt to analyze reality 'without presuppositions.' And even
this result is only seemingly possible. . . ." [4] The qualification of an
event, for example, as a socioeconomic phenomenon is nothing which
it possesses "objectively," but is conditioned by the orientation of our
cognitive interest, which for its part results from the specific cultural
meaning attributed to such events. This meaning is what it is in that
it exists for us as human beings, though not necessarily for us as separate individuals. "We cannot discover, however, what is meaningful for
and to us by means of a 'presuppositionless' investigation of empirical
data. Rather, perception of its meaningfulness to us is the presupposi-

---

Aufsätze zur Wissenschaftslehre which Loewith refers to as *W. L.* Several of the
articles in this collection have been translated and edited by Edward A. Shils and
Henry A. Finch under the title, *Max Weber on the Methodology of the Social
Sciences* (Glencoe, Ill.: The Free Press, 1949). Passages taken from the latter work are
identified as *M.*, otherwise as *W. L.* (Translator's note).]

[2] *M.*, p. 72.
[3] *M.*, p. 76.
[4] *M.*, p. 78.

tion of its becoming an object of investigation," [5] a perception of something in general becoming worthy of being known and questionable, thus, for example, the fact of the meaning of capitalism humanly so laden with presuppositions.

This human reality "worthy of being known" and meaningful to us in different possible respects, however, includes the significant fact of science itself, of scientific knowledge having become "historically so and not otherwise." The fact alone that Weber sees his own tendency to scientific understanding as something included and bound up with the historical uniqueness and problematical nature of the whole of modern life fundamentally distinguishes him from all scientific eagerness to know which is purely specialist in character and unaware of its own presuppositions, and from the naive faith in science professed by most Marxists. This knowledge of the unique character of our science induces Weber to raise the question of the "meaning" of specialized, rationalized science. This type of science, highly specialized and to that extent having become "positivistic," itself belongs within the "spirit" and "lack of spirit" of "capitalism." Whether such a type of science has a "meaning" at all, i.e., what kind of meaning it has, cannot—scientifically—be established from within its own self, especially since now it is neither a way to "God" nor to "pure Being," nor even to personal "happiness." Weber's "methodological" question respecting the value of science is, at bottom, the same question which Nietzsche posed to philosophy, when he asked about the meaning and value of "truth." For "what meaning would our existence have unless we became conscious of this 'will to truth' itself as a problem?" Starting out from the premise that "faith in the value of scientific truth" is the "product of definite cultures" and not a datum of nature, Weber also puts forward the demand for so-called "value-free" scientific judgments. This in no way signifies a retreat to the tenets of pure science: on the contrary it aims precisely to take into account the extrascientific standards operative in scientific judgment.

What this precept demands is not the elimination of determining "value ideas" and interests, but their objectification as a possibility of distancing ourselves from them. Science is separated from faith only by a "hairline." At bottom scientific judgments cannot really be divided from evaluative judgments; only both are to be kept separate. What can and should happen with scientific "objectivity" as the aim in view is not an illusory minimizing of "subjectivity," but a deliberate taking into account of and a pronounced emphasis on precisely that which is scientifically undemonstrable although it is scientifically relevant. So-

[5] *M.,* p. 75.

called "objectivity" (Weber always speaks of "so-called" objectivity, always placing the word between quotes) "rests exclusively upon the ordering of the given reality according to categories which are subjective in a specific sense, namely in that they present the presuppositions of our knowledge and are based on the presupposition of the value of those truths which empirical knowledge alone is able to give us." [6] Accordingly, Weber combats Marxism as a scientific "socialism" not because it is based upon ideas and ideals which are altogether undemonstrable scientifically, but because it presents the subjectivity of its fundamental presuppositions under the guise of their "objective" and universal validity, without distancing itself from them. Moreover, it confuses these two aspects and is scientifically "biased" in favor of its own value judgments and prejudices. "The foregoing arguments are directed against this confusion, not against the clear-cut introduction of one's own ideals into the discussion. An attitude of moral indifference has no connection with scientific 'objectivity.'" [7] Thus Marxism, according to Weber, does not have too little faith in science, but too much. What it lacks is "scientific" impartiality in respect to the questionableness of scientific objectivity.

On the basis of Weber's proposition, however, that binding norms and ideals are not demonstrable and that, consequently, there are no "formulas" as regards practice, it by no means follows that "value judgments are to be withdrawn from scientific discussion in general, simply because in the last analysis they rest on certain ideals and are therefore 'subjective' in origin. . . . Criticism is not to be suspended in the presence of value judgments. The problem is rather: what is the meaning and purpose of the scientific criticism of ideals and value judgments?" [8] Thus, for Weber, the main thing, finally, is to make understandable the ideas "for which men either really or allegedly struggle" through scientific criticism (as, for example, of Roscher and Knies) and through self-reflection. This exposure of the ideas and ideals that in truth guide and influence scientific investigations of what "in the last analysis is really wanted," Weber himself designates as social philosophy.

The final service that scientific reflection on this problem can provide is to bring to consciousness the "ultimate standards" which are manifested in concrete value judgments and thereby make room for a clear discussion and disputation on their nature.

This scientific self-reflection which leaves behind the naive positivism of specialized science *eo ipso,* to be sure, does not point to what

[6] *M.,* p. 110.
[7] *M.,* p. 60.
[8] *M.,* p. 52

one "ought" to do but to what one can do consistently with the given means in respect to a preconceived goal. Above all, it makes known what one in general really "wants." The always posited objective invalidity of our ultimate value-standards and the nonexistence of universally binding norms, however, does not belong to the general nature of science as such. This deficiency rather springs from the distinctiveness of those epochs whose fate it was to have "eaten from the tree of knowledge" and, in consequence, to have perceived "that we cannot learn the meaning of the world" but "must rather be in a position to create this meaning itself."

"Only an optimistic syncretism . . . can theoretically delude itself about the profound seriousness of this situation or practically shirk its consequences." [9] If "great communities" or "prophets" still existed, universal values could also still exist. But inasmuch as these are "not there," all that exists is a battle of many but equally true "gods," "ideals," "values" and "world views."

Whereas Dilthey in recognition of the same state of "anarchy in all our deeper convictions" and in renunciation of any "metaphysical university chair philosophy" tried to develop a basis for universal validities out of the "historical consciousness" itself, Weber not only renounced that, but straightway "breathed freely as soon as once again . . . the impossibility of pronouncing objectively valid value judgments had been proved" (Honigsheim), it being in keeping with his idea of the "freedom of man." Thus precisely because scientific inquiry is borne by unexpressed, but most particularly decisive, presuppositions of a human kind (analogous to man being the precondition of the specialist), Weber's concern is with what is no longer merely a specialized sociological task, but a philosophical one: to reveal expressly the "a priori" of the determining value ideas in all and in each specific individual inquiry. Such a quest must appear sterile to the specialized scientist—as Weber himself at times emphasizes—because it "produces" nothing—nothing, that is, in terms of positivistic-scientific progress. Indeed, it signifies a philosophical retrogression in the comprehension of the possible "meaning" of scientific objectivity and knowledge. The original motive of this reflection, however, is not a concern with an empty methodology; rather this return to the meaning of scientific objectivity springs, in its turn, from a wholly definite belief, namely from the disbelief in the traditional value ideas of scientific research. The most general characteristic of these traditional value ideas is, however, their claim to a humanly unconditioned objectivity. Thus what Weber is fundamentally attacking is the belief of science in ob-

[9] *M.,* p. 57.

jective norms in general and their scientific demonstrability in particular—with the means of science and for the "critical" procedure, and of both as the "truly human." In Weber, scientific impartiality, especially in respect to one's own prejudices, denotes the ethos of the theory. Truly worthy of man, according to Weber, is that procedure which upon perceiving what is "not there" draws from it positive conclusions. For this reason the purpose of his minute disclosure of what "in the last analysis is really wanted," that is the disclosure of the guiding value ideas of scientific research, is not merely to exhibit these presuppositions as existing and significant in order then to leave them be. Rather the much more specific purpose is to "de-magicize" and put into question their content.

The real and positive aim of Weber's scientifico-theoretical treatises is the radical demolition of "illusions." The two exemplary treatises on Roscher and Knies constitute a methodological destruction of wholly definite prejudices and value judgments, namely of those that violate "scientific impartiality" by contradicting a human-historical fact that the present time is a "religious weekday" and that science—as Nietzsche declared—is "scientific atheism." Weber's methodological considerations arise from his consciousness of this particular situation, namely that "our eyes have been blinded for a thousand years, blinded by the allegedly or presumably exclusive orientation towards the grandiose moral fervor of Christian ethics." Weber's methodology with an inner logic grows out of this central insight not only into the questionable foundations of modern science and culture, but of the contemporary life-orientation altogether. Weber was well aware of this principal motive of his methodological considerations, just as Marx had been of the basic meaning of his critique of Hegel's philosophy of law and its "method." Weber concludes his programmatic treatise on "objectivity in socio-scientific and socio-political knowledge" by warding off any possible misunderstanding that these methodological and conceptual investigations might have assumed any meaning whatsoever for themselves. No less does he reject the "subject-matter specialists" who are insensitive to the "refinement of a new idea." Finally, he justifies the necessity of his seemingly sterile investigations positively as follows: "All research in the cultural sciences in an age of specialization, once it is oriented towards a given subject-matter through settings of problems and has established its methodological principles, will consider the analysis of the data as an end in itself. It will discontinue assessing the value of the individual facts in terms of their relationship to ultimate value ideas. Indeed, it will lose its awareness of its ultimate rootedness in the value ideas in general. And it is well that it should be so. But there comes a moment when the atmosphere changes. The significance of the unreflectively utilized viewpoints becomes uncertain and the road is lost in the twilight. The light of the great cultural problems moves on. Then science too prepares to change its standpoint and its analytical apparatus and to view the stream of events from the heights of thought. . . ." [10]

* * *

. . . The constructional or, as it has also been called, the "nominalistic" character of Weber's fundamental methodological concepts and his whole scientific style does not arise from any direct exigency of science—neither can it be refuted with recourse to "phenomenon" for that would posit that the phenomena could be addressed only through a "logos." Rather it is a consistent expression of a quite definite attitude of man to reality. The ideal-typical "construct" has as its foundation a specific "illusionless" man who has been thrown back upon himself alone by a world become objectively meaningless and sober, and therefore, to that extent, emphatically "realistic." He is therefore forced to forge by himself any objective meaning and a meaningful relationship to things, and in particular the relationship to reality, as one specifically his own: in short "to create" a meaning, practically and theoretically. People, state, and the individual therefore can no longer be regarded and interpreted as uniform substances with deeper backgrounds—not merely because it would be unscientific but because such an attitude would be marked by transcendental prejudices and ideals, and the world view into which "we have been placed" no longer justifies such prejudices. Thus, for instance, Weber's exemplary definition of the existence of the State as arising from the "prospect" (*Chance*) that "definite types of social action (namely by individuals) occur" can be understood—fully understood!—only when we realize that it rests *de facto* upon a wholly definite political reality, namely the modern State into which we have been placed—inasmuch as it is itself a kind of rational "institution," an "establishment." In Hegelian terms it is the *Verstandesstaat*, the rational State; in Marxian terms an "abstract generality" above individuals as single private persons. It is a self-misunderstanding of Weber, the specialized scientist, when he asserts (vis-à-vis Spann) the purely "methodological" meaning of his "individualistic" and "rational" definitions and denies their substantive character together with their value-relatedness. Indeed what Weber has demonstrated in Roscher and Knies applies much more to himself: that the ultimate ideological presuppositions extend even into the logical structure. The ultimate presupposition of Weber's "individualistic" defini-

[10] *M.*, p. 112. [A detailed discussion of Weber's analysis of the implicit value assumptions in the work of Roscher and Knies is omitted here.]

tion of so-called social structures, however, is the following: since all kinds of objectivities, as a result of their disenchantment (through rationalization) can no longer be imputed an independent meaning, it is only the "individual," the single man dependent solely upon himself who is truly real and justified in his existence. On the other hand, if the State were still a *res publica* and man as such a citizen of the State or city and not primarily a private person responsible to himself, then it would certainly have made sense also to interpret the State itself as a substantive and "universalistic" entity and not only in terms of the prospects of its "existence." Thus Weber's scientific "impartiality" also here expresses itself as a permanent break with bias in the form of transcendental prejudices. Even the belief, shared by Marxism, in objective development and progress belongs to these "transcendental" prejudices, i.e., those going beyond the workaday prosaicness of a disenchanted world.[11] It poses itself as a necessity only "when the need arises to endow the course of humanity's fate, depleted of religiosity, with a this-worldly 'meaning' that is nevertheless objective." [12] But, according to Weber, this need is a contradiction of this-worldliness. "Reality" now stands in this "light" and the guiding thread for the interpretation of this reality is the process of rationalization through which reality has been disenchanted and rendered drab, flat, and matter-of-fact. The truly valuable standard, however, by which Weber himself judges this historical "factum" of rationalization is its seeming opposite, namely the freedom of the individual, dependent upon and responsible only to himself, the "human hero" in relation to the dominion of the "orders," "installations," and "establishments" of modern life which came into being through rationalization.

This thesis now calls for a closer elaboration, specifically through an analysis of the fundamental and comprehensive meaning of "rationalization" which, at the same time, is the opposite concept of Marx's interpretation of the same phenomenon in terms of "self-alienation."

"RATIONALITY" AS THE PROBLEMATIC EXPRESSION OF THE MODERN WORLD

We have established the singularity of the environing reality into which we have been placed as the fundamental and the whole theme of Weber's investigations. The underlying theme of their "scientific" research turns out to be the tendency towards this-worldliness. Weber, however, sums up the particular problematic character of our con-

[11] *W. L.*, pp. 203 ff.
[12] *W. L.*, p. 330, footnote 2; cf. p. 56 and pp. 61 ff.

temporary reality under the title "rationality." But Weber attempts to render intelligible this general process of rationalization of our entire life for the reason that the rationality springing from it is something specifically "irrational" and unintelligible. Thus, for example, whereas money-making for the purpose of self-preservation is rational and intelligible, the specifically rationalized money-making for money-making's sake—"conceived purely as an end in itself"—is specifically irrational. In his answer to one of Brentano's criticisms, Weber expressly establishes this elementary and decisive finding: every radical rationalization creates irrationalities with the necessity of a fate.[13] . . .

Weber has demonstrated the fact of rationalization in its universal as well as in its fundamental, world-historical, and anthropological meaning in his preface to the *Sociology of Religion*. The phenomenon of rationalization is "the great guiding line not only of his sociology but fundamentally of his whole system" (Freyer) and, not least, of his political writings. To Weber rationalization signifies the fundamental character of the occidental style of life. It is our "fate" in short, even though one may take different attitudes to this fate as exemplified by Weber and Marx and, accordingly, interpret it differently: religio-sociologically or socioeconomically. Even Weber's work in the sociology of religion purports to be nothing but a contribution towards a sociology of rationalism itself.[14] The originality of Weber's religio-sociological analysis of capitalism, in express contradistinction and, presumably, in opposition to Marx's "economic" analysis, lies in the fact that he does not view capitalism as a power of social relations, and of the means and forces of production, which has become an independent entity and from which we are then ideologically to interpret every other phenomenon deriving. Rather, according to Weber, it was possible for capitalism to become the "most fateful" force in human life only because it had already developed within the tracks of a "rational mode of life." "Rationality," claimed as a guiding thread for understanding, does not exhaust itself by being the rationality of something, the rationality of a definite area (which then as a "determining" factor spreads to other areas of life). Rather, Weber's "rationality," despite his specialized scientific procedure, in a kind of reversible causal imputation of definite "factors," is grasped as an original whole with no further causal imputation; that is, as the whole of a multiple conditioned but nevertheless unique "attitude towards life" and mode of life and as an occidental ethos. This normative ethos is manifested in

---

[13] *Soc. of Religion.*
[14] *The Protestant Ethic and the Spirit of Capitalism,* trans. Talcott Parsons, p. 26.

the "spirit" of (bourgeois) capitalism as well as in that of (bourgeois) Protestantism.[15]. . . A definite type of economics is not a direct outcome of a definite religious belief, nor is the latter an "emanative" outcome of a "substantive" type of economics. Both in fact form themselves "rationally" on the basis of an all-pervading rationality of the mode of life. On the other hand, so little can capitalism as such, in its preeminent economic meaning, be regarded as the independent cause of rationality, that, instead, we must view a rationality of the mode of life (originally religiously motivated) as having allowed capitalism, in an economic sense, to grow into a dominant life-force. Thus, wherever the tendency to "definite attitudes of practical rational mode of life" was missing, "the development of an economically rational mode of life also encountered serious internal obstacles."

In the past, however, religious forces and the "ethical ideas of duty," anchored in faith, belonged to the formative elements of the mode of life "to an extent hardly comprehensible today." Hence Weber raises the question of the inner relationship between the Protestant "ethic" and the "spirit" of capitalism. The inner "elective affinity" of both is one of an economic and religious view, and both rest upon a general "spirit" or "ethos" whose socially distinctive carrier is the occidental bourgeoisie.

. . . The upshot of this universal rationalization of life is a system of dependency on all sides, an "iron cage," a general "apparatization" of man, an inevitable regimentation of each one into an "enterprise" (*Betriebe*) which at the moment is determinative, whether in economics or science. And "in spite of all" (Weber concludes his lecture *Politics as a Vocation* with the exclamatory phrase "in spite of all!") this rationality, for Weber himself, is the site of freedom. This relationship between rationality and freedom postulated merely as a thesis here can be more directly inferred from the inner impulse of Weber's practical attitude towards all the rationalized institutions, orders, and organizations of modern life—he challenged their claim to any metaphysical reality and used them as a means to an end, i.e., as the object of his theoretical investigations. Thus it is all the more particularly important for us to lay bare Weber's thought also on this score.

In the essay on "Knies and the Problem of Irrationality" Weber discusses the bearing of the question of so-called free will in historical research: "One encounters in them again and again the 'unpredictability' of personal behavior which is a consequence of freedom, interpreted either explicitly or implicitly, as a peculiar dignity of man and

---

[15] Cf. *The Spirit of Capitalism and the Protestant Ethic,* op. cit., chap. 1.

therefore of history in which the 'creative' significance of personality is contrasted with the 'mechanical' causality of nature." [16]

In a footnote to this observation, Weber ironically comments on Treitschke's and Meinecke's "reverence" for a so-called irrational "remnant," an "inner sanctum" and "mystery" of the free personality. What Weber aims to show in the discussions that follow,[17] however, is not by any means "the unfreedom" of the individual but the "trivial self-evident fact"—although it perennially falls into oblivion or is obscured—that this "creative" freedom which is claimed as a specifically human attribute is not a hallmark of man, an objective datum, or to be read in him as in a book. Rather, it is something which can be "seen" only on the basis of a "value judgment," of a definite evaluation, on the basis of an attitude of subjectivity towards a fact which "in itself" is insignificant. For, in itself, incalculability, and consequently irrationality, is so little a hallmark of the freedom of human action (in contrast to the calculability of events in nature) that the predictability of the weather, for instance, can be less certain than the possibility of calculating and predicting human behavior.

> Every military command, every penal law, indeed every utterance that we make in intercourse with others, "calculates" on the ingress of definite effects into the "psyche" of those to whom it is directed—not on an absolute unequivocable internalization in every respect, but notwithstanding, on a degree thereof sufficient for the end that the command, the penal law, the concrete utterance in general aim to serve.[18]

In truth, the less free a human action is, the more unpredictable is human behavior, that is, the less a human being has control over himself and therefore the freedom of his own actions.

> The "freer" the decision to act—that is, the more this decision is a response to its "own" reflections rather than to "external pressures or irresistible affects"—the more completely, *ceteris paribus*, the motivations involved in the decision may be fitted into the categories, end and means; so much the more adequate will be the rational analysis of these motivations . . . but the greater the freedom of action—that is, the further removed from the processes of nature—the more there comes into play, finally, the conception of a personality that finds self-realization in the constant attunement of its inner being to definite ultimate values and life meanings; through the medium of an action these values and meanings are transformed into aims and purposes, and in the process this action becomes teleological and rational. Consequently there is less and

[16] *W. L.*, p. 46.
[17] Ibid., p. 64.
[18] *W. L.*, p. 64.

less place for the romantic-naturalistic conception of personality which, proceeding in the opposite direction, searches out the ethos of the personality in the dank, fallow subsoil of human, or rather animal, life. From such romantic obscurantism, with its indiscriminate attempts to immure the freedom of the will in the dark recesses of the natural world, emanates that mystery of personality as invoked occasionally by Treitschke and more frequently by many of his fellow romantics. The absurdity of this latter enterprise is obvious in direct experience: we "feel" ourselves either "necessitated" or codetermined in a "non-immanent" way in our "volition" precisely through those "irrational" elements of our action.

This is expressed even more clearly in the dispute with E. Meyer:

> The error in the assumption that any freedom of the will—however it is understood—is identical with the "irrationality" of action, or that the latter is conditioned by the former is obvious. The characteristic of "incalculability," equally great but not greater than that of the "blind forces of nature" is the privilege of the insane. On the other hand, we associate the highest measure of an empirical "feeling of freedom" with those actions which we are conscious of performing rationally—i.e., in the absence of physical and psychic "coercion," emotional "affects" and "accidental" disturbances of the clarity of judgment in which we pursue a clearly perceived end by "means" which are the most adequate in accordance with the extent of our knowledge.[20]

Thus rationality goes together with the freedom of action in that, as a "teleological rationality," it is a freedom to pursue, with a free choice of the adequate means thereto, an end predesignated by ultimate values or life "meanings." The "personality" is stamped concretely in this rational goal-oriented conduct as a constant relationship of man towards ultimate values. To act as a free person, therefore, means to act purposefully, that is, to adapt the given means to the pre-established end and to that extent to act logically or "consequently." The freedom of human action is evidenced concomitantly with rationality in the measuring and evaluation of the prospects and consequences inherent in the means available to a rational goal-oriented conduct. The more freely man considers and evaluates the necessary means to something (an end), the more he acts in terms of rational goal-oriented conduct and, therefore, acts all the more intelligibly. By the same token, however, free action is all the more strictly bound up with the recourse to a definite, purposive means (or, conversely, with the lack of adequate means and the abandonment of the goal).

[19] *W. L.*, pp. 132, 133; cf. pp. 69 and 137.
[20] *M.*, pp. 124–25.

It is precisely the empirically "free" acting person, i.e., the person weighing consequences, who according to the objective situation, is teleologically bound to inadequate . . . means for the attainment of his ends. The belief in his "freedom of will" is of mighty little help to the manufacturer engaged in cutthroat competition, to the broker on the exchange. He has the choice of being wiped out economically or of following very definite rules of economic behavior. If he does not follow them to his manifest loss, in explanation we will say . . . and perhaps we will use precisely this explanation . . . that he was lacking in "will power!" It is precisely the "laws of theoretical political economy" that necessarily posit . . . the existence of "free will" in every empirically possible meaning of the word.[21]

The freedom to bind oneself to the pursuit of one's ultimate ends in relation to specifically given means, however, signifies nothing more and nothing less than the responsibility of human action. But knowledge of the means—and only of the means, not the ends—is given by rational "science." [22] It thus makes possible the inner "consequence and therefore (!) the honesty" of our purposeful theoretical or practical conduct. The rational consideration of the given means in relation to a self-proposed end and of the end itself in respect to the prospects and the consequences of its realization constitutes the responsibility of free and rational action. The "tension," however, between the means and the end (the attainment of good ends can be bound up with the use of questionable means) makes of the rationality of responsibility itself a definite ethos. In contrast to an ethic of ultimate ends (*Gesinnungsethik*), which Weber expressly designates as an ethic of "irrational" conduct because of its indifference to "consequences" (in comparison to rational goal-oriented purposive-rational action, it is rational value-oriented) the "ethic of responsibility" always calculates the prospects and consequences of action in each case on the basis of the available means.[23] It is a "relative," not an "absolute," ethic since it is related to the knowledge of the prospects and consequences transmitted through a consideration of the means involved in the attainment of its ends. Thus along with a decision for the ethic of responsibility, one at the same time also decides for rationality as a means-to-an-end rationality. The contradiction between the preference for means-to-ends rationality and the theoretically equal weight given to the classification of rational goal-oriented conduct, rational value-oriented conduct, affectual conduct, and traditionalist conduct in the "system" is only an apparent one.[24] The intrinsic and primary reason for Weber's obvious

[21] *W. L.*, p. 133.
[22] *W. L.*, pp. 150 and 549.
[23] *Ges. Pol. Schr.* (Collected Political Writings), pp. 442 ff. and 447 f.
[24] *Wirtsch. u. Ges.*, II, pp. 11 ff.

preference for the "rational goal-oriented" schema is not that it affords to the highest degree an ideal type construct for the understanding of human action; it lies, rather, in the specific responsibility that characterizes rational goal-oriented conduct itself. While in this way rationality is rooted in the ethos of responsibility, as such, it refers back to Weber's idea of "man."

Weber, however, also sees the distinctive irrationality which forms itself in the process of rationalization, and which is the specific motive for its study, as likewise stemming from this relationship between means and ends, so fundamental for the concept of rationality and freedom, namely in the reversal of that relationship. As that which was originally merely a means (to an otherwise valuable end) becomes an end or an end-in-itself, actions intended as a means become independent rather than goal-oriented and precisely thereby lose their original "meaning" or end, i.e., their goal-oriented rationality based on man and his needs. This reversal, however, marks all of modern culture: its establishments, institutions, and enterprises are rationalized in such a way that it is these structures, originally set up by man which now, in their turn, encompass and determine him like an "iron cage." Thus *nolens volens* human conduct, from which these institutions originally spring, is forced to adjust to its own creations which have literally escaped its control. Weber himself declares that it is here that the cultural problem of rationalization towards the irrational lies together with the similarity as well as the differences, in the valuation of this problem complex by him and Marx. In his lecture on "Socialism," after an exposition of the so-called "separation" of the worker (the "intellectual worker" as well), Weber sums up: "All that which now socialism understands by the 'domination of things over man,' should mean the domination of means over the end (the satisfaction of needs)." The most pronounced manifestation, however, of this paradoxical inversion—this "tragedy of culture" as Simmel has called it—occurs when we encounter it, of all places, in a sphere which according to its own most particular intention aims to be a specifically rational one: in rational economic conduct. Here especially is most strikingly exhibited the fact—and the modality—of a conduct purely oriented towards a rational goal, transformed, with a fateful necessity, into its opposite, bringing forth the meaningless "irrationality" of independent and autocratic "conditions" which then rule over human conduct. The rational all-pervading organization of living conditions effects the organization's irrational autocratic rule. The aim of Marx's theoretical and practical work is the explanation and destruction of this general state of affairs, Weber's aim is its understanding. The Marxist economic equation for this inversion is C–M–C vs. M–C–M (commodity–money–commodity vs. money–commodity–money). For Marx, however, this economic perversion also signifies the economic form of a general inversion which consists in the fact that the "thing" in general, as well as the product produced (of any kind), rules over man as human being and as producer. Its direct human expression is the objectification and specialization of man himself—the man humanly compartmentalized through his specialized activity, the "particularized" specialist man whom—together with the highly specialized enterprise of any kind—Weber views as the typical man of the rationalized epoch and, in an ambiguous way, accepts.

The inexpressible yardstick, however, by which this irrationality of the rationalized as such is interpreted—both in Marx and in Weber —is the presupposition that the original and absolutely independent end, the ultimate end of all human institutions is *not* these institutions themselves, but only man himself—for whom everything else is a "means" for his ends. The economic temper of the bourgeois stratum of society which was "religiously" motivated originally, i.e., by definite human needs, becomes "irrational," for instance, not when it is transformed into a secular economy through the depletion of its religious contents so that what at first was a means for religious ends now serves other, if secular, ends. Rather, it becomes "irrational" by virtue of the fact that the economy becomes independent to such a degree that— in spite of all external rationality—there no longer exists any evident relationship to the needs of man as such. The predominance and the autonomy of the conditions which have grown into an independent fact of life is what it is—namely irrational—under the presupposition that the "rational" represents the independence and the autonomy of man—whether one determines his humanity in the horizon of his sociality, like Marx, or in the individuality of his self-responsibility, like Weber.

Weber's viewpoint for the interpretation of the humanity of man (by which that irrationality is measured) is not earthly happiness. This follows indirectly from the fact that he tries repeatedly to show that money-making, for instance, purely as an end in itself, is completely irrational when considered from the point of view of the "happiness" and "profit" of the individual, yet nowhere does he state that "this reversal of what we should call the natural relationship, so irrational from a naive point of view" is also utterly meaningless in his own opinion! The "we" here stands for the impersonal "one," for it is quite obvious that Weber's own sympathies lie precisely with those Puritans for whom the work of their callings and "business" with its incessant activity had become "indispensable to life." This, says Weber, is indeed the only fitting motivation and, at the same time, it gives expression to what is so irrational a mode of life "viewed from the standpoint of personal happiness."

It is just as obvious on the other hand, however, that Weber's own ethos was no longer that of a pious Puritan but of a completely secularized man, nevertheless, one who could not have been satisfied with a complete renunciation of the "meaning" and "interpretation" of human activity. If the idea of the duty to one's calling, which obviously stands behind Weber's "demand of the day," if this [idea] now haunts our life like a mere "ghost" of dead religious beliefs and "no one knows who will live in this cage in the future," the question that inevitably must be raised is, what was Weber's own attitude towards the irrational fact of universal rationalization whose human expression is this vocational and specialized humanity inasmuch as he, evidently, does not negate it in the Marxist manner or from the standpoint of happiness as "inhumanity," nor affirm it as a step forward in the progress of humanity? Why does he not, like Marx, fight against this universal "self-alienation" of man? Why does he not, like Marx, call this "same" phenomenon a "depraved materialism" of self-denial, rather than use the concept of rationality, scientifically neutral but ambiguous in its possible interpretation—ambiguous precisely because at one and the same time it gives expression to the specific accomplishment of the modern world and to the whole questionableness of this accomplishment? Does not Weber affirm and deny this fateful process of rationalization in a contradictory way? For after all, what he precisely and most sharply calls into question, and with the whole force of his personality, is precisely the planned, calculated "order," "security," and "compartmentalized specialization" of modern life in all its political, social, economic, and scientific institutions? Nevertheless how can he, conversely, from the first sentence of the *Sociology of Religion* up to his last manifesto, *Science as a Vocation,* call himself the "child of his age," "specialist," and "specialized" scientist, or in other words, deliberately place himself in this world and actually become the spokesman of this "devil" of intellectual rationalization and of the "flowers of evil"? Or with this quotation from Baudelaire has he allegorically disclosed the riddle of his attitude towards all and everything and thus also towards the irrational rationality of our world? "If anything we realize again today that something can be sacred not only in spite of its not being beautiful, but rather because and insofar as it is not beautiful," and he buttresses this assertion with a reference to biblical passages and to Nietzsche. And it is "commonplace to observe that something may be true although it is not beautiful and not holy and not good. Indeed it may be true precisely in these aspects." In another place he calls this the "ethical irrationality of the world" which, however, the absolute "moralist of ultimate ends" cannot endure. If from good only good can come and from evil only evil, "politics as a vocation" would not at all exist as a problem. But if this is "rationality," what then are the "flowers of evil"? Here indeed the crack seems to open through which it is possible to peer at the inner unity of this ambiguous attitude towards "the reality in which we move." The unity of this schism lies in the aforementioned interconnection between rationality and freedom, which we now have to develop more closely with respect to Weber's idea of man.

This freedom can be in inner accord with rationality only if it is not a freedom from this rationalized world, but a freedom in the middle of this "iron cage" which determines even individuals who are not directly concerned with economic acquisition "with irresistible force. . . ." But what is the nature of this "innerworldly" freedom on the basis of the rationalization of the world?

RATIONALITY AS FREEDOM FOR SELF-RESPONSIBILITY
OF THE INDIVIDUAL AMID UNIVERSAL BONDAGE

That the positive meaning of rationality, for Weber himself, lies in its seeming opposite does not follow from the investigations made in *The Sociology of Religion* which in their intentions are purely "historical," but from his political writings, particularly Chapter Two of "Parliament and Government" and from his *"Debattenrede."* Both writings fight rationalization in its political form of bureaucratization and nationalization. Here Weber asserts that World War One represents a further progress in the process of universal rationalization, i.e., of the rationally calculated, departmentalized, specialized bureaucratic human authoritarian organizations. This process extends to the organization of the army and the State as well as that of the factories, scientific technical schools, and universities. Highly specialized examinations of all kinds increasingly become a prerequisite for a secure official position. "This, as we know, was already before 'the demand of the day,' supported alike by the interest of the universities in enrollment and the mania of their students for sinecures and within the state as well as outside of it." This prosaic state of affairs inherent in bureaucratic specialization, he states, also hides itself behind the "socialism of the future." Even when it aims for the opposite, it strengthens the power of bureaucracy which places its stamp on the contemporary age and the foreseeable future.

A continuous elimination of private capitalism is no doubt theoretically possible—even though it is not such a trifling matter as many *literati,* who do not know it, dream. And it will certainly not be the consequence of this war. But let us assume that it succeeds for once: what would it signify practically? A destruction of the iron cage of modern wage-dependent labor? No! Rather the administration of any nationalized or "communal" enterprise would become bureaucratic.[25]

This "living machine," distinguished by "rational specialization" and "in-training" is exactly like a lifeless "curdled spirit."

Together with the dead machine it is at work to set up the iron cage of that bondage of the future, in which perhaps some day men, help-lessly, will be forced to integrate themselves if a purely technical good —and this means a rational administrative and maintenance officialdom, which is to decide over the direction of their affairs—is the ultimate and only value. For the bureaucracy can accomplish this incomparably much better than any other authoritarian organizational structure.[26]

An "organic," that is, an oriental Egyptian social structure would dawn —but in contrast to the latter as strict and rational as a machine. Who would deny that something of that kind lies as a possibility in the lap of the future . . . ? Let us even assume that precisely this possibility is an ineluctable fate—who then would not smile over the fear of our *literati* that political and social development in the future could give us too much "individualism" or "democracy" or the like and that "true free-dom" will first rise resplendent when the present "anarchy" of our eco-nomic production and the horsetrading among the parties in our Parlia-ment is overcome to the benefit of "social order" and "organic structure" —i.e., of the pacifism of social powerlessness under the wing of the only truly inescapable power bureaucracy in the state and in the economy! In view of the fundamental fact of the irresistible advance of bureauc-racy, the question of future political forms of organization in general can be posed only as follows: 1) How in view of the predominance of the tendency to bureaucratization is it altogether still possible, in some sense, to salvage some remnant of "individualistic" freedom of move-ment . . . ?[27]

*   *   *

The debate closes with a deliberately immoralist challenge: it is preferable today to have "private capitalist expansion, coupled with a purely business-type officialdom which is more easily exposed to corruption," rather than "governmental direction by the highly moral, authoritatively transfigured German civil service officialdom."

As regards the irresistibility of bureaucratic rationalization, accord-ing to Weber, we can ask only how it is possible in view of this over-

[25] *Pol. Schr.*, pp. 150 ff.
[26] *Pol. Schr.*, p. 151.
[27] *Pol. Schr.*, p. 152.

powering trend toward the rationalization of the totality of life to salvage any remnant of "individual freedom of movement" in any sense at all! It is also this same "freedom of movement," which Weber did not "salvage for himself," but incessantly battled for—almost for the sake of the battle itself. One who truly "salvaged" it for himself was a man like Jakob Burckhardt, through a deliberate withdrawal into the "private" sphere and the culture of "old Europe"; . . . whereas Weber had to conquer this freedom ever anew, without letup, ostensibly and spontaneously placing himself into precisely *this* world in order—while being in it—to work against it, in an "act of renunciation." The question, however, is *how* and *for what?* In order to answer this question we still require a comprehensive survey of the general context of meaning in which the phenomenon of rationalization stands.

Weber has demonstrated the most general and penetrating success of rationalization, particularly in the case of "science": a fundamental disenchantment with this world. The magic which governed the relation of man to the world in previous epochs was—rationally speaking —the belief in any "objective" meaning of any kind. With the stripping away of this "magic," the necessity arises to inquire anew after the "meaning" of our objectivities, and thus Weber in particular raises the question of the objectivity of science. Since all objectivities —through the rationalization effected by man—have lost their *objective* meaning, they are now—as it were, anew at man's disposal for the determination of their meaning. For the relationship of man himself to the world, this disenchantment with the world motivating the question of "meaning," signifies an all-pervading disillusionment; in other words: scientific "impartiality." The positive "opportunity" presented by this disillusionment of man and of the disenchantment with the world is the "sober" affirmation of everyday life and its "demands." At the same time, the affirmation of this everyday life signifies the negation of all transcendence, even that of "progress." Progress then means merely a moving forward along the predetermined rails of fate, with passion and resignation. In comparison with any transcendental faith, this belief in the fate of one's time and the passion of temporal activity constitutes a positive "disbelief." The positive factor, however, of this lack of belief in something that would transcend the "fate of our time" and the "demand of the day"—in objective, existing values, meanings, validities—is the subjectivity of a rational responsibility in the form of a pure self-responsibility which the individual assumes for and towards himself. The decisive characteristic of this "posited individualism" (the quotes are Weber's) lies in the distinction between two basically different kinds of responsibility. The specialized official, as any rationalized specialist, must be answerable to himself not as an individual, but always and only in regard to his office, to the respective institution, i.e., to "himself" as a member of this institution. On the other hand, the truly "executive" leading politician and the managing entrepreneur, those residues of the "heroic age of capitalism," *qua* human individuality acts on his own responsibility—and would act irresponsibly precisely if he felt answerable like a public official.[28] Hence the basic attitude which Weber assumes in this rationalized world, and which also determines his methodology, is one of an objective presuppositionless determination of the self-responsible individual through himself. Placed into this world of bondage, the individual as "man" belongs to himself and relies totally upon himself alone.

The presupposition of this position, however, is precisely this world of "statutes," institutions, enterprises, and securities against which it sets itself. Weber's position essentially is one of opposition; the opponents are an integral counterpart of the position. To achieve one's own purpose in this world and yet, in opposition to it, purposes which are not of this world and yet calculated for it, such is the positive meaning of this "freedom of movement" with which Weber was concerned. A "leader democracy with the 'machine,' " against a leaderless democracy but also against a leadership which has nothing to lead because it withdraws from the "machine": this is the crass *political* formula for Weber's fundamental movement in opposition. With this final affirmation of the productivity of opposition, Weber stands in the most extreme contrast to Marx, who on this score remained a Hegelian, because he wanted to abolish the "contradictions" of bourgeois society. And not, like Hegel, through their preservation within an absolutely organized State, but through their complete elimination in an absolutely classless society. The motive force of Weber's whole attitude, on the other hand, was the always newly overcome contradiction of the recognition of a rationalized world and the countertendency to achieve the freedom of self-responsibility.

The direct human expression of this fundamental contradiction is the inner human contradiction between man and specialist man. This unity of rationality and freedom is most impressively documented in the peculiar position which the man Weber himself assumed to his own humanity as a specialist. And even here the unity and divergency of its specialized interests correspond to the unity of a human contradiction. Weber never presented himself as an inseparable whole, but always as a member of a specific sphere—in this or that other role, as

---

[28] *Pol. Schr.,* pp. 153 and 415.

this or that other person: as an "empirical" individual scientist in (his) writings, as an academic teacher on the podium, as a politician on the rostrum, as *homo religiosus* in his most intimate circles. It is precisely in this separation of the life spheres—whose theoretical expression is value-freedom—that Weber's individuality in the uniqueness of its wholeness reveals itself. Even here the question for Weber was not the same as for Marx, namely to find a way by which the specific human type of the rationalized world, i.e., the specialist man, can be abolished along with the division of labor. Rather, Weber asks, by which way can man as such preserve the freedom of self-responsibility amid and in spite of, his inescapably compartmentalized humanity. Here too Weber affirms this self-alienated humanity (as Marx puts it) because it was precisely this form of existence which, while not affording or offering it, forced him into an extreme "freedom of movement." To act in the midst of this specialized and indoctrinated world of "specialists without spirit, sensualists without heart" with the passionate force of negativity, piercing now here and now there through some structure of "bondage"—this was the meaning of "freedom of movement." Just as Weber, in the sphere of politics, posits executives (as individuals) acting within the frame of the inevitable bureaucratization, so does the salvation of the human individual as such mean to him that it must take place within the ingrained attitude of the specialist humanity and with regard to it. By submitting to his fate, he at the same time already opposes it. But this counterposition has this previous subjection as its inevitable presupposition. In like manner, Weber's defense of the so-called anarchy in economic production corresponds—in purely human terms—to the defense of the right of *every* individuality as such (the "last human heroes"), yet Weber is neither, on one hand, an anarchist nor, on the other, an individualist in the usual sense. He wants indeed to save the "soul" from the predominance of the "man of order," yet this "soul" is not the sentimental soul of the "mechanic of the spirit" of Rathenau, but a soul existing amid the heartlessness of human calculations. Thus the individual as such, with which Weber was concerned as the "human element," also does not signify an indivisible whole above or outside the factual, compartmentalized mode of existence of the modern specialists. Rather, the individual is a "man" when he stakes his whole being in each and every separate role, great or small. On the strength of this kind of individualism, Weber could fix on anything and yet he fixed on nothing; place himself into any given situation and at the same time stand completely on his own. To be sure, this individualism which sums up his idea of man is not capable of destroying the iron cage of the general bondage, but it *is* capable of piercing it individually for one's own person. Thus Weber's deliberate renunciation of the "universal man," his restriction to the particularized work of the specialist—"in today's world, the presupposition for any serious work altogether"—is a renunciation which at the same time incorporates a great demand, namely, in spite of this "compartmentalization of the soul," man must ever be involved with his whole being—on the strength of passion—in all such acts which in themselves are isolated. "For nothing has any value for man as a man which he cannot do with passion." [29] With this "demon" of his passion—one might also call it the idol of a godless mankind—as the groundless ground of his purposes, Weber—in the midst of his strivings for a scientific and political objectivity—fought the belief in objectively valid aims, institutions, and concepts as idolatry and superstition—in order to salvage the human hero. As Honigsheim in his book *Max Weber as Sociologist* remarks, the sociological method of the destruction of all absolute value claims as put forth by the representatives of institutions ultimately serves this purpose. Sociology too, and in particular, served this freedom of movement. What Weber created for himself with his method was a "platform of negativity" on which the human hero "in a very plain sense of the word" should now bestir himself. The intellectual expression, however, of this human attitude is what Weber described as "simple intellectual integrity" which consists in giving account to oneself "of the final meaning of one's own actions."

Weber's idea of human freedom not only stands in contrast to the average individualism against which Hegel and Marx fought as the philistine freedom of private convenience, but it is also in extreme contrast to that "freedom" for which Marx wanted to emancipate man "humanly" and which, to him, was a freedom of "highest community." To Weber, this idea of Marx's was utopianism, while to Marx the human hero of Weber probably would have seemed a "conjuration of the dead," an isolated second edition of the heroic age of the bourgeoisie whose "sober reality" is "unheroic" and merely the ghost of its once great past. What for Weber was "ineluctable fate," for Marx was nothing more than the "prehistory" of mankind and that point which, for Marx, would mark the beginning of true history was, for Weber, the beginning of an ethic of irresponsible "conviction." This difference in their world views and ideas of man is spelled out in the dissimilarity of their determining point of view for the interpretation of the modern bourgeois capitalistic world— for Weber "rationality," for Marx "self-alienation."

[29] *W. L.,* p. 534.

PART THREE

SOCIOLOGY OF RELIGION

FIVE

ONCE AGAIN:

CALVINISM AND CAPITALISM

HERBERT LUETHY

MAX WEBER'S FAMOUS THESIS, *The Protestant Ethic and the Spirit of Capitalism*, appeared in 1904, and has remained the crowning glory of the historical and philosophical school of German sociology. The controversy provoked by this thesis has died down from time to time, but only to be rekindled again and again as new theses and supplementary subtleties are added to enrich the polemic. Throughout the last fifty years, most of the great scholars of the age have added either a comment or a book: Sombart, Troeltsch, and Brentano in Germany, Tawney and Robertson in England, Hauser and Sée in France, Amintore Fanfani (recently Prime Minister of his country) in Italy, Talcott Parsons in America, and Kurt Samuelsson in Sweden. The commemoration of the 450th anniversary of Calvin's birth has brought a new series of studies, and outstanding among them is a book by a Genevan theologian and national economist. This book[1] confronts

"Once Again: Calvinism and Capitalism," by Herbert Luethy. From *Encounter*, XXII (January, 1964), 26–32. Also appeared in Herbert Luethy, *From Calvin to Rousseau* (New York: Basic Books, 1969). Reprinted by permission of the author and *Encounter*.

[1] The fullest review, as I say, is to be found in André Biéler's *La Pensée économique et sociale de Calvin* (Geneva, 1959). The polemic was opened by Max Offenbacher, with his *Konfession und soziale Schichtung: Eine Studie über die wirtschaftliche Lage der Katholiken und Protestanten in Baden* (Tübingen, 1900). For

the various theses of this debate with the original texts of Calvin's massive teachings. Few historical arguments have produced a greater wealth of intellectually fertile, subtle, and often deeply disturbing *aperçus,* and raised deeper passions hidden under the calm surface of scholarship. Few arguments have borne a richer crop of basic misunderstandings; few a more meagre harvest of definite, tenable, unambiguous results (I mean results of which we can not only say: there's something in it, but: that's the way it is). The whole subject is lit by the flickering light of the illuminating, frequently obvious, but equivocal relationship between categories of concepts that are remote from one another and, furthermore, are themselves essentially vague: the *ethic* of a religious belief and the *spirit* of an economic system, the cure of souls and the balancing of accounts. The establishment of relationships between remote concepts is among the favourite games of the human mind, and perhaps one of its most fruitful, for it reveals surprising links and opens new perspectives— but also one of the most dangerous and seductively misleading ones.

In a short paper it is not possible to refer individually even to the most important matters in dispute which the polemic has aroused, not even in the broadest outlines: the result would be a pure chaos of ideas. Here, as elsewhere, the trouble begins with the terminology: what the problem is actually about is subject, on both sides of the equation, to misunderstanding and confusion. The explosive power of Weber's thesis derived from the correlation of two concepts, Protestantism and Capitalism. Yet when Weber comes to develop the thesis, it appears that the "Protestantism" referred to in his title is almost exclusively limited to a single one of its many manifestations, Calvinism; and Calvinism itself is examined principally in certain key texts which are only characteristic of certain specific periods and particular forms of *Puritanism,* such as the *Westminster Confession* of 1654 (a religious Civil War manifesto), or the utilitarian moral tracts of that Man of the Enlightenment, Benjamin Franklin (his advice "how to become rich") which reflect an entirely secular theory of virtue, but which can hardly be said to express a religious attitude. It is significant that fifty years elapsed after Weber's thesis before André Biéler set about examining the ensuing polemic in the light of what

---

an examination of the Puritan Revolution in England, see J. H. Hexter, *Storm over the Gentry* (published in *Encounter,* May, 1958, and commented on in the magazine's correspondence columns in subsequent issues); it has been reprinted in *Reappraisals in History,* published by Longmans. Invaluable is C. V. Wedgwood's *History of the Puritan Rebellion* in two volumes, of which the first appeared in 1955. As for "economics," "chrematistics," and the problem of usury, see the final pages of my own *Banque protestante en France* (Vol. II, Paris, 1961).

Calvin himself actually taught—and on this basis rejected most of what had been said on the subject. Perhaps even more deceptive and chameleon-like is the concept on the other side of the equation: Capitalism. In the century since Marx this word has been worked to death: it has been applied to every conceivable practice, epoch, and economic system; it has been degraded to a fashionable phrase and to a term of abuse, with the result that it is scarcely viable any more as an historical idea. There are as many definitions of capitalism as there have been economists and sociologists writing about it. The word as commonly used in European journalism is always available in order to express in an apparently concise term any passing feeling of uneasiness with existing society. That Weber spoke not of capitalism but of the *spirit* of capitalism—just as he wrote not about Protestantism as a theological doctrine but about the Protestant *ethic*—was a warning that has been invariably ignored. The word was there, malleable as putty, and the very next man to pick up Weber's thesis, namely Sombart, already made something entirely different of it.

For only in the whole context of his monumental, labyrinthine, and tormented work does Max Weber's thesis achieve its complete and subtle meaning. His great and questioning mind was never particularly interested in the facts of history, nor even in social and economic systems, but rather in the detection of the ultimate impulses behind man's attitude and behaviour. What he analysed were not the hybrid and wretched forms of an historically realised society (in which such ultimate impulses are never embodied in their purity), but rather the abstract and chemically pure "ideal types" which should provide the essences of a civilisation stripped of all the adulterations and accidents of actual history. His religio-sociological studies, and also his economic and social-historical works, whether he is writing the agrarian history of the Ancient World or dissecting the Indian caste structure, are in fact always concerned with the one problem posed by the historically unique nature of modern Western civilisation. And in this context the words "capitalism" or "spirit of capitalism" are used in a very particular sense: they mean no less than the entire inner structure governing Western society's attitudes, not only its economy but also its legal system, its political structure, its institutionalised sciences and technology, its mathematically-based music and architecture. Its economic modes of operation, works discipline, and accountancy methods are all regarded by him as the mere *pars per toto* of a whole civilisation-type for which Weber's final word is rationality (*Rationalität*)—a rationality which permeates all fields of social behaviour, the organisation of labour and management as well as the creative sciences, law and order, philosophy and the arts, the state and politics, and the dominant forms of private life. This rationality, driven by its own internal dynamic, has overthrown (or tamed) every form of resistance offered by pre-rational human nature, magic and tradition, instinct and spontaneity. Finally, with the Reformation, it has forced its way into the innermost temple wherein the motives behind human behaviour are generated, into the very heart of religious belief, there to destroy all the dark, magical, mysterious tabernacles—image, cult, and tradition—for which it substitutes the Bible as the authentic truth, supposedly unshakeable, accessible to critical examination, and susceptible of proof.

This is what the Reformation means for Weber and this is the knot with which he linked economic theory and religious doctrine. Weber rightly insists upon the historically well-nigh monstrous uniqueness of this civilisation, which cannot be explained in terms of its material bases alone. Those material and technical pre-conditions on which Europe started to build her civilisation after the late Middle Ages, existed equally or even more richly in other high cultures, in Hellenism, in ancient Rome, in India, China, and the Arab Caliphate; yet in no other case did they cause a similar leap from the merely static to the irresistibly dynamic. We know to-day how right Weber was to insist on the precedence of inner spiritual and cultural pre-conditions over all external and economic forms. He was right against almost all his contemporaries, liberals and Marxists alike, who accepted the availability of capital and of labour force as adequate pre-conditions for economic progress and thus believed that a Western-type civilisation could be transplanted or imposed virtually anywhere. And how right he was, too, to be tormented with worry about the future prospects of a fully and finally rationalised civilisation in which the impulses inherited from its pre-rational past should have died once and for all. The fact that he thought he could summarise the nature of this civilisation in the ambiguous term "capitalism" (the catchword for a purely materialistic dynamic) demonstrates the tension in his thought, a tension close to breaking-point between highest admiration and utter rejection of the achievements of Western civilisation at the time of its greatest *hubris*.

A similar inner tension marks his attitude towards Protestantism. He respected what he called its ethical and moral "values"—an expression which itself reveals the problematic nature of his attitude—while regarding its religious roots as desiccated and doomed. Having first broken through the paganism of image, rite, cult, and tradition to find a sure source of nourishment in the Holy Scriptures, Protestant rationalism (he thought) must eventually hollow and empty these too.

It is this inner ambivalence towards them both that enabled Weber
to draw his connection between the Protestant ethic and the spirit of
Capitalism and to create the paradox of his functional equation. It
is both the greatness and the tragedy of Weber—a positivist and a
sceptic, a universal spirit and an ardent German nationalist, who died
in 1920 when his world lay in ruins—that he had attempted to pursue
the insoluble contradictions both within his being and his age in all
directions down to their deepest roots, without ever finding the
answer. And it is the obverse of his greatness that his powerful and
fragmentary life's work did not lay the foundations of "a science of
society" but rather has become an inexhaustible mine for glittering
esoteric formulas and slogans, many of which have been more misleading and harmful than the one here under discussion.

All this is only a preliminary remark to our subject, yet it has to be
stated in order that the complex starting-point of the polemic becomes comprehensible: and it allows me to anticipate my conclusion.
In the debate that Weber began no one else has employed the term
"capitalism" as he did, *i.e.*, to denote a whole pattern of civilisation.
The argument was immediately transferred to the lower plane of economic management, accumulation of capital, or even of the simple
profit motive. And precisely because of this misunderstanding, the
isolated essay on "Capitalism and Protestantism" (which is the one
fragment of Weber's work known by hearsay at least to all educated
persons) has produced its powerful and irritating effect. If Weber had
not so wilfully substituted one single feature for the totality, if he
had given his work a title that expressed his actual purpose in common language (such as *Protestantism and Modern Society* or *The
Reformation and the Spirit of Western Civilisation*) he would, in a
new form and tone, have only been stating what no one has ever
questioned, and it would have caused no such excitement—that the
Reformation marks a profound spiritual breach between the Middle
Ages and the modern world, bringing a ferment into Western history
which has changed its course irreversibly, far beyond the domain of
the Protestant churches and communities, to imprint its mark upon
the whole Western world; that without Calvin we could not imagine
Cromwell, or Rousseau, or the Founding Fathers; that the modern
industrial society, as well as creative science, the rule of law, constitutionalism, in brief the free society, first appeared (and have flourished
best) in those countries which were moulded by Calvinism; and that an
indissoluble internal bond links all these aspects of our Western
society.
Had this provided the substance of the polemic, it could be termi-

nated here and now without further ado. This development in its factual manifestations is the content of our history during these last four hundred years, and it provides an inexhaustible subject for research and speculation; but that it is so no one can doubt. And also that this was not the whole story: that the Reformation was not alone and in itself the turning-point, but merely one of its elements intimately linked with others of the age which *together* altered the whole spiritual and material picture of the world—humanism, the Copernican revolution, the mastery of the seas and the discovery of new continents, the sudden emergence of global powers and global trade, all the splendour and chaos, worldly triumph and metaphysical despair engendered in a world that would be henceforth boundless but that had lost all security and all familiarity. And we also know that all this was not a totally new start from the void. The closed world of the Middle Ages had been burst asunder by powerful forces created within that very world, forces that led from the Crusades to the Spanish-Portuguese *Conquista,* from the scholastic universities to humanism, from the mediæval schisms and heresies to the Reformation. In a certain sense, Martin Luther's revolt against the worldliness of Renaissance Rome was the revolt of a mediæval spirit against the modern world, and not the obverse.

However the key word, capitalism, had been inserted, and the debate became limited to this one aspect of the relationship between the teachings of the Reformation and economic behaviour, and this not as one among many interconnecting links supporting a civilisation's entire history but as a direct and causative relation between religious doctrine and economic practice. It was as though the essential thread had suddenly been discovered which would lead dialectically from the nailing of Luther's ninety-five theses on the Wittenberg church door to the assembly lines of Detroit and the ramifications of Standard Oil. It is hardly necessary to add that this entire debate took place beneath the long shadow of Karl Marx, whose challenge no historian and no social scientist of the past hundred years has been able to ignore. Weber's thesis stressing the decisive influence of the spiritual fundamentals upon economic behaviour, rather than *vice versa,* is itself only comprehensible in the context of his intensive debate with historical materialism. The whole ensuing polemic on the primacy of the spiritual or the economic motivations has an odd chicken-and-egg quality: did the Reformation produce the spirit of Capitalism, or did the spirit of Capitalism produce the Reformation? Only the second thesis, which makes Protestantism the "subjective superstructure," or "the ideology" of capitalism, accords with historical

materialism—and in the hands of many a bourgeois historian, historical materialism has become far more vulgar than ever it was in Marx's
own version. Thus did the Reformation acquire its place in a very
categorical picture of the historical process, considered as "a history of
class struggles." In all these versions of modern history, satisfactorily
reconstructed on the great lines of the rise to power of the bourgeoisie
and the decline of feudalism, the Reformation takes its place as "the
first bourgeois revolution." By analysing the English Puritan Revolution of the 17th century as the second bourgeois revolution, Tawney
skilfully constructed a bridge to the third and greatest, the French
Revolution at the end of the 18th century.

So it is that the second catchword was inserted, a twin to the concept
of capitalism, equally iridescent and equally ambiguous: "the bourgeoisie." And with it comes its opposite, the counter-concept of "Feudalism," and even more hopelessly worked to death, if that be possible.
In an interpretation of history which reduces acting and thinking
historical human beings to the simple function of conscious or unconscious instruments and exponents of class forces, the leaders of the
Reformation become spokesmen for the aspiring bourgeoisie, the class
that bred capitalism. So self-evident has this interpretation become to
a whole generation of historians that we must start all over again if
we are to rescue the history of the Reformation and of its endlessly
complex effects from the preconceived schemata now deeply embedded
in popular history and school textbooks.

For this interpretation, quite simply, is not true.

Let us return once more to the starting-point of the whole polemic.
At the back of Weber's thesis there is one established and supporting
set of facts, and this set of facts, be it noted, dates not from the period
of the Reformation but from the turn of the 20th century. Weber's
starting-point was a statistical survey carried out in 1900 by the German sociologist, Max Offenbacher, into "the economic condition of
Catholics and Protestants" in the religiously mixed (60 per cent
Catholic) Grand Duchy of Baden. Offenbacher established that the
Protestant citizens of the Grand Duchy owned a disproportionately
large percentage of capital assets and occupied more than their share
of leading positions, of educational qualifications, academic positions,
and skilled labour jobs. This was the sort of research then being carried out in the very early days of German sociology. At about this time
Offenbacher and others had established that the Jews played a disproportionately large role in the commercial and liberal professions. A
few years earlier Max Weber himself had carried out research into the
Polish "infiltration" (*Unterwanderung*) in the East Prussian territo-

ries; and the whole complexity of Weber's personality is evident in the fact that his anti-capitalist anger was first aroused by East Prussian agrarian capitalism which, he said, was de-Germanising the East German territories by recruiting cheap Polish labourers instead of more expensive Germans. These researches were carried out with true German thoroughness, propriety, and scholarliness; and yet, in retrospect, we cannot but feel uneasy about the spirit in which they were conducted, a spirit which finally brought disaster to Europe.

Be that as it may, here was the problem, and now this historian set about discovering the causes. Where was he more likely to find the reason for the economic success of Baden's Protestant minority than in the Protestant doctrine itself? Offenbacher's researches in the Grand Duchy of Baden were directed explicitly and exclusively at the economic status of the members of the two Churches; but they nevertheless established not merely a Protestant predominance in "capitalist activity" but a generally higher degree of ambition and achievement in all fields such as science, academic life, the professions, the civil service, as well as in business. Now this exclusive interest in the Protestants' economic condition, which is implicit in the formulation of the questions in this statistical enquiry, becomes in Weber's interpretation the essence of the whole much larger problem, to the extent that he totally neglects the evidence of Protestant successes in all other fields except as capitalists or *entrepreneurs*. Acting in all good faith, yet with consequences that were to weigh heavily throughout the whole polemic, Weber thus distorted from the start the entire premise upon which the problem rested.

Similar statistics could obviously have been established for all areas with religiously mixed populations, and quite independently of the economic system or the level of industrialisation would have produced similar results. My own country, Switzerland, would provide one excellent field for such research, thanks to its preservation of mediæval geo-political autonomies and its mixture of adjoining religious self-governing communities. The dividing boundaries between highly developed and (in modern parlance) under-developed areas of this country correspond almost exactly to the old boundaries between the two religious communities, the adherents of the new and the old faith. This is striking evidence; but these boundaries were already practically the same *before* the Reformation, and thus show us the extreme complexity of establishing cause and effect. Even more striking is the case of a country such as France, where since the 18th century a tiny Protestant minority had played a leading part grotesquely out of proportion to its numerical strength, not only in industry and finance, but equally in political and intellectual life. Nor are these spectacular achievements limited to the modernised or "capitalist" parts of France. In the poor peasant lands of the south, which since the 16th century have been the centre of resistance for politically defeated French Calvinism, the Protestant peasants remain to this day a nobility and an élite. And, in spite of entirely different power relationships throughout history, and in spite of the more recent reversal of this power relationship, the same statement applies to agricultural, Catholic, clerical Ireland where the small Protestant minority was and has remained the active élite.

But here I wish to warn against the drawing of hasty conclusions. There can be no doubt of the ethical, intellectual *and* economic role played by dissenting minorities as an élite (and a "yeast") but this fact seems to be quite unconnected with the actual form of their dissent. To quote the Church Father: *Opportet haereses esse!* Let us recall the Jews of Central and Eastern Europe, the religious minorities of the Near East and of India, groups whose achievements obviously have nothing whatever to do with the Protestant ethic and which yet have certain features in common with those of the Protestants in other parts of the world. In each case these are the response to a challenge imposed by legal or social discrimination which produce or evoke a higher level of activity and of discipline whenever the subjective conditions for such a response exist. The fact that Protestant doctrine, in its Calvinist variety, was more suited to the production of such endeavour and self-discipline than was Catholic doctrine, is shown to be true by the comparison between the Catholic minority in England and the Protestant minority in France—the general situation and conditions of life were almost identical through four centuries, and yet the English Catholics, unlike the French Protestants, have never acted as "the yeast" within their society. The Protestant teaching that the believer's behaviour as an individual is subject to no sanction by any external spiritual authority but only to the inner sanctions of his own conscience has undoubtedly armed and equipped them better for life in a "hostile" environment, without the paternal protection of established church authority, and it strengthened those virtues of responsibility, self-control, and spiritual independence which even the bitterest enemies of the Reformation have recognised in the Protestant minorities. Another equally important factor of spiritual as well as economic history is that for centuries the Protestant minorities living in Catholic countries, regardless of class, were a Bible-reading people, a "people of the book," like the Jews, and thus constituted a literate minority amidst illiterate masses. Yet we need not depend exclusively on such micro-sociological comparisons between different religious groups living within one and the same countries. Much more striking is (and was already for Weber) the global evidence furnished by the comparison of whole countries and continents. Consider the case of the two parts of the old Low Countries Belgium and Holland, once a single nation, but the development of which has diverged radically since 1600; no natural or historical pre-conditions except their different fate in the Reformation can explain why these two sections of one country, living side by side, should have diverged as obviously and to the extent they have. Similarly, on a continental scale, there is the image and counter-image of Anglo-Saxon and Latin America, the sociologist's textbook-example of development and under-development. . . .

And here another question arises, which strangely enough has scarcely ever been mentioned in all this polemic. The Reformation took place at the very height of a period of almost breath-taking growth in Europe, of development in all the fields of the mind, of technology, of the liberation of human personality, of economic and imperial expansion. In no single one of these fields is there a scrap of evidence to show that the Reformation was a fresh start or that it gave birth to anything fundamentally new. All the evidence advanced in favour of Weber's thesis is taken from the 18th and 19th centuries—that is to say, from a period so remote in time from the age of religious division as to make direct and unambiguous connection with the Reformation quite impossible of proof, and all such examples are but further developments of what in fact started in all Europe towards the end of the Middle Ages.

One can go further: specifically in the field of capitalist organisation, Catholic Europe in the 15th and early 16th centuries (the age of the Fuggers) reached a level of structural and organisational development which was not to be achieved again for a further two centuries. Precisely in this domain a startling decadence and stagnation began in the middle of the 16th century. So does the Reformation represent a breakthrough from which a fresh progress can be dated? Or was it not rather the Counter Reformation, as an authoritarian and total reaction against all manifestations of the free heretical spirit, which stopped all further progress and which, after the spiritual and material catastrophes of the Wars of Religion, prevented a resumption of such progress wherever it had been triumphant?

Before the Counter Reformation this progress had not only been common to all Europe but had had as its matrix those very parts of Europe which had now fallen to the Counter Reformation and which now subsided into a sleep of death both economically and (even more) intellectually, and where only the arts continued to flourish in the service of throne and altar. Think of the powerful *translatio imperii* of the sciences from Italy to England in the 17th century, or the astonishing absence of Catholic Germany from the re-birth of German philosophy and literature that followed the Thirty Years War.

And the exception which proves the rule is the confusing special position occupied by France. There the Catholic State Church had long been subordinated to the French crown and served as an instrument of the absolute monarchy which needed no reformation to establish a national church sovereignty. It refused to accept the Counter Reformation, the Tridentine Council, the Inquisition, and clerical control of all intellectual life. During the decisive struggles of the 17th century His Most Christian Majesty of France was invariably allied to the Protestant states against Catholic Spain, and despite Louis XIV and the persecution of the Huguenots, Calvinism's imprint remained far stronger in France than its external history reveals.

It is probably the most absurd failure of this whole discussion concerning the historical role of Protestantism, a discussion carried on in a sort of intellectual incest behind closed windows, that it has quite simply ignored the other side of its problem: the historical part played by the Counter Reformation (which was itself a reformation and which in its own way marked the end of Catholicism as a universal church), as if the sudden breaking of an ascendant curve of development did not constitute a far greater problem than its continuance. In the period of the Reformation all the bases of the modern world—capital, wealth, the highest technological and artistic level of development, global power, world trade—all these were almost exclusively present in countries that were and remained Catholic. Italy was the uncontested centre of material and intellectual culture. Spain and Portugal enjoyed the monopoly of colonising and exploiting both the Indies, the most important field of enterprise and the greatest source of wealth in the opening years of the modern age. It was *here*, and not among the poor and half-barbarian Protestant states on the fringe of northern and north-western Europe, that all the material and technical pre-conditions for the creation of modern economy and modern society were to be found.

One century later all this was petrifaction and decay. Catholic historians have shown us what an appalling break the Counter Reformation was in the cultural history of Europe, and how deadly was the shadow cast by Inquisition and heresy trials across the lands where this reaction had triumphed. It was as if a spell had been laid upon this half of the continent from which it was not to awake until two centuries had passed, under the spur of enlightened, anti-clerical absolutism (or, even later, as a sequel to the Revolutionary Wars). During these centuries, in *one* half of Europe, an intellectual ferment, general and active throughout the *whole* continent on the eve of the Reformation, was extinguished and destroyed. The existential minimum of a free society, without which neither intellectual nor industrial pioneers, neither scientific research nor economic progress, are possible, was there totally uprooted. This is a cross-road of history which becomes caricature when we reduce it to a mere economic phenomenon.

Yet even in this narrow perspective we should raise the question *why* the Reformation permitted the free northern Netherlands to preserve and develop the great heritage of industrial and mercantile achievement while in the Spanish Netherlands it was destroyed—instead of reversing the terms of the problem and trying to discover *why* the Reformation produced achievements for which it was not, in fact, responsible. For the splendour and glory of Amsterdam flowed from the same factors that had made the splendour and glory of Antwerp in an earlier age. Amsterdam did not so much invent new commercial and financial devices as inherit what the Spanish wrath destroyed in Antwerp and attract those who fled the Inquisition (Jews, heretics, etc.). It is certainly legitimate to single out in the complex course of history *one* line of development (the development of the modern market and of a competitive economy in north-west Europe) as a subject of specialised research. But to believe that this will reveal the essence of the Reformation and of its effects, to wave a bank account book or a balance sheet and to cry: "Here is the quintessence of Calvinism!"—this is nonsense. And it is as much the duty of the economic historian as of the theologian to protest against such nonsense.

SIX

RELIGIOUS OUTLOOKS
AND CLASSES

CARLO ANTONI

WEBER'S STUDIES IN THE economic ethics of world religions (*Versuche einer vergleichenden Religionssoziologie*) have a nonhistorical character insofar as they are an attempt to group the various religious ethics into unitary and systematic frames which admit of no development. Here in all its boldness is seen Weber's ability to deduce logical transitions, the practical and theoretical consequences through which a religious dogma is passed to a social class, from this to a legal order, to an art form, to an educational ideal, to a logical system, to a sexual ethic, to an industry, and so forth. Here cultures assume the character of isolated and almost impenetrable geometrical forms constructed with crystalline coherence and rationality according to different formulae. In fact, at one point Weber calls these studies "contributions to a sociology of rationalism."

Above all, the aim of these studies was to furnish a confirmation of the Puritan origin of the modern capitalist spirit. Here also the different religious ethics are examined in relation to the economic attitudes which they engender, so as to give better insight into that type of economic rationalism which came to prevail in the West during the sixteenth and seventeenth centuries. In sum, the studies were intended to be a series of negative experiments which would serve to establish how, given the economic, social and political conditions

"Religious Outlooks and Classes" (editor's title). From Carlo Antoni, *From History to Sociology*, trans. Hayden V. White (Detroit: Wayne State University Press, 1959), pp. 161–67. Copyright 1959 by Wayne State University Press. Originally published as *Dallo Storicismo alla Sociologia* (Florence: G. C. Sansoni, 1940). Reprinted by permission of the translator and Wayne State University Press. Some footnotes have been omitted for reasons of space.

favorable to its development, a capitalism of the modern type could not have been realized had the Calvinist ascetic element been lacking.

Another value of these studies lies in their having revealed the economic *ethos* in all its importance. Weber derived his conclusions, not in a bookish and scholarly manner from philosophical tracts, but from all of the documents which might give insight into the moral and religious life of the people. Here, truly, the distance between East and West and the basic reasons for their different destinies is measured in grand perspective.

Thus, Weber describes Confucianism as more of a doctrine and a rite than a religion, one which was imposed upon China by its bureaucratic class of literati-calligraphers. It is seen to embrace a utilitarian and rationalistic ethic of conventions, self-control and rank and to be opposed to any form of mystic contemplation and orgiastic ecstasy as an irrational disorder or vulgar barbarity. Here thought remains bound to practical problems and bureaucratic interests. One abandons all attempts to communicate with the masses and dedicates himself to the mastery of a difficult calligraphy. Hence, there is no development of the art of definition or reasoning. War is disparaged as mere brigandage; the world is seen as the best possible—provided that its eternal order is not disturbed; all men are held to be naturally equal and capable of perfection; the only possible redemption is held to be that which liberates one from barbarity and ignorance; the only sins are those committed against the authority of parents, ancestors, one's hierarchical superiors, the ceremonial, and the traditional customs; the only prize of virtue is a long life, health, wealth, and (after death) a good name. With this mandarin ethic, tenaciously bound to tradition and hostile to any reform, China remained further from the capitalist spirit than classical antiquity itself. Weber was thus able to establish the fact that in precisely the country of parsimony and spirit of gain, in spite of its glorification and utilization of wealth as a means of moral perfection, in spite of the peace, tolerance, freedom of business and commerce, freedom of choice of profession and methods of production found there, China developed no rationally organized business activity, monetary system or commerce.

India seemed to offer all the conditions favorable to the development of a rational business activity. In India commerce and usury flourished; the profit instinct was never wanting; war, politics and finance were rational; public debts, tax assessment, supply and monopolies were similar to those of the West. There the rational number system was invented, rational sciences such as grammar and mathematics were cultivated, tolerance was almost an absolute and the professions were specialized. The merchant class was as autonomous as in the medieval West, and cities were developed. Nevertheless, modern capitalism did not arise in India, and when it was imported, it found no indigenous points of contact. According to Weber, this was because of the magico-ritualistic division of the populace into castes. A ritual which regarded any change in profession or even in techniques as embodying a danger of pollution and degradation was bound to frustrate any technico-economic transformation. In fact, it was the outcastes and the pariahs, not the members of the older artisan castes, who manned the modern industry of India.

A different situation obtained in Japan, where the population had received its *ethos*, not from a class of literati, such as the mandarin and the Brahmin, but from the warlike and chivalric samurai. Thus, even if it were unable to develop a rational economy by itself, Japan could easily adapt itself to modern capitalism because of the spirit of individualism which informed the feudal contract there.

For Weber, however, the study of the ascetic or redemptive religions of India constituted an essential test for his thesis. Buddhism, the most radical of these religions, freed man from the "wheel," from the eternal cycle of death and rebirth, through pure contemplation and the destruction of the individual will. Consequently, it represented a type of asceticism diametrically opposed to that of the Calvinist. One Indian religion which did have a positive effect upon economic activity was that of the Jains, a monastic sect devoted to trade and labouring under a severe *ascesis* of controlled, methodical conduct, non-enjoyment of wealth, business honesty, and a strong group solidarity. But Weber does not explain why this sect of "Indian Puritans" did not create its own capitalist spirit similar to that found in the West.

One might argue that it is precisely through this examination of the Orient that the specific thesis of Weber concerning the origin of the capitalist spirit in the psychological need of the Calvinist for some sort of confirmation is shown to be invalid. The whole of Western cultural development, as opposed to the traditionalistic Orient, is shown by these studies to have been moving towards the realization of a rational economic progress from the beginning. Precisely through a comparison with the Asiatic world is modern capitalism revealed to be anything but a paradoxical, unforeseen occurrence. The Orient, with its idea of a sacred and eternal order of things, lacked the idea of the duality of ethics and politics which is presupposed in the dialectic of the condemnation of the world and its ethical reconsecration. To see this development as a kind of psychological deviation is to reduce this grandiose phenomenon to rather shabby proportions.

Even Judaism lacked these presuppositions. Against the celebrated thesis of Sombart, Weber himself denied a capitalistic spirit to the Jews. Their contribution to the development of the West rests, according to him, only in their character as a guest people who follow the petty bourgeois ethic of the prophets and psalmists towards the members of their own sect, an ethic which reflects the ancient rule of good neighborliness and solidarity, while practicing usury and speculation in their relations with the stranger. This form of capitalism is viewed as in itself reprehensible and is only conceded as a practice to be used upon strangers. Such an idea could never give birth to a professional and commercial ethic such as that which came out of Calvinism.

The real problem of these studies is not the way in which the economic ethic determines a given socio-economic order but the way in which the socio-economic order determines the ethic. Here Weber's attention is directed, not to the relation between dogma and economic activity, but to the opposite side of the cycle, to the relations between social conditions and dogma. He reascends, as it were, to the stratum which gives to the ethic its characteristic traits. That class which in his essay was only adumbrated here becomes the protagonist. Thus envisaged, Confucianism is the ethic of a class of bureaucratic literati which lives off prebends and perquisites; Hinduism is the religion of a hereditary caste of ritualist-literati who are the custodians of the sacred doctrine informing the caste hierarchy; Buddhism is the product of a patrician class and is a religion of mendicant monks completely detached from the world; Judaism was originally the religion of a confederation of semi-nomadic tribes, then of free peasants and shepherds, and finally of a petty bourgeois pariah people led by a class of intellectual ritualists; Christianity was the doctrine of a displaced artisan craftsman class and remained a bourgeois religion with its centers in the cities—political organisms peculiar to the West; Islam is the religion of a knightly order of warrior-conquerors, and its heresy, Sufism, was the religion of a petty bourgeois confraternity directed by plebian practitioners of an orgiastic mysticism.

Thus, even the most profound difference between East and West is, below all the differences of faith, primarily a question of classes.

In fact Weber makes the fortunes of Christianity—from the first isolated communities to the medieval mendicant orders to the modern sects of Methodists and Quakers—dependent upon the city, the center of the middle class, having its own freedom and politico-military power, a political organism unknown to China. For Weber, China is essentially an agrarian culture, ultimately dependent upon a vast network of canals and dams for the control of the rivers and therefore dependent upon a patrimonial and bureaucratic monarchy. Hinduism, for Weber, is linked to a monarchical political system and it is in the service of this system that the Brahmins legitimize social rank by the ritualistic division of society into castes, thereby impeding the fraternization of the corporation and the solidarity of the bourgeoisie with the magical concept of impure contact.

However, Weber hastens to protest that he does not intend at all to consider religiosity as an ideology or a mere reflection of the material and ideal interests of a class. However deep these influences may be, he declares, the religious ethic proceeds from religious sources, and even if it adapts itself to the needs of the community, those needs are above all religious in nature. Actually, in these studies the religious life assumes concrete historical individuality only insofar as it is determined by the economico-political exigencies of a class. Its autonomy is postulated as that of an irrational and incommunicable mystical experience which acquires a physiognomy in the degree to which it is confiscated by ideas. What are the origins of these ideas? In Weber's exposition they would seem to emanate for the most part from class interest.

Except for that prejudice this sociology of religion would be differentiated from materialism only by its substitution of the concept of social class for that of economic class. Class is defined by Weber as a human group not always organized but always in some way associated through its mode of life, conventional ideas of honor, and legally monopolized economic "chances" or opportunities. It is a concept which he worked out during the agrarian inquest when he was confronted with the crisis of the Prussian peasant and the *Junker* aristocracy. And just as the German political problem seemed to him to be a problem of the ruling class, so in the field of religion and ethical history he is concerned with the problem of the "carrying" class.

However, the character of this sociology remains analogous to that of materialist historiography. The spiritual life is explained in terms of its causes, that is, is considered objectively, as a nature deprived of any intrinsic truth. Having denied to himself any value judgment, Weber could not construct any sort of hierarchy and was therefore unable to perceive any sort of development. Typical in this respect is his concept of the history of Jewish religion, which in its various phases appears to be determined solely by external political contingencies. In spite of Weber's protestations, the various ethical systems here appear only as projections of class interest—they are indelibly stamped with designations such as "bureaucratic," "warlike," "bourgeois," and "petty bourgeois."

Nietzsche had juxtaposed a master morality to a slave morality. Weber lists more moralities, as many in fact as there are social types, and since he seeks to be objective he shows no preference for any particular one. But since under the terms of such a view even our moral life appears relative to the class to which we belong or to the classes which have formed and led it (in Judaism and Christianity the carrying class is the petty bourgeoisie), to liberate it from such class bonds would be to push it into a void. And one would be left with that sense of drift which Weber himself reflects in calling himself a polytheist— at least if one does not try to find a norm, as he himself did, in the technique of one's own profession, in responsibility to the vocation assigned by fate.

PART FOUR

BUREAUCRACY

SEVEN

WEBER'S THEORY
OF BUREAUCRACY

PETER M. BLAU

IN HIS CLASSICAL theory of bureaucracy, the German sociologist Max
Weber outlined the distinctive characteristics of formal organizations
that are bureaucratically organized. The most important of these
characteristics are:[1]

1. Organizational tasks are distributed among the various positions
as official duties. Implied is a clear-cut division of labor among positions
which makes possible a high degree of specialization. Specialization in
turn promotes expertness among the staff, both directly and by enabling
the organization to hire employees on the basis of their technical qualifications.

2. The positions or offices are organized into a hierarchical authority
structure. In the usual case this hierarchy takes on the shape of a pyramid
wherein each official is responsible for his subordinates' decisions and
actions as well as his own to the superior above him in the pyramid and
wherein each official has authority over the officials under him. The scope
of authority of supervisors over subordinates is clearly circumscribed.

"Weber's Theory of Bureaucracy." From Peter M. Blau, "The Study of Formal
Organization," in Talcott Parsons, ed., *American Sociology* (New York: Basic Books,
1968), pp. 57–62. Copyright © 1968 by Basic Books, Inc., Publishers, New York. Reprinted by permission of the author and the publisher.

[1] Max Weber, *Essays in Sociology* (New York: Oxford University Press, 1946), pp.
196–204, and *The Theory of Social and Economic Organization* (Glencoe, Ill.: The
Free Press, 1947), pp. 329–36.

3. A formally established system of rules and regulations governs official decisions and actions. In principle, the operations in such administrative organizations involve the application of these general regulations to particular cases. The regulations ensure the uniformity of operations and, together with the authority structure, make possible the coordination of the various activities. They also provide for continuity in operations regardless of changes of personnel, thus promoting a stability lacking in many other types of groups and collectivities, such as social movements.

4. There is a specialized administrative staff whose task it is to maintain the organization and, in particular, the lines of communication in it. The lowest level of this administrative apparatus consists of the clerical staff responsible for keeping the written records and files of the organization, in which all official decisions and actions are embodied. Whereas the "production" staff contributes directly to the achievement of the organization's objectives, whether this involves producing cars, collecting taxes, fighting wars, or curing patients, the administrative staff contributes to goal achievement only indirectly by keeping the organization itself going.

5. Officials are expected to assume an impersonal orientation in their contacts with clients and with other officials. Clients are to be treated as cases, the officials being expected to disregard all personal considerations and to maintain complete emotional detachment, and subordinates are to be treated in a similarly impersonal fashion. The social distance between hierarchical levels and that between officials and their clients is intended to foster such formality. Impersonal detachment is designed to prevent the personal feelings of officials from distorting their rational judgment in carrying out their duties.

6. Employment by the organization constitutes a career for officials. Typically an official is a full-time employee and looks forward to a lifelong career in the agency. Employment is based on the technical qualifications of the candidate rather than on political, family, or other connections. Usually such qualifications are tested by examination or by certificates that demonstrate the candidate's educational attainment—college degrees, for example. Such educational qualifications create a certain amount of class homogeneity among officials, since relatively few persons of working-class origin have college degrees, although their number is increasing. Officials are appointed to positions, not elected, and thus are dependent on superiors in the organization rather than on a body of constituents. After a trial period officials gain tenure of position and are protected against arbitrary dismissal. Remuneration is in the form of a salary, and pensions are provided after retirement. Career advancements are "according to seniority or to achievement, or both." [2]

Weber presents an implicit functional analysis of the interdependence between the characteristics of bureaucracy, with rational, efficient

[2] Ibid., p. 334.

administration as the criterion of function. Effective accomplishment of complex administrative tasks on a large scale requires that they be subdivided into specialized responsibilities, which can be readily handled by individuals, and that professionally qualified experts be appointed to discharge these responsibilities. This pronounced division of labor creates serious problems of coordination, particularly in a large organization. A special administrative staff is needed to maintain channels of communication and coordination, and a strict hierarchy of authority serves to effect the coordination of diverse tasks in the pursuit of organizational objectives by enabling superiors on successive levels to guide, directly or indirectly, the performance of increasingly wider circles of subordinates. But close supervision of all decisions is inefficient and produces strains. The system of official rules is designed to standardize operations and restrict the need for direct supervisory intervention largely to extraordinary cases. Professional training and official rules notwithstanding, however, strong emotions and personal bias would interfere with the ability to make rational decisions. The emphasis on impersonal detachment has the function of precluding the intrusion of such irrational factors into official decisions. Lest the impersonal discipline in the hierarchical bureaucracy alienate its members, secure careers lessen this burden and promote loyalty to the organization.

In brief, the problems created by one condition in the organization stimulate the development of another to meet them. A number of interdependent processes of this kind give rise to the constellation of features characteristic of the typical bureaucracy, as conceptualized by Max Weber. He held that these features of an administrative organization and, especially, their combination are "capable of attaining the highest degree of efficiency." [3]

INFORMAL ORGANIZATION

Weber has been criticized for presenting an idealized conception of bureaucracy. His implicit functional scheme addresses itself to the problem of how a given element of the organization contributes to its strength and effective functioning. What is missing is a similar systematic attempt to specify the *dysfunctions* of the various elements[4] and to examine the conflicts that arise between the elements comprising the system. Thus, even if it is true that the hierarchy of au-

[3] Ibid., p. 337.
[4] See Robert K. Merton, *Social Theory and Social Structure* (Glencoe, Ill.: The Free Press, 1957), pp. 50–54, who calls attention to the importance of systematically investigating dysfunctions as well as functions.

thority promotes discipline and makes possible the coordination of activities, does it not also discourage subordinates from accepting responsibility? Or, granted that promotion should be based on objective criteria rather than on personal considerations or family connections, which of the two major criteria is to be selected—seniority or merit? When questions such as these are raised, it is seen that Weber's one-sided concern with the functions of bureaucratic institutions blinds him to some of the most fundamental problems bureaucratization creates.

Another criticism of Weber's analysis that has been advanced is that he is preoccupied with the formally instituted aspects of bureaucracies and ignores the informal relations and unofficial patterns which develop in formal organizations. Selznick has emphasized that the formal structure is only one aspect of the actual social structure and that organizational members interact as whole persons and not merely in terms of the formal roles they occupy.[5] Many empirical studies of work groups in formal organizations have called attention to the importance of the informal organization that emerges in these work groups and that constitutes a dynamic force in the organization.

To be sure, Weber realized that actual practice does not follow in every detail the formal blueprint. The new discovery was, however, that these departures from official procedures are not idiosyncratic but become socially organized. The social patterns that are informally organized by the participants themselves complement those formally organized for them by management. Furthermore, the informal organizations that always arise in formal organizations, as Barnard pointed out, are essential for operations.[6] Simultaneously with Barnard, a research team arrived at the same insight from its study of industrial workers in an electric plant.

Roethlisberger and Dickson[7] found that the informal relations in a work group assumed a distinctive structure, with subgroups and status differences, and that informal norms emerged that regulated the performance of workers. Specifically, workers were expected by their fellows neither to produce too fast nor to produce too slowly, and deviations from these group norms were penalized by ridicule, loss of status, and, eventually, ostracism. In other words, workers informally organized themselves to control output, and an informal status structure

[5] Philip Selznick, "Foundations of the Theory of Organizations," *American Sociological Review*, XIII (1948), 25–35.

[6] Chester I. Barnard, *The Functions of the Executive* (Cambridge: Harvard University Press, 1958), pp. 115–23.

[7] Fritz J. Roethlisberger and William J. Dickson, *Management and the Worker* (Cambridge: Harvard University Press, 1939).

complemented this organized social control. The informal organization, therefore, had important implications for production.

Research on human relations in industry proliferated widely after this pioneering study, and a number of case studies of bureaucracies have attempted to apply its insights in order to refine Weber's analysis. Gouldner, for example, shows that managerial succession in an industrial organization promoted bureaucratization, as implied by Weber's theory, because a new manager unfamiliar with informal practices is constrained to rely on official procedures to implement his directives. But such exercise of authority that rests on bureaucratic rules and discipline should be distinguished from professional authority that rests on technical expertness, a distinction Weber failed to make explicit.[8]

The general conclusion that emerges from these case studies of informal organization in bureaucracies is that procedures formally instituted for specific purposes in organizations recurrently create disturbances in other respects and the informal patterns that typically arise to cope with these disruptions often produce a basic reorganization of operations. Whereas the focus on informal practices and relations permitted some refinement of Weber's theory, it also led investigators increasingly away from the study of the fundamental structural features of complex organizations.

[8] Alvin W. Gouldner, *Patterns of Industrial Bureaucracy* (Glencoe, Ill.: The Free Press, 1954).

PART FIVE

POLITICAL SOCIOLOGY

EIGHT

CRITICAL REMARKS
ON WEBER'S THEORY
OF AUTIIORITY

PETER M. BLAU

. . . THE PURPOSE OF this paper is to examine critically Weber's theory of authority. After briefly summarizing the main concepts and analysis, a methodological criticism of Weber's procedure and some substantive criticisms of this theory will be presented.

THE CONCEPT OF AUTHORITY

Power is defined by Weber as a person's ability to impose his will upon others despite resistance.[1] He distinguishes two basic types of power, the domination of others that rests on the ability to influence their interests, and the domination that rests on authority, that is, the power

From "Critical Remarks on Weber's Theory of Authority," by Peter M. Blau. From *The American Political Science Review*, LVII (June, 1963), 306–16. Reprinted by permission of the author and the publisher. Ellipses indicate deletions from the text.

[1] Weber presents slightly different definitions of power (*Macht*) in two parts of *Wirtschaft und Gesellschaft*, 2 vols. (Tuebingen: J. C. B. Mohr, 1925), which are translated, respectively, in *The Theory [of Social and Economic Organization* (New York: Oxford University Press, 1947),] p. 152, and in *Max Weber on Law in Economy and Society* (Cambridge: Harvard University Press, 1954), p. 323.

to command and the duty to obey.[2] Weber does not explicitly consider coercive power in his analysis of domination,[3] nor does he deal with such forms of personal influence as persuasion, but it is convenient to clarify his concept of authority by contrasting it with these opposite extremes.

A fundamental ~~criterion~~ rule of authority "is a certain minimum of voluntary submission."[4] An army commander may impose his will upon the enemy, but he does not have authority over enemy soldiers, only over his own, since only the latter obey his commands because they are duty-bound to do so, while the former merely yield to the coercive force of his superior arms. Since authority entails voluntary compliance with the superior's directives, it obviates the need for coercive force or for sanctions. Resort to either positive incentives or coercive measures by a person in order to influence others is *prima facie* evidence that he does not have authority over them, for if he did their voluntary compliance would serve as an easier method of control over them.

Voluntary obedience is not a sufficient condition for authority, however, since other forms of personal influence also rest on willing compliance. In persuasion, for example, one person permits the influence of another to influence his decisions or actions. Authority is distinguished from persuasion by the fact that people *a priori* suspend their own judgment and accept that of an acknowledged superior without having to be convinced that his is correct. The subordinate in an authority relationship "holds in abeyance his own critical faculties for choosing between alternatives and uses the formal criterion of the receipt of a command or signal as his basis for choice."[5] In Weber's words, the "ruled" act as if they "had made the content of the (ruler's) command the maxim of their conduct for its own sake."[6]

Authority, then, involves unconditional willing obedience on the part of subordinates. It is not easy, however, to distinguish authority ~~by these criteria~~ from other forms of control. The slaves who blindly

[2] The term *Herrschaft* (domination, translated by Parsons as imperative control) is apparently intended by Weber as a subcategory of power and as a more general concept than authority, but he does not use the term consistently, sometimes including under it the power that rests on constellations of interest, and sometimes confining it to the power of command that rests on the duty to obey; see *Wirtschaft und Gesellschaft,* pp. 603–12, translated in *Max Weber on Law . . . ,* ch. xii.

[3] This criticism is the basis of Amitai Etzioni's typology of power in *A Comparative Analysis of Complex Organizations* (New York: Free Press, 1961), pp. 4–19, esp. p. 14.

[4] Weber, *The Theory . . . ,* p. 324.

[5] Herbert A. Simon, *Administrative Behavior* (New York, 1952), pp. 126–27.

[6] *Max Weber on Law . . . ,* p. 328.

obey their master although he does not use a whip, for fear that he
may do so, are not very different from the soldiers who obey their
commander or the officials who obey their bureaucratic superior, since
they too know that the superior may otherwise invoke sanctions to
penalize them. But if we consider the slave's obedience to be *voluntary*
compliance, then the distinction between this concept and coercion
loses all its meaning. Many borderline cases exist, according to Weber,
both because the distinction is an analytical one and because coercion
or other forms of control often later develop into authority.[7] For this
transformation to occur, however, a belief system must emerge that
socially legitimates the exercise of control,[8] and this legitimating value
system furnishes the final and basic distinguishing criterion of authority. We speak of authority, therefore, if the willing unconditional
compliance of a group of people rests upon their shared beliefs that
it is legitimate for the superior (person or impersonal agency) to impose his will upon them and that it is illegitimate for them to refuse
obedience.

Before turning to the three types of authority Weber differentiates,
let us briefly note some problems raised by his central concept. Authority denotes imperative control, from which there is no easy escape,
yet a major criterion of it is voluntary compliance. While I may have
stressed the voluntary element in authority more than Weber does
himself, I have done so deliberately to call attention to the implicit
paradox between voluntarism and authoritarian control, since by
making it explicit we can hope to clarify it. Weber ignores this paradox, despite his interest in paradoxical phenomena, because his focus
on types of legitimacy leads him to take the existence of legitimate
authority for granted [9] and never systematically to examine the structural conditions under which it emerges out of other forms of power.

Another problem concerns the specific referent of Weber's concept
of authority. When he presents his abstract definitions, he seems to
refer to authority in interpersonal relations. In his analysis of empirical situations, on the other hand, he is concerned with political
systems or institutions, such as feudalism. Moreover, in his analysis
of historical cases where he applies and develops his concepts he sometimes treats them as concrete types and sometimes as analytical ele-

[7] Ibid., pp. 325–27.
[8] *The Theory* . . . , p. 325.
[9] Even as sympathetic an interpreter as Bendix notes that Weber takes the existence of traditional and legal authority as given; see [Reinhard Bendix, *Max Weber*
(Garden City: Doubleday & Company, Inc., Anchor Books, 1962),] pp. 386–87. While
Bendix adds that Weber traces how legal authority develops from the other two
types, even in this case Weber's concern is not with the development of legitimate
authority out of other forms of power.

ments. Feudalism, for example, can hardly be considered an analytical element that can be found in all kinds of historical situations, but charisma can be, and Weber sometimes, although not always, treats it as an analytical element. To ignore the important methodological difference between these two kinds of concepts confuses the analysis. These difficulties stem from Weber's abstract conception of action[10] and from the particular procedure he employed to derive generalizations about historical reality.

TYPES OF AUTHORITY

The distinctive feature of authority is a belief system that defines the exercise of social control as legitimate. Three types of authority are consequently distinguished by Weber on the basis of differences in the legitimating belief systems that validate them.

The first type is authority legitimated by the sanctity of tradition. In "traditional authority" the present social order is viewed as sacred, eternal, and inviolable. The dominant person or group, usually defined by heredity, is thought to have been pre-ordained to rule over the rest. The subjects are bound to the ruler by personal dependence and a tradition of loyalty, and their obedience to him is further reinforced by such cultural beliefs as the divine right of kings. All systems of government prior to the development of the modern state would seem to exemplify traditional authority. Although the ruler's power is limited by the traditions that legitimate it, this restriction is not severe, since some arbitrariness on the part of the ruler is traditionally expected. Generally, traditional authority tends to perpetuate the *status quo* and is ill suited for adaptation to social change; indeed, historical change undermines its very foundation. The spirit of traditional authority is well captured in the phrase, "The king is dead—long live the king."

The values that legitimate "charismatic authority," Weber's second type, define a leader and his mission as being inspired by divine or supernatural powers. The leader, in effect, heads a new social movement, and his followers and disciples are converts to a new cause. There is a sense of being "called" to spread the new gospel, a sense of rejecting the past and heralding the future. Devotion to the leader and the conviction that his pronouncements embody the spirit and ideals of the movement are the source of the group's willing obedience to his commands. Charismatic leaders may appear in almost any area of

[10] As noted by Paul F. Lazarsfeld, "A Duality in Max Weber's Writings on Social Action," paper delivered at the meetings of the American Sociological Society, Detroit, 1956.

social life—as religious prophets, political demagogues, or military heroes. Indeed, an element of charisma is involved whenever a person inspires others to follow his lead. Charismatic authority usually acts as a revolutionary force, inasmuch as it involves rejection of traditional values and a rebellion against the established order, often in reaction to a crisis. There is also an anarchistic streak in charismatic movements, a disdain for routine tasks and problems of organization or administration, since the leader's inspiration and the sacred mission must not be profaned by mundane considerations. For Weber, the innovating spirit of charisma is symbolized by Christ's words, "It is written . . . but I say unto you. . . ."

The third type, "legal authority," is legitimated by a formalistic belief in the supremacy of the law whatever its specific content. The assumption is that a body of legal rules has been deliberately established to further the rational pursuit of collective goals. In such a system obedience is owed not to a person—whether traditional chief or charismatic leader—but to a set of impersonal principles. These principles include the requirement to follow directives originating from an office superior to one's own, regardless of who occupies this higher office. All organizations that have been formally established—in contrast to the organizations of social life that have slowly emerged in the course of history or that have spontaneously erupted—illustrate legal authority structures. The prototype is the modern government which has a monopoly over the legitimate use of physical coercion, and the same principles are reflected in its various executive agencies, such as the army, and also in private corporations, such as a factory. While superiors have authority over subordinates, the former as well as the latter are subject to the authority of the official body of impersonal regulations. Legal authority may be epitomized in the phrase, "A government of laws, not of men."

At one point, Weber outlines these three plus a fourth type of belief that legitimates a social order, namely, "rational belief in an absolute value [which creates the legitimacy] of 'Natural Law.' " [11] This fourth type of legitimate *order,* however, is not included in the subsequent more detailed analysis of legitimate *authority,* while the other three are. Does this imply that Weber considered a *wertrationale* orientation toward natural rights a possible basis of political institutions but not a basis of political authority? He makes no explicit statements to help us answer this question.

Although his typology of authority involves three main types and not two, it also reveals the Hegelian practice of Weber to refine con-

[11] *The Theory . . . ,* p. 131.

cepts by juxtaposing opposites; only it entails a more complex combination of contrasts. The traditional authority which maintains the *status quo* is defined by contrast with two dynamic forces that threaten it, the revolutionary ideals advocated by a charismatic leader, and the rational pursuit of ends guided by abstract formal principles in disregard of historical tradition and time-honored convention. The personal submission to a charismatic leader is defined in juxtaposition with two impersonal forces that tend to undermine it in the course of historical developments, the crystallization of the revolutionary movement into a traditional order, and its bureaucratization into a rational formal organization. The formal acceptance of legal principles as authoritative is characterized in contradistinction to two irrational forces which must be overcome for such formal rationality to be realized, the power of tradition, and the power of charisma. Extrapolation from these contrasts yields two important features of each authority system. The power of tradition is neither rational nor strictly personal. (While there are personal elements in traditional authority, analytically traditionalism should be considered an impersonal force.) The power of charisma is dynamic and nonrational. The power of rational law, finally, is impersonal and dynamic.[12]

Weber's extensive analysis of authority structures follows somewhat different directions in the case of each type. His discussion of traditional authority focuses upon differences between sub-types, notably between patrimonialism and feudalism. Although "both types have in common rulers who grant rights in return for military and administrative services," [13] patrimonialism is an extension of the patriarchal authority of the master over his household to include a group of dependent officials, whereas feudalism originates in a contract between independent knights and an overlord. "If a knight enters the service of a ruler, he remains a free man; he does not become a personal dependent like the patrimonial retainer." [14]

In his analysis of charismatic authority, on the other hand, Weber is not concerned with different sub-types or with historical antecedents but primarily with subsequent developments. He traces in detail the ways in which charisma tends to become routinized in the course of time and to develop into traditional or bureaucratic institutions. The personal significance of the leader makes charismatic structures inherently unstable.

[12] The term "dynamic" is used in the specific sense of "producing social change."
[13] Bendix, op. cit., p. 369.
[14] Ibid., p. 361; see pp. 329–81 for an excellent summary of the contrast between patrimonialism and feudalism, which is based on discussions of Weber that are dispersed in different parts of his writings.

Weber's discussion of legal authority deals both with the historical conditions that led to its development and with its implications for subsequent developments, but there is again a difference in focus. In his treatment of charisma, his concern is with its transformation into *other* systems. In his treatment of legal rationality, however, his concern is with the way in which *this* system increasingly penetrates all institutions and becomes more fully realized throughout society. In short, Weber's theory encompasses only the historical processes that lead from charismatic movements to increasing rationalization and does not include an analysis of the historical conditions and social processes that give rise to charismatic eruptions in the social structure. He has no theory of revolution. . . .

THE IDEAL TYPE

* * *

In one respect, according to Weber, the method of sociology is unlike that of the natural sciences and like that of social philosophy. Since values give social life its meaning, it is not enough to show that two social conditions occur together or that one produces the other. It is also necessary to interpret these observations in terms of existing values. This is the gist of Weber's concept of *Verstehen,* as I understand it. In another respect, however, the method of sociology parallels that of the natural sciences and contrasts with that of history. Sociology is a generalizing science. Although every historical event is unique, the sociologist must ignore these unique aspects of social events and subsume them under general categories or types in order to generalize about them. Even if history furnishes us only with one instance of a social system, as in the case of modern capitalism, Weber treated it as an ideal type in an attempt to explain its development by deriving generalizations about it rather than by interpreting the configuration of historical conditions that led up to it. This procedure was his solution to the issue posed in the German *Methodenstreit,* notably by Dilthey, Windelband, and Rickert.[15]

The ideal type is an abstraction that combines several analytical elements which appear in reality not in pure form but in various admixtures. In actual bureaucracies, for example, officials are not completely impersonal, not all official business is recorded in writing, and

[15] See Wilhelm Dilthey, *Einleitung in die Giesteswissenschaften* (Leipzig: Duncker & Humbolt, 1883); Wilhelm Windelband, "Geschichte und Naturwissenschaft," lecture given in Strassburg, 1894, published in his *Praeludien* (Tuebingen: J. C. B. Mohr, 1907); and Heinrich Rickert, *Die Grenzen der naturwissenschaftlichen Begriffsbildung* (Tuebingen: J. C. B. Mohr, 1902).

the division of responsibilities is not always unambiguous. To be sure, the ideal type does not correspond to any empirical case or to the average of all cases, but it is intentionally designed in this form, as Weber stresses.[16] It is not a substitute for empirical investigation of historical situations but a framework for guiding the research by indicating the factors to be examined and the ways in which the observed patterns differ from the pure type.

A criticism of the ideal type advanced by Schelting is that implicit in Weber's procedure are several different constructs.[17] The two basic ones are the individualizing ideal type, which refers to a specific social system that occurred only once in history, such as Western capitalism, and the generalizing ideal type, which refers to a category that includes many social systems of the same kind, such as bureaucracy. In my opinion, Weber's use of the same procedure in the analysis of these different problems was quite deliberate. He tried to extend Rickert's conception and break through the dilemma posed by Windelband's postulate that one cannot generalize about unique events by treating Western capitalism, a unique historical phenomenon, as if it were a general type, that is, just as he treated bureaucracy. The attempt, however, is doomed to failure. One case cannot yield a general principle. For, as the very term implies, a generalization must refer to more than one case. But how can we possibly know that it does if there is only one case to examine? The relevant requirement of a generalizing science is that it abstracts those elements of unique occurrences that many have in common, thereby transforming them into non-unique cases in terms of the conceptual scheme and making it possible to subsume them under general categories. This is not accomplished by Weber's very different procedure of abstracting those elements of a historical system that reveal its most distinctive features in pure form. The analytical category and the ideal type are two entirely different abstractions from reality. Had Weber selected a few distinctive elements of modern capitalism that it has in common with other economic systems, he could have derived a generalization about the analytical elements of religious systems that promote these characteristic features of capitalism. But he was too interested in the unique aspects of Western capitalism to formulate his problem in this sociological manner, and his ideal type is no adequate substitute for doing so.

The generalizing ideal type is also subject to criticism. Parsons notes that it implies a fixed relationship between various elements, say, specification of responsibility and legal rationality—although these

[16] *The Theory* . . . , p. 111.

[17] Alexander von Schelting, *Max Weber's Wissenschaftslehre* (Tuebingen: J. C. B. Mohr, 1934).

elements may in fact vary independently of one another.[18] Friedrich's objections are that the ideal type is neither derived by systematic induction from empirical observations nor by deduction from more abstract concepts and that it implicitly led Weber to introduce value judgments into his analysis.[19] Bendix points out that the procedure of constructing ideal types obscures the very contradictions, conflicts, and compromises in which Weber was especially interested.[20] . . .

A fundamental shortcoming of the ideal type, which underlies many criticisms of it, is that it is an admixture of conceptual scheme and hypotheses. Take the ideal type of bureaucracy. In part, it is a conceptual scheme which calls attention to the aspects of organizations that should be included in the investigation, and which supplies criteria for defining an actual organization as more or less bureaucratized. In addition, however, Weber indicates that these characteristics tend to occur together, that certain historical conditions promote them (such as a money economy), and that the specified characteristics and, in particular, their combination increase administrative efficiency. These are not elucidations of concepts but statements of fact which are assumed to be correct. Whereas concepts are not subject to empirical verification, hypothesized factual relationships are. Only empirical research can ascertain, for instance, whether authoritarian management and impersonal detachment, singly and in combination, always promote administrative efficiency, as predicted, or whether they do so only under certain conditions, or perhaps not at all. But what bearing would such empirical findings have on the ideal type? If we modify the type in accordance with the empirical reality, it is no longer a pure type, and if we do not, it would become a meaningless construct. Since the ideal type confuses statements that have different significance for empirical investigation and theoretical inference, it has serious limitations compared to analytical conceptual schemes.

Ignoring that Weber's analysis of bureaucracy is assumed to represent an ideal type, it can still be considered a sophisticated conceptual scheme and a set of interrelated hypotheses, which furnish guidelines for the study of bureaucracies of various kinds, and which can be refined on the basis of research as well as conceptual clarification. In Weber's ideal bureaucracy, for instance, the official's legal authority rests on technical expertness, but in actual bureaucracies, the professional standards of the expert often come into conflict with the admin-

---

[18] Talcott Parsons, *The Structure of Social Action* (New York, 1937), pp. 606-9; and his comments in the introduction to Weber, *The Theory* . . . , pp. 13 and 75.

[19] Friedrich, ["Some Observations on Weber's Analysis of Bureaucracy," in R. K. Merton et al., eds., *Reader in Bureaucracy* (Glencoe, 1952)], pp. 27-33.

[20] Bendix, op. cit., p. 275.

istrative requirements of the managerial official, even if the two are the same person. Professional and bureaucratic authority must be distinguished, as Parsons and Gouldner point out,[21] to clarify some of the central issues and conflicts in today's organizations which tend increasingly to be both professionalized and bureaucratized. Another problem is the specification of conditions under which the bureaucratic characteristics Weber delineated further operating efficiency. To cite only one illustration, it is highly questionable that strict lines of authority in an organization have the same significance for effective administration in a hospital as in an army, or in a country where an egalitarian ideology prevails as in Weber's imperial Germany. To refine Weber's theory by the investigation of such problems entails dispensing with the notion of the ideal type.

ELABORATION OF THE CONCEPTION OF AUTHORITY

Turning now to a substantive analysis and clarification of Weber's conception of authority, the focus is on some issues his theory has not resolved. The first question is posed by the description of authority as voluntary imperative control. How can compliance be imperative if it is voluntary? The second problem is that of the origins of authority, especially of the processes through which other forms of power become transformed into legitimate authority. Closely related is a third issue, namely, that of the structural conditions that give rise to authority systems, of the existential determination of the beliefs that legitimate authority.

Authority often originates in other forms of power; for example, the conqueror later becomes the king. In a bureaucracy, with which I am most familiar, and which I therefore shall use as an illustration, the situation is somewhat more complex. The legal contract into which officials enter by becoming members of a bureaucracy legitimates the authority of superiors over subordinates. Although employees assume the contractual obligation to follow managerial directives, the scope of the formal authority that has its source in the legal contract is very limited. The legal authority of management to assign tasks to subordinates is rarely questioned—there is willing compliance—but this legal authority does not and cannot encourage willingness to work hard or to exercise initiative. Managerial responsibilities require more influence over subordinates than that which rests on their legal obligations.

The bureaucratic manager has the official power of sanction over

[21] Parsons, op. cit., pp. 58–60 (footnote 4), and Alvin W. Gouldner, *Patterns of Industrial Bureaucracy* (Glencoe, 1954), p. 22.

his subordinates, a typical manifestation of which is the civil service efficiency rating, on which the career chances of officials may depend. He may use his sanctioning power directly to impose his will upon subordinates. Such domination does not, strictly speaking, involve the exercise of authority, since his orders are followed to avoid penalties or attain rewards rather than simply because doing so is an accepted duty. An alternative strategy is for the manager to try to expand the scope of his influence over subordinates by obligating them to follow his directives and requests. This strategy involves essentially relinquishing some of his official power in exchange for legitimate authority.

The official position and power of the bureaucratic manager give him opportunities to furnish services to subordinates and, thereby, create social obligations. His superior administrative knowledge, on the basis of which he presumably was promoted, enables him to train newcomers and advise even experienced officials in difficult cases. His managerial status gives him access to top echelons and staff specialists, making it possible for him to channel needed information to subordinates and, what is of special importance, represent their interests with the higher administration or the legislature. In brief, he has many occasions to benefit subordinates and win their appreciation. His formal prerogatives and powers make it possible for him to earn their good will merely by not exercising them—for instance, by not enforcing an unpopular no-smoking rule. The manager who discharges his responsibilities by refraining from resort to his coercive powers and by devoting effort to benefiting subordinates obligates them to himself. The advantages they derive from his mode of supervision obligate them to reciprocate by willingly complying with his demands and requests.

This type of personal influence over *individual* subordinates does not constitute the exercise of authority in the specific Weberian sense either. For authority requires social legitimation. Only the shared values of a social collectivity can legitimate the power or influence of a superior and thus transform it into authority. The bureaucratic superior whose managerial practices further the *collective* interest of subordinates creates joint social obligations. Hence, the group of subordinates has a common interest in remaining under this manager and maintaining his good will, which finds expression in shared feelings of loyalty to him and in group norms making compliance with his directives an obligation enforced by the subordinates themselves. The prevalence of such a normative orientation among subordinates legitimates the superior's authority over them.

The distinguishing criterion of authority suggested here is that structural constraints rooted in the collectivity of subordinates rather than instruments of power or influences wielded by the superior himself enforce compliance with his directives. To discharge its joint obligations[22] to the superior, the group of subordinates is under pressure to make compliance with his directives part of the common norms, which are internalized by its members, and which are socially enforced by them against potential deviants. Such normative constraints require even the individual who does not feel personally obligated to the superior to submit to his authority. This conception helps to resolve the paradox posed by the definition of authority as a form of social control that is both voluntary and imperative. Voluntary social action is never devoid of social constraints. From the standpoint of the collectivity of subordinates, compliance with the superior's directives is voluntary, but from the standpoint of the individual subordinate it is the result of compelling social pressures. The compliance of subordinates in authority relationships is as voluntary as our custom of wearing clothes.

Let us recapitulate the main points of the argument and somewhat refine them. Authority usually has its source in other forms of power, specifically, in a situation where a group of people are dependent in vital respects on one person (or another group). Their dependence enables him to coerce them to do his bidding. He can, however, use his power and the resources from which it derives—whether these are superior physical force, wealth, knowledge, or charisma—to furnish services to subordinates and thus obligate them to follow his directives, which makes it unnecessary for him to coerce them. In this manner, coercive power is transformed into personal influence. If the superior's actions advance the common interests of subordinates and make them collectively obligated to him, a further transformation tends to occur as group norms enforce compliance with his directives to repay the joint obligations to him. This is the process by which personal influence turns into legitimate authority. The influence of one individual over another in a pair relationship cannot become legitimate authority, because only the shared norms of a collectivity can legitimate social control and only the collective enforcement of compliance makes the compliance independent of the superior's personal influence over the individual subordinate. But once an authority system has become institutionalized, it can find expression in apparently isolated pairs. A father exercises authority over an only child, since culturally defined

[22] The closely related concept of joint liability is used by Max Weber in his discussion of the Jews' relation to God, which is translated in *Ancient Judaism* (Glencoe, 1952), pp. 215–16, and to which my attention was called by Bendix. op. cit., pp. 230–41.

role expectations, which are enforced by members of the community, such as teachers and neighbors, constrain the child to obey his father. Such institutionalized authority is typically supplemented by other forms of influence.

The power of sanction formally invested in the bureaucratic official has paradoxical implications for authority. In terms of the conception advanced, the direct use of sanctions by a manager to compel subordinates to carry out his orders does not constitute the exercise of authority. Quite the contrary, it shows that his directives do not command their unconditional compliance. It is this official power of sanction, on the other hand, that makes subordinates dependent on the bureaucratic superior, and this dependence, in turn, is the ultimate source of his authority over them. This paradox is not confined to bureaucracy but is characteristic of all power: its use to coerce others destroys its potential as a source of authority over them. What is distinctive about the bureaucratic case is that the instruments with which an official readily can extend his authority over subordinates beyond the narrow confines of the legal contract are placed into his hands by the formal organization.

In general, a situation of collective dependence is fertile soil for the development of authority, but its development is contingent on judicious restraint by the superior in the use of his power. If he alienates subordinates by imposing his will upon them against their resistance, they will obey only under duress and not freely follow his lead. If, on the other hand, he uses some of his power to further their collective interests, the common experience of dependence on and obligation to the superior is apt to give rise to shared beliefs that it is right and in the common interest to submit to his command, and these social values and the corresponding social norms of compliance legitimate and enforce his authority over them, as has been noted.[23] In brief, coercive power and authority are alternative forms of social control, which are incompatible, but which both have their roots in conditions of collective dependence.

The question arises, what are the various kinds of collective dependence in which authority has its ultimate source? Weber calls attention to the importance of "the *monopoly* of the *legitimate* use of physical force" for the power of the state.[24] The transformation of this

---

[23] See Friedrich's discussion of authority as resting on the "potentiality of reasoned elaboration" of a communication in terms of existing beliefs and values, on the one hand, and as related to the exercise of discretionary power, on the other, in Carl J. Friedrich, ed., *Authority* (Nomos I), (Cambridge: Harvard University Press, 1958), pp. 28–48.

[24] *The Theory* . . . , p. 154 (italics in original).

coercive power by political values and norms produces political authority. Note that this type cuts across Weber's distinction between legal and traditional authority, since traditional political structures as well as rationalized legal ones ultimately rest on the force of arms. The dependence of the followers on a charismatic leader, in contrast, is due to their ideological convictions. Their firm belief in the mission the charismatic leader represents and symbolizes makes his approval and disapproval more important to them than any other sanctions. This is similar to the dependence created by any personal attachment, such as a boy's infatuation with a girl, except that the ideology makes an entire collectivity dependent on the leader and is, therefore, an essential condition for the development of charismatic authority. A very different source of domination is technical knowledge (real or attributed; quackery will do if superstition gives it credence) which makes people who suppose they need it dependent on a person. Socially acknowledged superior competence may be considered the basic source of professional authority. Finally, people are dependent on others for their material well-being, notably on their employer and his representatives. This dependence gives rise to managerial authority.[25]

The purpose of presenting these types is not to make a claim for a definitive typology of authority but merely to illustrate that a classification on the basis of the dependency conditions in which authority is rooted does not yield the same types as Weber's classification in terms of legitimating beliefs. Although differences in these legitimating value systems have significant implications for social systems, as Weber's analysis shows, a theory of authority should also come to grips with the structural conditions in which it originates.

DEMOCRACY AND BUREAUCRACY

What is the referent of Weber's concepts of authority? In some discussions, he appears to deal with three analytical principles that underlie conformity—convention, ethics, and law.[26] At other times, he seems to refer to political systems—traditional political institutions, revolutionary movements, and modern governments based on rational law. (The limitations of the ideal type may be responsible for Weber's switching between these different conceptualizations.) If his analysis is considered an approach to a theory of political institutions, it is amaz-

---

[25] This conceptualization was suggested by, although it differs from, the classification of organizations in terms of incentives in Peter B. Clark and James Q. Wilson, "Incentive Systems." *Administrative Science Quarterly*, VI (1961), 129–66.

[26] See *The Theory* . . . , pp. 126–32.

ing that it does not include a systematic treatment of democracy or the general conception of sovereignty, its locus and its distribution. Democracy is subsumed under the legal order, although Weber makes it clear that a legal order is not necessarily democratic.[27] On the contrary, the prototype of the legal order is the autocratic bureaucracy. "Experience tends universally to show that . . . the monocratic variety of bureaucracy . . . [is] capable of attaining the highest degree of efficiency and is in this sense formally the most rational means of carrying out control over human beings." [28] It is this kind of unsupported and questionable value judgment that Friedrich undoubtedly has in mind when he states that Weber's discussions of bureaucracy "vibrate with something of the Prussian enthusiasm for the military organization." [29]

Weber examines the relationship between democracy and bureaucracy from several perspectives, but he never systematically differentiates the two concepts in the manner in which he distinguishes the legal order from the two other types of authority structures. One theme in Weber's analysis is the paradoxical relationship between the two institutions. Some legal requirements further democracy as well as bureaucracy, such as the principle of "equal justice under law," and the emphasis on technical knowledge rather than inherited status prerogatives (achieved instead of ascribed status), both of which help produce a levelling of status differences.[30] Nevertheless, " 'democracy' as such is opposed to the 'rule' of bureaucracy, in spite and perhaps because of its unavoidable yet unintended promotion of bureaucratization." [31] A major reason for this is that bureaucracy concentrates power in the hands of those in charge of the bureaucratic apparatus and thereby undermines democracy.[32]

A related problem with which Weber is concerned is the contrast between political and bureaucratic domination. Under the rule of law, as Bendix notes, "success in the struggle for power becomes manifest in decisive influence upon the enactment of binding rules. To exercise

---

[27] Ibid., p. 310: This legality . . . may derive from a voluntary agreement of the interested parties on the relevant terms. On the other hand, it may be imposed on the basis of what is held to be a legitimate authority." A circular argument is involved in defining the legal order here as possibly resting on accepted authority and then using the existence of such an accepted order to account for the legitimacy of the legal authority.

[28] Ibid., p. 337.

[29] Friedrich, op. cit., p. 31.

[30] *From Max Weber: Essays in Sociology* (New York: Oxford University Press, 1946), pp. 224–28.

[31] Ibid., p. 231.

[32] Ibid., pp. 232–35.

such decisive influence a politician must contend with others like himself in the competition for votes, in political organizations, and in the legislative process of enacting laws and supervising their execution." [33] Political power is apparently viewed as containing elements of the two opposite prototypes, economic power which rests on constellations of interests and authority which rests on beliefs in its legitimacy. Power in the political struggle results from the manipulation of interests and profitable exchanges—for example, of commitments or "spoils" for votes—and does not entail legitimate authority of protagonists over one another. Success in this struggle, however, leads to a position of legitimate authority. The political struggle occurs not only among politicians but also between them and the executives of bureaucratic organizations to prevent the latter from exploiting their dominant administrative position to usurp political power. A final complication arises in mass democracies, where the political struggle is carried out through large party organizations which tend to become bureaucratized, with the result that the conflict between political and bureaucratic principles manifests itself again in the struggle between the politician who directly appeals to the voters and the regular party official, once more creating the danger that democratic processes become submerged by bureaucratic considerations.[34]

These brief excerpts show that Weber discusses the differences and interrelations between democracy and bureaucracy extensively; nevertheless, he never makes a systematic analytical distinction between them. Let me attempt to draw such an analytical distinction. Two reasons why men organize themselves and others and form an association can be distinguished. First, their purpose may be to settle on common courses of actions, on objectives to be collectively pursued. Second, their purpose may be to implement decisions already agreed upon or accepted, to work together on attaining given objectives. There are other reasons for establishing a social association, for instance, giving common expression to shared values, as in religious congregations, but the discussion here is confined to the first two kinds. The principle of organization must be adapted to its purpose.

If men organize themselves for the purpose of reaching common agreement on collective goals and actions by some form of majority rule, they establish a democratic organization. The specific mechanisms and institutions through which the democratic rule of the majority is effected can differ widely and pose important problems in a large social structure. Whatever the particular institutional solution

---

[33] Bendix, op. cit., p. 439.

[34] See Max Weber, *Gesammelte Politische Schriften* (Muenchen: Drei Masken, 1921), pp. 182–83, 201–11, summarized in Bendix, op. cit., pp. 446–47.

to these problems, however, the fundamental principle that is expected to govern a democratic organization is freedom of dissent. For tomorrow's majority will not be able to emerge unless today's majority —and, indeed, every majority—relinquishes the right to suppress dissenting minorities, however extremist their views.

If men organize themselves and others for the purpose of realizing specific objectives assigned to or accepted by them, such as winning a war or collecting taxes, they establish a bureaucratic organization. The exact form best suited for such an organization depends on a variety of conditions, including notably the kinds of skills required for the tasks.[35] Strict lines of authority, for example, are probably not conducive to the exercise of responsibility and initiative in a research organization. In any case, the fundamental principle that is expected to govern the specific character and administration of a bureaucratic organization is that of administrative efficiency, that is, the achievement of specified objectives at minimum cost.

In sum, the differentiating criteria between democracy and bureaucracy proposed are whether the organization's purpose is to settle on common objectives or to accomplish given objectives, and whether the governing principle of organizing social action is majority rule rooted in freedom of dissent or administrative efficiency. The distinction is an analytical one, since many organizations have the dual purpose of first deciding on collective goals and then carrying out these decisions. As a result, the two principles come into conflict. Unions are a typical example. Democratic freedom of dissent and majority rule are often set aside in the interests of administrative efficiency and effective accomplishment of union objectives. Even if Michels erred in considering this process inevitable, it is undoubtedly prevalent.[36] Another illustration is the tendency of party bosses to circumvent primaries and other democratic processes in the interest of building an efficient machine for winning elections. Although some specific conflicts may be due to corrupt or domineering union or party officials, there is a fundamental organizational dilemma which is independent of individual motives. Democratic decisions are futile without an administrative apparatus strong enough to implement them, but the requirements of administrative efficiency frequently are incompatible with those of

[35] See the typology developed in James D. Thompson and Arthur Tuden, "Strategies, Structures, and Processes of Organizational Decision," in Thompson et al., (eds.), *Comparative Studies in Administration* (Pittsburgh: University of Pittsburgh Press, 1959), pp. 195–216.

[36] Robert Michels, *Political Parties* (Glencoe, 1949); for a case study of an exception to the tendencies Michels describes, see Seymour M. Lipset et al., *Union Democracy* (Glencoe, 1956).

democratic decision-making—if only because one organization cannot be governed by two distinct ultimate principles of social action.

In our political system, we have attempted to resolve this dilemma by separating the process of deciding on collective goals and the process of accomplishing these goals into two distinct sets of political institutions—the party and election machinery and the legislative branch of the government, on the one hand, and the executive branch of the government, on the other. The former institutions are expected to be governed by majority rule and freedom of dissent, while the latter are expected to be governed by administrative efficiency. Democratic values demand not only that political objectives be decided by majority rule but also that they be implemented by the most effective administrative methods, that is, by executive agencies whose operations are governed by the principle of efficiency and not by majority opinion. Despite the institutional separation, however, the fundamental dilemma between democracy and bureaucracy recurrently reasserts itself, especially in the form of demands for suppressing freedom of dissent in the interest of national security.

CONCLUSIONS

This paper has presented a critical review of Weber's theory of authority and bureaucracy. The ideal-type procedure Weber used in his analysis has been criticized for failing to differentiate between conceptual elaborations and hypotheses concerning the relationship between facts, and also for confusing the distinction between analytical attributes of social systems and prototypes of the social systems themselves. The substantive theory has been criticized for focusing primarily on the beliefs that legitimate authority while neglecting to conceptualize systematically the structural conditions that give rise to it. Finally, the lack of a systematic theory of democracy as well as of revolution was noted, despite the prominent part these two problems play in Weber's thinking and writing. Having focused in the paper deliberately on what appear to be limitations of Weber's theory, I would like to close by putting these criticisms into proper perspective.

Perhaps the most difficult task for a scholar is to develop a new approach to the study of reality, a new conception and perspective that fundamentally changes the development of theory and research in a discipline for generations to come. It is no exaggeration to say that Weber was one of the rare men who has done just this. He has shaped the course of sociology, not alone but together with a few others, and it would not be what it is today had he not lived. It is the fate of every scientist, but particularly the great innovator who blazes new trails and points in new directions, that his very success in clearing the path for others makes his own work soon appear crude and obsolete. While this does not hold true for the philosopher, it does for the social scientist, and Weber clearly and self-consciously was a social scientist rather than a philosopher. Much of Marx's work seems crude today; so does much of Freud's; and if much of Weber's does too, as I have suggested, it is because he belongs to this august company.

NINE

REFLECTIONS
ON CHARISMATIC LEADERSHIP

REINHARD BENDIX

"THE TERM 'CHARISMATIC LEADER' has recently attained widespread and almost debased currency. In the past, it was occasionally applied to Gandhi, Lenin, Hitler, and Roosevelt. Now nearly every leader with marked popular appeal, especially those of new states, is indiscriminately tagged as charismatic." [1] Difficulties in the use of this term arise not only from indiscriminate labeling but also from conflicting theories of societies. Two recent discussions are especially instructive in this respect.

In an assessment of Max Weber's political writings Karl Loewenstein has raised the question of whether or not the term "charisma" can properly be applied in contemporary politics. Charismatic leadership depends upon a widespread belief in the existence of extraordinary or supernatural capacities, but such beliefs are at a discount in secular contexts. Though democratization has increased the plebiscitarian component of modern politics, the qualities of personality which attract voters indicate the popularity, but not necessarily the charisma, of a successful political leader. Accordingly, Loewenstein feels that today "charisma" in the proper sense is likely to be found in those

---

"Reflections on Charismatic Leadership," by Reinhard Bendix. Originally published in *Asian Survey*, VII (June, 1967), 341–52. Revised for Reinhard Bendix, ed., *State and Society* (Boston: Little, Brown and Company, Inc., 1968). Reprinted by permission of the author and the publishers. Some footnotes have been omitted for reasons of space.

[1] Ann Ruth and Dorothy Willner, "The Rise and Role of Charismatic Leaders," *Annals of the American Academy of Political and Social Studies*, 358 (March 1965), 78.

areas of the world in which a popular belief in supernatural powers is still widespread, as in some parts of Africa or Asia.[2]

Quite the opposite position has been formulated by E. A. Shils, who sees a charismatic element in all societies. Shils notes Weber's distinction between the disruptive or innovative effects of charisma and the continuous and routine character of tradition or the legal order; this parallels Loewenstein's distinction between the magico-religious contexts that encourage and the secular contexts that discourage charisma. As Shils points out, Weber himself did not confine his use of the term to magical or religious beliefs, and he analyzed the institutionalization of charisma through kinship, heredity, and office. But he also believed that the opportunities for genuine charisma had diminished in the course of an increasing rationalization and bureaucratization of Western society. Shils takes issue with this last point. He maintains that men in all societies confront exigencies of life which demand a comprehensive solution. Man's position in the cosmos, birth, death, marriage, basic ideas of equity are among these central concerns. The need for establishing some order with reference to these concerns may vary among men, but the point is that charisma attaches itself to those individuals or institutions which satisfy that need or promise to do so. Such ordering may involve philosophical or artistic representations, religious doctrines, interpretations of the law, or the authority of government. Charisma has necessarily a protean character, since it may become a focus of belief whenever ultimate concerns are given an authoritative ordering.[3]

This is not the place to discuss these larger questions substantively, but it is appropriate to refer briefly to one rather topical application of the term "charisma." The new nations provide a setting of rapid change in which charismatic leaders may achieve new forms of political integration. In his analysis of *Ghana in Transition* David Apter has suggested that charismatic leadership helps to undermine tribal authority and thus helps to make way for the creation of secular, legal institutions in a nation-state. He notes, however, that charismatic leadership is not easily reconciled with secular systems of authority. Perhaps a charismatic leader like Nkrumah can transfer some of the loyalty, traditionally accorded to tribal chiefs, to the agents and symbols of a secular government—as long as he is the leader. But then the problem is: How can the loyalties of a personal following be transferred to the institutions of government ("routinized" in Weber's

[2] Karl Loewenstein, *Max Weber Staatspolitische Auffassungen in der Sicht unserer Zeit* (Frankfurt: Athenaum Verlag, 1965), pp. 74–85.

[3] E. A. Shils, "Charisma, Order and Status," *American Sociological Review*, XXX (April 1965), 199–213.

terminology)? Without such transfer governmental stability is not assured.[4]

In a critique of writings on Ghanaian and African politics Claude Ake has raised the basic question whether or not in the new nations charismatic leaders can fulfill any such constructive functions. They often command a large percentage of the vote, but this may involve a fleeting acclamation and an engineered consent rather than widespread public support. Since in the new nations political instability is rife and integration difficult to achieve, any leader may at times obtain considerable political power, if he can command a certain degree of loyalty. Modern means of publicity can give such leadership all the appearance of charisma: the singular gifts of the leader and the unquestioning devotion of his followers. But such appearances can be misleading. The popular celebrations at Nkrumah's overthrow (in 1966) suggest either that his charisma had disappeared by then, or that it had been on the wane for some time past, or indeed that there had been little of it in the first place. Such uncertainties only point up the evanescent qualities of "charisma," which may come to the fore in times of rapid change but which are neither a substitute for regular leadership nor easily reconciled with enduring political institutions.[5]

These contemporary uncertainties in the use of the term suggest that there are special hazards in drawing analogies between new nations, then and now. In his analysis of *The First New Nation* S. M. Lipset has noted that George Washington was a source of unity in the early years of the United States and that his commanding military success inspired widespread veneration of his person. But Lipset also notes that Washington was oriented to the rule of law, permitted the growth of an embryonic party system, and established a precedent for succession to office by voluntarily stepping down in favor of President-elect Adams. Genuine as Washington's charisma probably was, it was acted out in a framework of received political and legal institutions— and it is just the absence of such a framework which jeopardizes analogies between this early American and the contemporary experience in the new nations.

I have cited the large interpretative questions raised by Loewenstein and Shils and the uncertainties of the contemporary application of the term because I believe that the proper definition and use of the concept "charisma" must be clarified, before these larger issues can be addressed. My purpose in this paper is, therefore, to restate Weber's

---

[4] See David Apter, *Ghana in Transition* (New York: Atheneum, 1966), pp. 303–306. See also pp. 168, 173–174, 233, 296–297, and 323.

[5] See Claude Ake, "Charismatic Legitimation and Political Integration," *Comparative Studies in Society and History*, IX (October 1966), 1–13. . . .

original formulation of the concept and emphasize its dynamic implications. Secondly, I shall comment briefly on some analytic problems which arise when the term "charismatic leadership" is applied to four Asiatic leaders, whose careers illustrate different facets of the problem.

In referring now to Weber's specification of the term "charisma" I confine myself to the concept of "charismatic leadership," leaving out the "routinization of charisma" (through its association with kinship, heredity, and office) as well as the positive or negative relations between charisma and social structure. An analysis of individual political leaders need not be concerned with routinization, except in so far as it bears on the problem of succession. Also, the leaders under consideration are politically active in societies undergoing rapid change, i.e., in contexts presumably favorable to charismatic appeals.

Weber defines "charisma" as

> a certain quality of an individual personality by virtue of which he is set apart from ordinary men and treated as endowed with supernatural, superhuman, or at least specifically exceptional power or qualities. These are such as are not accessible to the ordinary person, but are regarded as of divine origin or as exemplary, and on the basis of them the individual concerned is treated as a leader.[6]

Five specifications are added to this basic definition. Weber notes first that "charisma" is probably the greatest revolutionary power in periods of established tradition, and second that it typically neglects considerations of economic efficiency and rationality. Thirdly, he emphasizes that the charismatic leader and his followers constitute a congregation (Gemeinde); he has no officials assisting him but rather disciples or confidants, who have no career or qualifications in the bureaucratic sense and no privileges. They are personally called by their leader based on his peremptory judgment of their own charismatic gifts; they may be as summarily dismissed when he judges that they have failed his trust in them.

Weber's fourth and fifth specifications are of special interest to us here. For that reason it may be best to quote him verbatim:

> It is *recognition* on the part of those subject to authority which is decisive for the validity of charisma. This is freely given and guaranteed by what is held to be a "sign" or proof (Bewährung), originally always a miracle, and consists in devotion to the corresponding revelation, hero worship, or absolute trust in the leader. But where charisma is genuine, it is not this which is the basis of legitimacy. This basis lies rather in the conception that it is the *duty* of those who have been called to a charismatic

---

[6] Max Weber, *The Theory of Social and Economic Organization* (New York: Oxford University Press, 1947), pp. 358–359.

mission to recognize its quality and to act accordingly. Psychologically this "recognition" is a matter of complete personal devotion to the possessor of the quality, arising out of enthusiasm, or of despair and hope.

No prophet has ever regarded his quality as dependent on the attitudes of the masses toward him. No elective king or military leader has ever treated those who have resisted him or tried to ignore him otherwise than as delinquent in duty. . . .

If proof of his charismatic qualification fails him for long, the leader endowed with charisma tends to think his god or his magical or heroic powers have deserted him. If he is for long unsuccessful, above all *if his leadership fails to benefit his followers*, it is likely that his charismatic authority will disappear. This is the genuine charismatic meaning of the phrase "by the grace of God" (*Gottesgnadentum*).[7]

A first reading of this passage might suggest that a leader is charismatic when his followers recognize him as such, because they see "powerful results achieved in the absence of power." [8] But closer examination suggests that both the recognition by followers and the leader's own claims and actions are fundamentally ambivalent.

For the charisma of a leader to be present, it must be recognized by his followers, and in the ideal typical case this recognition is a matter of *duty*. But a personal devotion arising from enthusiasm, despair, or hope is easily contaminated by the *desire for a "sign"* which will confirm the existence of charisma. In turn, the leader demands *unconditional devotion* from his followers, and he will construe any demand for a sign or proof of his gift of grace as a lack of faith and a dereliction of duty. Yet his "charismatic authority will disapper, . . . if *proof of charismatic qualifications* fails him for too long." It appears then that charismatic leadership is not a label that can be applied but refers rather to a problematic relation between a leader and his followers which must be investigated. For it is in each case a question of fact: To what extent and in what ways has the followers' desire for a sign—born out of their enthusiasm, despair, or hope—interfered with, modified, or even jeopardized their unconditional devotion to duty? And similarly it is a question of fact: To what extent and in what ways has the leader's unconditional claim to exceptional powers or qualities been interfered with, modified, or even jeopardized by the actions which he construes as proof of his charismatic qualifications?

[7] Ibid., pp. 359–360. The translation has been modified slightly. I have also rearranged the sequence of Weber's specifications.

[8] The phrase in quotation marks has been suggested by Dankwart Rustow, *The World of Nations* (Washington, D.C.: The Brookings Institution, 1967), p. 165. It is a succinct paraphrase of the miraculous element in the followers' perception of charisma.

The following sketches of four political leaders in Asia may be considered with these questions in mind.

PRINCE NORODOM SIHANOUK, CAMBODIA (1923——)

Prince Sihanouk exemplifies in his own person the transition from prince to plebiscitarian leader. He was called to the throne in 1941, at the age of eighteen, presumably because the French colonial rulers considered him submissive. Yet at an early time, Sihanouk faced up to the problem of procuring Cambodia's independence from French rule, while dealing with the leading political party, which was not only nationalist and anti-French but also opposed to the monarchy. The Prince recognized the difficulties which would surround the emerging state and did not want to foreclose the possibility of appealing to France for assistance. Therefore he chose to negotiate the achievement of independence rather than win it through open revolt. But by winning independence as a monarch in 1953, Sihanouk also succeeded in countering anti-monarchical sentiments. Because the throne was customarily above national politics, Sihanouk recognized that in an independent Cambodia he had to choose between his monarchical position and an active political role. Accordingly, he abdicated in favor of his father in 1955 and founded a party, the *Sangkum*, in order to arouse greater public interest in political affairs. Originally, the party was not intended to be "political"; however, the people responded enthusiastically, and eventually all other parties were dissolved, and their leaders and followers joined the *Sangkum*. In 1960, upon the death of his father, Sihanouk was requested to ascend the throne once again, but he refused. Instead, his mother became Queen, while the Prince suggested that the National Assembly amend the Constitution and create the position of Chief of State. The amendment was passed, and Prince Sihanouk was elected to the newly created position.

In this way the charisma of the royal family was transferred in good part to the position of a plebiscitarian political leader. The concept of the *Sangkum* party as a loyal following of the entire people may be considered similarly: a transmutation of subjects into citizens with the ideology of the people's loyalty to the king virtually intact. The subsequent dissolution of all competing parties may have the same significance; while pressure was no doubt exerted, it may have involved to a great extent an appeal to loyalty which even the opponents of the Prince could not ignore. The same populist approach is evident in the National Congress. Originally designed to provide a forum for the people to voice their opinions and complaints, the agenda of the Congress are arranged in practice by the *Sangkum*. Prince Sihanouk presides over the meetings of the Congress, while the people in attendance are a largely passive audience. The Prince is generally able to influence the course of the meeting which becomes in effect a royal audience in plebiscitarian disguise.

In his new role of plebiscitarian leadership the Prince has reenacted the attributes of a benevolent ruler with a strong emphasis on good works and modernity. The populist stance, the jokes to get people relaxed, human warmth and personal solicitude, the appeal to the people at large and to the grandeur of the country's traditions, even the Prince's exemplary actions such as the design of textiles or well-publicized acts of manual labor—all these are instances of symbolic identification with the people in a context of popular affection and deference. Reactions are not unequivocal, however. There are signs of discontent among competing groups within the *Sangkum,* which are critical of the Prince's foreign and domestic policies; there is also unrest among the educated youths who cannot find the opportunities for which they feel themselves qualified. Nevertheless, the Prince apparently uses his protean talents to show his solidarity with the people rather than to manifest his exceptional powers as a leader. And accounts of popular reactions present the people as, on the whole, content and deferential rather than devoted or eager for signs and miracles. In sum, this is a case of institutionalized charisma, with the aura and potential terror of royalty mellowed by populist appeals and an adaptation of plebiscitarian methods of government.

This classification is suggested also by Prince Sihanouk's personnel policy. The men he has employed are not disciples but rather men distinguished by their experience and independent judgment. His present advisors include men who formerly opposed him but whom he appointed apparently because he valued their talents. However, two of the chief advisors are relatives of the Prince. It is speculated that the future leaders of Cambodia will be recruited from this group of advisors, perhaps under the direction of Prince Monireth, Sihanouk's uncle. But the question is whether or not any successor can achieve anything like Prince Sihanouk's very personal combination of royalist tradition and plebiscitarian methods. As long as Sihanouk is still "King" to the people at large, no one is likely to question his right to name his successor; indeed some years ago the Prince designated one of his sons as the future head of the *Sangkum* party. But how long will this belief in the institutionalized charisma of royalty remain intact? The Prince's son, for example, would succeed not to the throne but to the position of party leader. And unless he is quite as successful as his father in holding the warring party factions at bay by an appeal to the people and by successful actions in their behalf, his image will get tarnished more quickly than it would in the presence of comparable intrigues at a royal court with its base in the sacred blood ties of the royal family.

The strength of institutionalized charisma (as in royalty) is that succession is solved through inheritance; its weakness is that personal qualification for office is a matter of chance. In the case of charismatic leadership proper the assets and liabilities are reversed: there is no rule for succession, while personal qualifications can be decisive. The relation between Gandhi and Nehru is a case in point.

JAWAHARLAL NEHRU, INDIA (1889–1964)

Among the four leaders considered here, Nehru is the only one who is clearly a disciple and a publicly designated successor. Since in the eyes of his followers at least, Nehru's charisma was derived from Gandhi, we are obliged to examine the transfer of charisma from teacher to disciple, in order to assess the latter's charismatic appeal. Weber discusses the transfer of charisma as an aspect of "routinization." Since by definition charisma is out of the ordinary and dependent upon manifestations of strictly personal qualities, it exists in pure form only in the person in whom it originates. Yet the disciples of the leader and his followers at large share a strong desire to perpetuate that "gift of grace" and its real or presumed benefits, and efforts at such perpetuation come to the fore when the problem of succession must be solved. In this respect Weber distinguishes six typical alternatives; the one of interest here is that the original charismatic leader designates his own successor, who is then accorded recognition by the community.

Nehru's long schooling in England had prepared him to become a junior member in his father's legal firm, but he found this prospect dull. In 1919, at the age of thirty, he became actively involved in the Indian independence movement. The designation of Nehru as a successor to Gandhi took place over a number of years. During this early period, Nehru emerged as a young, conspicuously Western, relatively wealthy, and intensely theoretical member of the inner circle of disciples. All the disciples were held together by their faith in Gandhi's political and moral leadership. Yet there were divisions among them, for the specific goals of Hindu-Moslem harmony, the elimination of untouchability, and the improvement of village life were broad enough to allow considerable variation with regard to means and ends. In the context of the movement for independence the most noteworthy division concerned nonviolence, which was a creed to some and a tactic to others. This tells us something about

Gandhi's tolerance for diversity among his immediate followers, suggesting the permissive preaching of the *exemplary prophet* which "says nothing about a divine mission or an ethical duty of obedience, but rather directs itself to the self-interest of those who crave salvation, recommending to them the same path as he himself traversed." [9]

Nehru's tie to Gandhi was based on deep respect and acceptance of Gandhi's tactical skill, but these sentiments did not affect Nehru's own wide-ranging ideological and political explorations and commitments. Such world-political preoccupations separated Nehru from things Indian even in the midst of intense political activities. Gandhi commented in 1924 that Nehru was one of "the loneliest young men of my acquaintance in India." [10] This personal and cultural isolation was directly related to the articulation of Nehru's political position. His views on international affairs sharpened his conflict with the older Congress leaders including his father, but these views also enabled Nehru to appeal effectively to labor groups and radical youth, among whom some had lost faith in Gandhi. In this setting Gandhi, choosing to withdraw from the Congress presidency in favor of Nehru (1930), used Nehru to keep the young rebels in line. Gandhi also induced his chosen disciple to accept policies that bewildered him so that Nehru was forced for the sake of party unity to represent as his own a position in which he did not believe. This pattern recurred during the long years of discipleship, from Gandhi's reconciliation between Nehru and his father in 1919 to his formal designation of Nehru as his political heir in 1942. For Nehru these were also years during which he was pulled in several directions, dedicated to the man in whose charisma he believed, but at odds with him in his style and judgments. Yet Nehru served him and the cause of independence with complete devotion despite the false positions and humiliating experiences into which Gandhi's tactics forced him from time to time.

A lesser man might have succumbed to the strain of that relationship, compounded as it was by Gandhi's cooperative and antagonistic relations with Nehru's father. But Nehru was an intense and ebullient man, who apparently overcame the ambiguities of his position and his own ambivalence. He was aided not only by his courage and idealism for India but also by Gandhi's patient trust in his qualities of

[9] Max Weber, *The Sociology of Religion* (Boston: The Beacon Press, 1963), p. 55.

[10] In a letter to Motilal Nehru, September 2, 1924. Quoted from B. R. Nanda, *The Nehrus: Motilal and Jawaharlal* (New York: The John Day Co., 1963), p. 247, in Margaret Fisher, "India's Jawaharlal Nehru," *Asian Survey*, VII (June 1967), 367.

mind and character despite outbursts of temper, doctrinaire views, and repeated clashes with other Congress leaders. Nehru's relationship with Gandhi reflected his ambivalence to India as a whole. Admiring Gandhi's tactical "magic" and his uniquely Indian means of achieving independence, Nehru still saw non-violence only as a tactic to achieve a political purpose; thus at the same time he identified with, and dissociated himself from, this symbol of India. While he enjoyed Gandhi's trust during the long years of his discipleship, Gandhi still mixed expressions of confidence with fatherly admonitions, giving Nehru his blessing but withholding his mandate. There is some suggestion in this context that Nehru's successful campaigns among the Indian masses were an escape from an enervating tutelage as well as a discovery of India. Contacts with the Indian people were a means of attaining confidence in his mission, for he witnessed the unconditional devotion with which they viewed him as the embodiment of Gandhi's charisma and the charisma of his own sacrifices for independence. There is an almost tragic irony in the paradox that what his personality represented to the people was largely independent of what he said to them. Nehru's effect on the masses inspired his confidence in India while increasing the scepticism of his colleagues. Yet this mass enthusiasm and Nehru's continued isolation among the disciples provided Gandhi again and again with the opportunity to weld the factions of the Congress together. And then, at the age of fifty-three, once more in jail, Nehru learned from the book of an Englishman what it was that distinguished him from Gandhi. The book distinguished between the prophet, who pursues the truth relentlessly, and the leader, who strikes a compromise between truth and the views of the average man. Nehru thought his own role to be that of the leader but believed Gandhi had confused the two roles. Apparently Nehru did not recognize Gandhi's unique fusion of prophecy and teaching, which was a part of that specific charisma of India's holy men that was beyond his own grasp. By separating the teacher's role from the educative function of exemplary conduct, Nehru revealed his own Western acculturation as well as the discrepancy between his self-image and the Indian people's recognition of his charismatic gift. He wanted to be their teacher, while they sought in him the exemplary prophet.

In this all too brief consideration I have emphasized the problem of succession, highlighted by the great charisma of Nehru's mentor. It may be noted that the charismatic appeal of Gandhi and of Nehru is entirely the by-product of their personal gifts in the context of the Indian independence movement. In turning now to a discussion of two leaders in Communist countries, we must attempt to disentangle the relationship between the leader and his people from the manipulated representation of that relationship by the mass media.

KIM IL-SŎNG, NORTH KOREA (1919———)

It is difficult to separate the fact from fiction in the life history of Kim Il-sŏng. Kim has concentrated in his hands all power of decision-making in the party, the government, and the army. To account for this fact, and to celebrate it, North Korean historians have written hagiological accounts which twist the story of Kim's childhood, his role as a guerilla leader, and the first phase of his party leadership into so many anticipations of his present preminence. For that reason it becomes difficult to assess the rather meagre descriptions of Kim's leadership. The Korean party appears to model its mobilization of the people after a shock-troop pattern, giving its civilian appeals and organizational efforts the appearance of simulated combat under conditions of guerilla warfare. For example, Kim approaches production problems in the manner of a self-confident guerilla leader who himself masters whatever he asks of his soldiers and by his example encourages them to greater effort. He reportedly learns the technicalities of the factories or collectives he will visit, thus living up to the reputation of the omniscient leader. In this way he emphasizes by his example the Party's mission as the teacher of the people. Organized propaganda shows this leadership in action and seeks to enhance its exemplary effects by the testimony of "awed witnesses." But this inevitably raises questions, as does Kim's power to divert resources to those farms and enterprises which have been selected for exemplary success in their production efforts. Propagandistic manipulation of this kind can give a hollow ring to the claim of exceptional powers on behalf of the leader, and a mere joke or derisive comment aimed at such manipulation can turn a follower's devotion into a sceptic's "withdrawal of efficiency" (Veblen).[11]

Here we come to a lacuna in Weber's approach to charisma, due to the time at which his analysis was written (1913–14). He did not foresee that it would be possible to *simulate* publicly all aspects of charismatic leadership—the manifestations of the leader's extraordinary

---

[11] According to Chong-sik Lee biographical data detrimental to Kim's official image have been suppressed, such as his flight to Siberia to escape the Japanese invasion, which makes his subsequent political prominence largely the result of Russian or Chinese influence. There is some question, of course, whether the manipulation of such biographical details enters into people's awareness; but even in the absence of knowledge, suspicions and rumors can spread quickly if they project people's feelings.

gift, the unconditional devotion of his disciples, and the awed veneration of his large following—saturating all channels of communication so that no one could escape the message. Modern dictatorships have used such centrally organized, public hagiology extensively; and, given the possibilities of the "great lie" and the "will to believe," a widespread belief in charisma can be created under favorable conditions. Yet the built-in limitations of "charisma by publicity" should not be overlooked. All hagiological writings contain paeans to the virtues of the saints; in the eyes of the believers the credibility of these writings is enhanced, rather than diminished, by stories showing "powerful results achieved in the absence of power," and such stories are also a regular feature of dictatorial propaganda. But then the authors of conventional hagiology were true believers themselves, who expressed their own sense of the miraculous for the edification of their readers, in the absence of any claim to be believed other than the authenticity of their own religious experience. In this respect, a manipulated hagiology differs. Where all media are saturated with news of the leader's great deeds and the devotion of his followers, ordinary people may begin to resist the message by various strategies which help them escape the din and the drive to mobilize them. For the saturation of the media *means* manipulation and can suggest even to the unlettered that "powerful results are 'achieved' in the presence of power" and hence in the absence of miracles.

Nevertheless, it would be mistaken to infer that charismatic leadership cannot occur under these conditions. First of all, central manipulation of news is still compatible with credibility. All totalitarian regimes have an interest, for example, in obtaining testimonials to the leader by prominent individuals with a reputation for probity and independent judgment. Whether or not pressure is used to obtain such testimonials, they can be turned to good account by the mass media—at least for quite a time. Again, the leader himself may use the media to project his supreme confidence in his mission, while pomp and circumstance can enhance the effect of that message. In this respect it is quite wrong to suppose that charismatic leadership implies the absence of deliberate manipulation on the part of the leader. On the contrary, a sense of personal mission will justify the manipulative enhancement of the charismatic appeal, so long as this does not conflict with the appeal itself.[12] Secondly, the leader's career may exemplify his charisma in the eyes of the people, and the mere

---

[12] It is probably more difficult to make testimonials to the leader appear genuine, when these are given by his direct collaborators, because the secular context militates against the image of the disciple who is moved by unselfish devotion to duty and who partakes of the leader's charisma.

fact of media manipulation will not necessarily undermine their belief in him. Indeed, a people's recognition of that charisma—born of "the will to believe" and manifest in their devotion to duty—may endure long after they have begun to discount the credibility of the leader's entourage and of the whole apparatus of media manipulation. This consideration may have some bearing on the case of Mao Tse-tung.

MAO TSE-TUNG, CHINA (1893————)

The evidence of Mao Tse-tung 's leadership is overwhelming, and there is little doubt that this leadership deserves the attribute "charismatic." Stuart Schram points out that Mao gives the appearance of an "average Chinese peasant." [13] The peasant is traditionally a symbol of weakness; Mao's success has made him a symbol of strength. For great power to develop out of universal weakness is indeed a miracle in the literal sense. Since in this case identification with the peasant also symbolizes the nation, Mao personifies the whole transformation of his country. His grand and remote appearance only intensifies the impression of mystery associated with miracles—whether or not this appearance is a personal trait, a manner acquired during a dramatic life spent in revolutionary politics, an impression created by party propaganda, or a sign of old age, or some combination of these.

Three main aspects of Mao's thought are directly related to his rise to power. His nationalism is exemplified in the mobilization of the Chinese against Japanese aggression. His concern with military action is related to his long experience in guerilla warfare with its combination of militancy and populism. And his emphasis on voluntarism and conscious action (though related to Leninist ideas) reflects the special importance he has attributed throughout his career to moral and psychological preparedness as the principal basis of revolution. These themes were articulated in Mao's early writings, and his continued adherence to these basic ideas conveys an impression of extraordinary consistency. In his own mind and those of his devoted followers these ideas are directly related to the success of the Chinese revolution. Accordingly, Mao's outlook is seen as the cause of "powerful results achieved in the absence of power." It is not surprising that an aging leader relies on this inspiration of his successful achievements of the past, when his revolutionary regime begins to encounter the resistance of men and the complications of circumstance, as all established revolutionary regimes do.

[13] See Stuart R. Schram, "Mao Tse-tung as a Charismatic Leader," *Asian Survey*, VII (June 1967), 383–384.

A number of factors have been cited to explain the excesses of the Mao cult in recent years: a struggle for power within the highest ranks of the party, senile vanity, echoes of traditional emperor worship, Mao's penchant for a personalist approach to problems of leadership despite his awareness of the importance of organization, and last but not least his conscious manipulation of his own personality-cult as a political weapon. To this plethora of causes an outsider hesitates to add further possibilities. But if the evidence for Mao's charisma is as strong as has been suggested, then it is probable that mounting complexities bring out both the supreme leader's fear of losing his extraordinary powers and that mixture of hope and fear of despair with which the young generation reacts to a charisma placed in jeopardy. As the difficulties of the regime mount, the populist desire for a "sign" or proof of charisma is increasing, just at the time when the leader who embodies that charisma is visibly aging. After all, the paradox is that a personality cult centering on a seventy-four-year-old man comes to a crescendo at a time when he must solve the most difficult problem of charismatic leadership—the problem of succession. The more the cult centers on him personally, the more insoluble that problem becomes, and Mao appears to be quite aware of this fact. Referring to organizational changes involving the delegation of his power to Liu Shao-ch'i and Teng Hsiao-p'ing in 1956, Mao stated in October 1966:

> When I retreated into the second line by not conducting the daily work and by letting others execute it, my purpose was to cultivate their prestige so that when I have to see God, the country can avoid great chaos.[14]

In now reversing that earlier decision according to his own interpretation, Mao is apparently attempting to transform the people's recognition of his personal charisma into a cult of sacred objects. It remains to be seen whether such a transformation can capture the imagination of the people and also preserve their devotion to duty—in the absence of visible miracles and eventually in the absence of the charismatic leader himself.

All this is without precedent in the history of Communist movements only in the sense that a career of leadership which spans the entire period from the beginning of the revolutionary movement until eighteen years after the seizure of power is also without precedent.

[14] Quoted in Gene T. Hsiao, "The Background and Development of 'The Proletarian Cultural Revolution,'" *Asian Survey*, VII (June 1967), 392. Mr. Hsiao has suggested to me that the reference to "God" is meant ironically, and the statement itself is clearly polemical. But these considerations do not, I think, affect the interpretation suggested here.

This factor must be recognized in making comparisons between Mao and either Lenin or Stalin. Lenin's early death removed him from the contentions arising later so that the deification of his person and the canonization of his writings became weapons for his immediate followers in their struggle over the succession and in subsequent policy disputes. Mao's position is quite different. Still being alive, he has become the leading participant in struggles in which he uses his own deification and canonization in order to resolve the problem of succession and the policy disputes associated with that problem. Again, Stalin was the disciple who won out in the struggles for the succession following Lenin's death and in the absence of any clear settlement of that succession by Lenin himself. The purges instigated by Stalin in the 1930's were well removed from that question; they could be compared to Mao's present situation only if instead Lenin had lived and had instigated these purges in order to designate his successor and make certain basic policy decisions binding upon him and the Party leadership.

There is reason to anticipate some deification of Mao after his death, as old and young followers alike seek to preserve the power of his charisma for themselves and the community at large. At present Mao appears to anticipate just such a development. By laying the ground work not only for the choice of his successor but for the terms in which that successor will be obliged to implement the legacy of Maoist revolutionary achievements, he may be attempting to foreclose the gross misuse of his charisma by followers whose interest in institutionalization is greater than his own. It is an arresting thought that Mao's effort to replace the party elite with new men and to employ the Red Guards as an instrument of "permanent revolution" is in part an old man's struggle over the use that is to be made of his work and his person by those who will live after he is gone.

In conclusion it is appropriate to consider the distinction between charismatic leadership and leadership *sans phrase,* to which I alluded earlier. The term "charisma" is used indiscriminately, because this distinction is difficult to make in practice, though not in theory. All types of leadership are alike in that they involve an ambivalent interaction between leaders and led. A leader demands unconditional obedience, because he does not want his performance to be tested against criteria over which he has no control. Such tests jeopardize his authoritative right to command. On the other hand, the led withhold an ultimate surrender of their will (if only in the form of mental reservations), because they do not want to forego their last chance for a quid pro quo, i.e., for a gain through effective leadership in exchange for the obedience shown. Yet to withhold unconditional obedience in this way always runs the risk that leadership will fail us, because we have not shown our ultimate devotion to duty. The interactions between leaders and led probably trace an erratic path between this Scylla and Charybdis. The hazards of cumulative causation (as actions and reactions reenforce each other) and the reluctance of most men to face the ultimate consequences of their acts frequently lead to a tempering of demands and expectations on both sides. By not claiming ultimate authority and demanding unconditional obedience leaders can avoid being challenged and yet hope to accomplish a modicum of success. And the led are ready to obey when no ultimate commitment is demanded of them, because a mixture of acquiescence and performance leaves them free to hope for benefits with only a moderate inconvenience to themselves. In theory it is easy to see that "charisma" makes its appearance when leaders and led are convinced that these easy accommodations are no longer enough, when consummate belief, on one side, and the promptings of enthusiasm, despair, or hope, on the other, imperatively call for unconditional authority and obedience. In theory it is even easy to see that "charisma" appears to be present and yet is in jeopardy, when such convictions animate the leader *or* the led, but not both simultaneously. There are many historical examples of a leader who feels the call but cannot find a following, or of people at large searching in vain for a leader who will satisfy their longing for a miracle. Thus, charisma appears to occur frequently because the search for it continues. But genuine charisma is a rare event, born as it is of a belief in the mysterious gift of one man which that man shares with those who follow him.

PART SIX

WEBER'S PHILOSOPHY
OF HISTORY AND POLITICS

TEN

MAX WEBER'S
POLITICAL SOCIOLOGY
AND HIS PHILOSOPHY
OF WORLD HISTORY

WOLFGANG MOMMSEN

IN BRINGING ABOUT and accelerating the process of universal rationalization, which Max Weber considered so ineluctable, spiritual factors played a vital part, in particular the spirit of modern capitalism which had grown out of the religious thinking of Puritanism, and modern science. But, historically, the decisive factor was that, as it progressed, rationalization no longer required these impelling ideals, the less so as it advanced further.

This historic duality of charisma and rationalization, which is the basic theme of Weber's sociology, might at first sight seem to correspond—on the 'ideal type' plane—to a linear development of world history proceeding from charisma via the traditional to the bureaucratic form of dominance. We should then have an elaboration of

From "Max Weber's Political Sociology and His Philosophy of World History," by Wolfgang Mommsen. From *International Social Science Journal*, XVII, no. 1 (1965), 35–45. Reprinted by permission of the author and UNESCO. Some footnotes have been omitted for reasons of space. Ellipses indicate deletions from the text.

Wilhelm Roscher's theory of history, which . . . was the subject of
Weber's close analysis. It is common knowledge that he dismissed any
such interpretation as a vulgar error. Charismatic dominance was in
no way to be found exclusively at primitive stages of development,
but was generated also in societies classifiable in principle as of the
bureaucratic type, "an extremely important element of the social structure." Perhaps not without the incidental purpose of excluding constructions like the linear process of historical development here attempted, Max Weber elaborated his typology of the "three pure types
of legitimate dominance" in the reverse order. It is clear therefore that
there is no sort of logical sequence in the types of mastery or dominance, still less any fixed cycle of these. As depicted in Weber's typology, the historical process may more correctly be described as a descent
from a predominantly charismatic form, through traditional, to bureaucratic forms of life and dominance, interrupted again and again
and directed into new courses by further eruptions of charisma. In
these charismatic "eruptions," which on occasion amounted to "charismatic revolutions," a decisive part was played by great men, "prophets"
and "leaders" (*Fuehrer*).

Unquestionably, there is a kinship between this historico-philosophi-
cal conception and Nietzsche's. The latter interprets history as a process of natural growth and decay, in which great personalities also
play the parts of creative elements. It can easily be shown that Max
Weber was extraordinarily impressed and influenced by Nietzsche's
aristocratic individualism, which in its absoluteness did not hesitate
to challenge the two-thousand-year-old tradition of Western civilization. Weber's concept of the great individual setting objectives for
society out of his own unmotivated conviction, reminds one distinctly
of Nietzsche, whose basic argument rested on absolute freedom for
great men in their choice of values.

Yet Weber disagreed strongly with Nietzsche's view that the great
man must dominate the mass, not for its own good, but solely from
love of that power which is the indispensable basis of his aristocratic
vitality. Weber condemned the errors of the prophecies derived from
Nietzsche, the belief that only by stepping into "aristocratic buskins"
could one stand out from the multitude. His liberalism and keen
sense of responsibility towards the masses could not but oppose this
authoritarian variant of individualistic thinking.[1] The individual be-

---

[1] Cf. also a marginal note of [Eduard Baumgarten, ed., *Max Weber—Werk und
Person* (Tuebingen, 1964),] p. 615, to Georg Simmel's *Schopenhauer und Nietzsche*,
p. 236: "Nietzsche should at least have clearly distinguished his 'will to power' from
the appetite of the common man by stating explicitly that it was not dominance and
might as external realities that constituted the value of this will to power, but the

comes great not against, but with the masses. It is among the essential characteristics of the great charismatic leader that he is able to convince his followers of his capacity to lead. It is true that, in line with Nietzsche, he is thus inwardly responsible only to himself and his own cause, but there is all the same a certain responsibility for the wellbeing of the "others," whom Nietzsche cynically dismissed as "the sheep."

Thus Max Weber's theory of history was in no way simply a matter of great men "who make history"; and he certainly would not have accepted Nietzsche's dictum that "the goal of mankind does not lie in its ends" but "only in its highest exemplars." Nevertheless Nietzsche's call for great men, for whom the fetters of their time have become too tight to burst, to arise and to point the way to new shores, clearly left an imprint on Weber's sociology of dominance. Weber, it is true, turned against those of his contemporaries who would have a new Caesar at any price; he realized that the dominance of great men invariably meant a loss of internal and external freedom.[2] But even in his sociology of dominance it is the great charismatic leader figures who spearhead the traditional or bureaucratic systems and who, whether to perpetuate or perfect the existing order, set new goals—men like Napoleon, Bismarck, Gladstone (the "dictator of the election battlefield"), or Theodore Roosevelt. In this, Max Weber would wholeheartedly have endorsed the words: "Society is measured exclusively by what the individual does."

According to Weber, historical development, whose principal content was "the shifting battle between discipline and the individual charisma," was in principle open to the future. But this rational construction of historical evolution was overshadowed by a deeply pessimistic fear of a new enslavement to come. Looming through the mists of an as yet unspecified time ahead Max Weber perceived the outlines of a petrified society similar to that of late Antiquity, in which Western concepts of freedom and the personal responsibility of the individual would have lost all meaning. Max Weber agreed with Nietzsche's "devastating critique of those 'ultimate men' who had invented happiness." His own feelings closely approached the gloomy forebodings of Zarathustra when he announced to his people: "Woe, the time

character of the sovereign soul the manifestation and expression of which play their part in every sociological relationship." To this Weber remarked: "But that was *not* Nietzsche's idea! In this respect he was himself a German *petit-bourgeois*."

[2] See the inaugural address in which he derides the German *bourgeoisie* because "it is looking for the appearance of a new Caesar," *Politische Schriften*, p. 21. Regarding the negative effects of the dominance of great Caesar figures, see "Die Herrschaft Bismarcks," ibid., pp. 299 et seq., and [Wolfgang Mommsen, *Max Weber und die Deutsche Politik, 1890–1920* (Tuebingen, 1959)], pp. 97 et seq.

is coming when man will no longer speed the arrow of his desires beyond mankind, and will have forgotten how to draw his bowstring." [3]
Weber was afraid lest the historical development of man might lead
to something very similar, to the total victory of "technical man" over
"cultured man." To the disciplined professional willing to take his
destined place in the machinery of modern industrial society, to busy
opportunists who are always ready to conform to existing circumstances
and are directed exclusively by purely rational (*Zweckrationalen*) aims
—to these, it would seem, the future belonged, not to the creative
individuals animated by spiritual ideals.

In the endless struggle between creative charisma and rationalizing
bureaucracy the latter, in Weber's opinion, was bound to win, if only
because it had every material condition on its side. In particular,
modern capitalism, which forced everyone to become a professional,
led irresistibly to the rationalization and bureaucratization of all aspects of life. ". . . The rationalization of political and economic needs
is accompanied by an irresistible process of disciplining which increasingly constricts the influence of charisma and of individually differentiated action." Weber noted with an undertone of resignation that "the
charismatic glorification of reason" was "the ultimate form" which
"charisma had assumed in its fluctuating course." He thought he
already discerned a foretaste of the coming age of unfreedom in the
social realities of his day: ". . . in the "benevolent feudalism" of the
Americans, in Germany's so-called "welfare institutions," in the Russian factory-made constitution—the new House of Enslavement stands
everywhere ready for occupation."

We have now surveyed the basic universal-historical premises on
which Max Weber's political sociology has been built, and from which
the full meaning of his views on political practice can be determined.
Assertion of the value of the individual personality in a world-
historical setting that is basically antagonistic to it, was the keystone
of his thinking. "We individualists and partisans of democratic institutions are swimming against the tide of materialist forces," Weber
noted in connexion with the Russian revolution of 1905; and again in
his studies on the future constitution of Germany in 1917 he asked

---

[3] [*Also Sprach Zarathustra*, chap. 5]; cf. Max Weber's paraphrase of this Nietzschean
thought in *Religionssoziologie*, I, 204, speaking of the mechanical edifice erected by
a triumphant capitalism: "No one yet knows who will inhabit that abode and
whether this prodigious development may end in entirely new prophets arising or in
a mighty rebirth of ancient thoughts and ideals—or if neither happens, in a
mechanized petrifaction decked out with a sort of obsessive self-importance. Then
indeed could it be said of these 'ultimate' men of that stage of cultural development:
'Technicians without souls, sensualists without hearts—this nothingness imagines
it has climbed to a level of humanity never reached before.' " . . .

this fundamental question: "How is it, in view of this overwhelming tendency towards bureaucratization, *at all possible still* to save *anything* of what is meant by individual freedom of movement?" How could modern society be preserved from "mechanical" petrifaction? Such was Weber's general formulation of a problem which deeply disturbed him. What could be done to avert this menace? That thought was uppermost in Weber's mind in his economic no less than in his political reflections; the maintenance of a dynamic society in which the individual retains the maximum personal initiative is the central idea determining his attitude towards concrete political and economic problems.

In the political field the burning question was how there could be any real or permanent leadership in the context of a modern, bureaucratically organized industrial society. Weber was already disturbed by what Karl Mannheim was later to call "the trend towards leaderlessness in the last days of liberalism." The fear that "professional politicians without a profession," in other words opportunists void of any high ideals, might monopolize the leadership of society and the State, formed the core of his politico-constitutional considerations. It was not his specifically democratic feeling based on the law of nature or otherwise which had made him since the turn of the century a pioneer of parliamentary democracy, but the recognition that this was the best form of selected leadership within an industrial society. His "democracy under a leader and subject to a plebiscite" which is the ripest formulation of his views on modern democracy, was largely modelled on the British system, though quite un-British in content. That system, he thought, could allow a plebiscite-controlled dominance by great, charismatic leader figures, while as far as possible obviating the disadvantages of pure Caesarism. In Weber's terminology, "plebiscitory leader-democracy," in contrast to the established "leaderless democracy" consisting of professional politicians without a profession, is a variant of charismatic dominance which in fact assumes the form of a purely rational (*Zweckrational*) and formally legal constitutionalism.[4]

This corresponds with the picture drawn by Max Weber of the democratic political leader. The features are those of his own ideal personality. The politician is exclusively responsible to himself and to the task selected by him with regard for certain ideal personal values. His responsibility is restricted to "proving his worth," i.e., he must give proof by results that the unquestioning dedication of his followers to himself purely as a person is its own inherent justification.

[4] Compare my study "Zum Begriff der plebiszitären Führerdemokratie bei Max Weber," op. cit., pp. 398 et seq.

As against this there is no obligation towards the material goals of the masses; Weber emphatically repudiated any suggestion that the democratic leader had to carry out a mandate entrusted to him by the electorate. Attachment of the masses to his own person, and not any objective conviction on his part of the value of the ends to be achieved, is what according to Weber characterizes a "plebiscitory leader-democracy." It is not objective aims as such that determine the outcome of an election, but the personal-charismatic qualities of the candidate leader. This was the only way in which Weber could conceive the independent dominance of a strong personality under modern conditions. He described "leadership democracy" as a continual competition between politicians for the favour of the masses. It is conducted principally by demagogic means; a system of formal "rules of the game" requires that the successful politician prove his worth and in the event of defeat be prepared to step down.

At the same time, the principle of struggle as an essential element of all voluntary political "business" is accepted, together with the concept of "dominance" or "mastery." Contrary to traditional liberalism Weber strongly emphasized that the business of a politician was to exercise power. To him pacifism was a weak and contemptible gospel which in a politician was totally irresponsible.[5] In contrast to "leaderless democracy," which tends towards minimizing the dominance of men over men, "leader democracy" aims at a maximum degree of dominance, which nevertheless must be exercised with the formally free consent of the dominated. For only really strong leadership is capable of great creative achievements in the social field, whereas a business administration can never hope to exceed the limits of the established order. From the universal-historical standpoint, freedom is won, not by a reduction of personal authority in favour of the rule of law, but on the contrary only by all possible enhancement of personal authority under conditions which guarantee the necessity for the political leader constantly to prove his worth while excluding the decline of his dominance into sterile tyranny. Only the dominance of the great statesman can ensure a permanently viable society and prevent "freedom" from becoming a meaningless term.

In view of the above it will be understood why Max Weber, even in

---

[5] The well-known address of 1919 entitled "Politik als Beruf" contained in its second part a strongly-argued justification of power politics as against the humanitarian pacifism of the time. In his draft of the speech (an extract may be found in Baumgarten, op. cit., Table 16), it is significant that at one point, instead of the pair of opposites "Affective policy and responsible policy" (*Gesinnungspolitik und Verantwortungspolitik*) there stood originally "Affective policy and power policy," from which it may be assumed that in Weber's opinion responsible politics was normally synonymous with power politics.

the field of domestic politics, came down so strongly on the side of the "will to power." His attitude may be summed up in the following paradox: *"The utmost possible freedom through the utmost possible dominance."* To this must be added the influence of the Puritanical idea of original sin. It is here, and not so much in his efforts to describe reality empirically and free of all value judgement, that we find the real reason for the almost insufferable placidity with which Max Weber treated the problem of violence in domestic politics. He took over in its entirety the traditional doctrine of "reasons of State," and described the constitutional State as the typical modern form of power dominance but without much attention to its basis of rational values. This was also the case when he said that between ethics and politics there is an unbridgeable gulf and spoke of a formal competition between political and ethical standards. He denied in principle any possibility of introducing ethics into politics and considered the strict separation of the two spheres as the only honest solution. From the standpoint of his extreme individualism, which regarded itself as bound exclusively by personally chosen values, the political world was a mechanism run by strict rationality whose laws had to be taken into account by the individual—and above all by a political leader—if he wished to use them in accordance with his ultimate aims. This means that in certain contexts the practical politician unavoidably comes into conflict with the commands of a non-political ethic, particularly in cases where politics generate normative claims of the same intensity as those generated by religious ethics.

This holds good in particular of political postulates of such apparently compelling force as that of modern nationalism. It is known that Max Weber regarded nationalism and with it the claims of a rational power policy as matters of faith; he never questioned their absolute or relative justification. On the contrary, he postulated the primacy of national interest, as opposed to the entire complex of political and legal institutions, as a further strictly rational instrument in the same way as the Puritan considered the material environment as a mere apparatus furnishing ever-fresh support for his religious views.

This absolute national principle seems to have stood in stark contrast to Weber's democratic and individualistic assumptions. Yet even here there were inner links. Just as he approved unreservedly the competition between politicians for power in the area of domestic politics, since it represented a dynamic in social life, so he also approved the struggle for power between the nations as bearers of autonomous cultural ideals and the extension of their influence throughout the world. He was convinced that every civilization would remain "nationally tied" for a long time yet. To this extent therefore the great nation-States were called upon to defend, if necessary by force of arms, the validity and prestige of their cultures and, if necessary, also to expand them. Weber regarded as a matter of principle the struggle between nations and their values as a built-in factor of a dynamic world order. The counterpart to this was seen in the Mediterranean society of late Antiquity, when a supranational world State dictated peace with an iron hand, obstructed the political evolution of separate national groups, and in this way brought about the gradual paralysis of all social life. It was entirely in keeping with Weber's universal-historical view that during the First World War he endorsed the world mission of the German Empire to fight for a German-oriented middle European cultural sphere, between "Anglo-Saxon convention," "Latin reason," and the "Russian knout."

From this position Max Weber went so far as to espouse a policy of forthright national imperialism. It must be borne in mind however that he shared the then common belief that nations had in the end a chance to maintain their national and cultural identity only provided they were strong enough to become world powers. This is the sense in which we must interpret his famous saying that ". . . Germany's unification was a youthful prank which the nation was indulging in old age, and the cost of which it would have done better to forego if it was to prove the end and not the beginning of Germany's bid for world power."

The approval of conflict as an essential element of dynamic international action, even at the expense of certain cultural values, held equally in the economic field. Weber was convinced that the mobility of an industrial society largely depended on maintaining the impetus of economic development. To restrain technical and economic progress would in his opinion bring a modern society appreciably closer to "petrifaction." From this universal standpoint and not merely on economic grounds, Max Weber attached the utmost importance to the principle of economic competition based on private enterprise. Not only was competition indispensable as the best form of market control, but above all as the source of economic impetus; free competition and private enterprise, working together, ensured to modern industry that forward drive which was the secret of its tremendous achievements. According to Max Weber's system of values intensive economic activity was for universal-historical reasons—as explained earlier—specifically advocated, in contrast to the mere euphoria of a *rentier* class, on which he poured contempt.[6] His personal ideal found expression in the restless energy of the classic Puritan entrepreneur.

[6] Compare the supporting documents, pp. 111 et seq., in: Mommsen, op. cit.

To this extent we can agree with Ludwig Marcuse who sees in Max Weber the classic exponent of *bourgeois* individualistic capitalism, without necessarily accepting his conclusion that Weber has nothing more to say to us in that late phase of capitalism in which the irrationalities of the capitalistic system appeared in intensified form.[7] Actually, Max Weber described himself on occasion as a "class-conscious bourgeois."[8] It was not by chance that in the days before the First World War he fervently championed the development of Germany into a modern industrial state. He regretted that the German *bourgeoisie* lacked the same self-confidence, based on sober economic achievement, that he found so admirable in the middle-classes of the Anglo-Saxon countries.[9] Even in those days he favoured Germany's modelling itself in every way upon the social type that had developed in its purest state in the industrial West and which he saw as the dominant type of the future. During and after the First World War, too, when ideas of a planned economy began to circulate in Germany even in non-socialist circles and came in for much discussion, he clung firmly to the principle of individual enterprise. He held that in this generation of big business the great industrial entrepreneur was indispensable.[10]

Even when, during the German revolution, he made certain oratorical concessions to socialism, Max Weber nevertheless strongly rejected any idea of a socialist economy whether now or in the future. Every "rational socialistic economy," he maintained, would magnify the power of the bureaucrats—who ultimately controlled the means of production—to extraordinary proportions and as a result would immeasurably increase the dependency of the workers. What this meant will be apparent in the light of his concern regarding a "new enslavement of the future."

Nor was Max Weber by any means a *bourgeois* capitalist in any reactionary sense. His passionate denunciation of the "patriarchal" lust for power of the German entrepreneurs excludes any such interpretation. He supported the incorporation of the workers as equal partners in the system of modern industrial capitalism. But eudaemonistic con-

---

[7] Compare the long report presented by Marcuse to the Heidelberger Soziologentag, 1964.

[8] See: Mommsen, op. cit., pp. 118 and 123.

[9] Cf. ibid., pp. 106 et seq.

[10] See also *inter alia* Joseph Redlich, *Das politische Tagebuch*, II (Cologne, 1954), 120 et seq.; also Weber's speech at Nuremberg on 1 August 1916 in which he stressed the accomplishments of the German entrepreneurs during the war (according to articles in the *Nürnberger Zeitung* and *Fränkischer Kurier* of 2 August 1916); further, *Gesammelte Aufsätze zur Soziologie und Sozialpolitik*, p. 503. Documentary evidence on the revolutionary period, Mommsen, op. cit., pp. 295 et seq.

siderations were as foreign to him as sentimentality. Even in this field he upheld the principle of conflict. Emancipation of the working class should not derive from any benevolent or welfare policy of government, but should be brought about by the power and initiative of the workers themselves. Political and trade union organizations, and especially the weapon of strikes, were the predestined means. State social policies should be restricted to channelling the struggle between the social partners through a system of legally enforced rules of the game ensuring equal chances for both sides. The ideal of a welfare state was, so far as we can see, something for which Max Weber had no use, being persuaded that it did not foster individual initiative or progress through personal service within the framework of the existing social system.[11] Thus even in the social field Weber's concrete proposals for solving social problems were guided by a conception of the struggle for power as a struggle confined within legal bounds and waged objectively.

We approach the end of this exposé. Throughout Max Weber's sociology we meet with the ideal of an individualistic personality of aristocratic and at the same time rational type. He viewed all social phenomena first of all from the standpoint of what they represented for the individual. This is the governing idea underlying his universal theory of ideal types (*Idealtypenlehre*). That is why he rejected the use of all collective conceptions in sociology, and demanded that this science should always proceed from the behaviour of the individual and the motives that had prompted it.[12]

It may be objected to this interpretation that Max Weber wanted to undertake only empirical research. Indeed, as we have seen, he passionately opposed all global theories of civilization of a philosophical character. Empirical science must abjure all forms of speculation which "seek to interpret the universe." But this does not mean that it can or should renounce the orienting power of ultimate ideals and convictions. On the contrary, "the study of all civilization rests on the transcendental assumption that we are civilized beings, endowed with the capacity and will to face the world and find a meaning in it." Even empirical science therefore is in a sense governed by the highest cultural ideals.

[11] Cf. attack on "German so-called social welfare institutions" ["die deutschen sogenannten Wohlfahrtseinrichtungen"], *Politische Schriften*, p. 60.

[12] *Wissenschaftslehre*, p. 415; cf. also letter to Robert Liefmann dated 9 March 1920 (Weber bequest): ". . . if I have become a sociologist (according to my letter of accreditation), it is mainly in order to exorcise the spectre of collective conceptions which still lingers among us. In other words, sociology itself can only proceed from the actions of one or more separate individuals and must therefore adopt strictly individualistic methods.". . .

Max Weber refused to consider explicitly the question of the meaning of history. In his scientific work however he proceeded from a certain conception of cultural evolution in the centre of which stands the world-historical phenomenon of the ever-recurring struggle of the creative individual with the forces of rationalization. Although he feared that in this combat the individual would finally be overcome, he did not simply take refuge in the cult of irrationality, but acclaimed rationalization as foredestined. For it was precisely within the rational environment that the individual was presented with the challenge of asserting his individuality and establishing its validity by all available means.[13] The principle of individuality and the principle of rationality were in Weber's mind dialectical quantities. They belonged together: a rational, methodical way of life was in his opinion an essential feature of the personality. Nevertheless, Weber repeatedly stressed the fundamental antagonism between the ideal of individual responsibility and the products of rationalization, with particular reference to the modern disciplined working world and its bureaucracies. The conflict between the two principles was in his view the great theme of world history.

The concern about a new "enslavement of the future," but withal the recognition that mankind could not simply turn back on the path leading ultimately to the rationalization of all living conditions, greatly influenced Weber's socio-political ideals. His political views were conditioned by the knowledge that the self-responsible initiative of the individual in a modern industrial society was more than ever in danger. His attempts at a solution were those of an aristocratic liberal who wished to unite two opposite poles. His idea of a "plebiscitory leader-democracy with machinery" is a typical example: the capacity of the charisma to command was to combine with the technical accomplishments of rational bureaucracy to keep the "open-ended society" "open" in its world-historical context—which promised it small chance of survival—and thereby prevent it from sinking slowly but surely into a condition of social ossification. The attitude was one of heroic pessimism. Optimistic ideals such as abolishing the domination of man over man were not in Weber's line. He unreservedly approved of power play in political and social life and wanted to channel it along legal ways—and not too much even of that. In line with Nietzsche he did not want to see the dynamism of "will to power" eliminated entirely from human evolution, for the concept of freedom would thereby also largely lose its meaning. Without power there could be no such thing as political leadership in the true sense, and

[13] This view has been expounded in particular by Karl Loewith, ["Max Weber und Karl Marx," in Loewith, *Gesammelte Abhandlungen* (Stuttgart, 1960), pp. 32 et seq.]

without this there could be no dynamism in society. It was therefore necessary to preserve society from a state of leaderlessness. It must not be delivered up to professional politicians without a profession; for the field must not be entirely given over to "organization men," whose one ideal in life was to conform.

ELEVEN

POLITICAL CRITIQUES
OF MAX WEBER:
SOME IMPLICATIONS
FOR POLITICAL SOCIOLOGY

GUENTHER ROTH

COMMEMORATIONS ARE FREQUENTLY polite and somewhat stately affairs, but the centenary of Weber's birth has attested both to his great influence and to the still controversial character of his person and work. Weber was a passionate advocate of political rationality and, literally, a "radical" sociologist with a world-historical vision: two features which—in the world as it is—are bound to engender political and scholarly controversy. His case also shows, duly magnified, some of the typical tensions between political ideology and political sociology. Weber has been a major target for a series of critiques aimed at political sociology in general, if not at most of social science. These critiques either use a sociological approach for political purposes or deny altogether the present rationale of political sociology, and to some extent even the viability of Western pluralist society. Because Weber had a highly articulate view of politics and took his stand on political issues that have remained controversial to this day it is not always easy to distinguish specific critiques of Weber's politics and scholarship from the general implications for political sociology. There is considerable room for different historical interpretations; it is, of

From "Political Critiques of Max Weber," by Guenther Roth. From *American Sociological Review*, XXX (April, 1965), 213–23; revised version of a paper read at the annual meeting of the American Sociological Association, Montreal, 1964. Reprinted by permission of the author and the publisher. Some footnotes have been omitted for reasons of space. Ellipses indicate deletions from the text.

course, also possible to put different accents on the definition of politics. At any rate, the major intent of this presentation is not an historical defense of Weber but a review of critiques insofar as they seem to have a bearing on the *raison d'être* of political sociology. In my judgment, this rationale is imperiled if Weber's insights into the nature of politics are denied.

Since sociological analysis properly endeavors to look at the world dispassionately or, more correctly, from a "theoretical" perspective in the strict contemplative sense of the word, it must appear relativist and Machiavellian to all those who, for ideological reasons, cannot recognize any dividing line between political sociology and political ideology. Weber emphatically insisted on such a distinction. He always made it clear that he did not claim scientific support for his political views. Of course, in his political writings he drew on his sociological learning; he also put concrete political issues into the universal historical context with which his studies were concerned. But since his critics refuse to distinguish between his scholarship and his politics, they can quote sociological statements—his own or that of any other person— as articulations of political views.

WEBER'S SOCIOLOGICAL ETHIC

The vehemence of various critiques must be attributed not only to Weber's insistence upon a detached scholarly study of power and authority, but also to his own political decision that politics is the art of the possible—a rational craft. Here indeed is a connection between Weber's sociological work and his political commitment, which may be said to imply a *sociological ethic:* it was sociological because he considered it empirically indisputable that recurrent ideological conflict was as basic a fact of social life as the impossibility of reconciling any Is with any Ought, insofar as large-scale social structures were concerned; it was an ethic because he advocated moral stamina in the face of these "iron" facts.[1] His recognition of the realities of power was not identical with the glorification of the state and of *Realpolitik* by many of his contemporaries. Rather, his views were a secular counterpart of the age-old Christian dualism, revived as a major literary

[1] This seems to me related to what Benjamin Nelson has called the "social reality principle," in derivation from Freudian terminology. The term "sociological ethic" follows Weberian vocabulary and is gleaned from Carlo Antoni, *From History to Sociology,* Hayden V. White, trans. (Detroit: Wayne State University Press, 1959), 141. Since Antoni is a follower of Benedetto Croce's idealist intuitionism, the object of his study must appear to him as "the decline of German thought from historicism to typological sociologism" (see his preface of 1939).

topic by Dostoevski and Tolstoy, about whom Weber planned to write a book. Those who would remain "pure and innocent" must stay out of politics altogether, yet even this is not entirely safe since values may be compromised by a refusal to act—witness the pacifists who refuse to fight the enemies of humanitarianism. Whoever enters politics encounters the need to exercise power, and this implies ethical as well as political compromise.

These sociological insights did not shake Weber's resolve that man should act decently toward his fellow man, even if there was no absolute supernatural or scientific justification for it. For him this was a simple rational affirmation of the humanitarian element in Western civilization. He had no illusions about the dark side of Progress, and this was one reason for his aversion to abstract moralizing. He was convinced that responsible political leadership cannot afford to adhere to moralistic, legalistic or any other kind of ideological absolutism, since these are inherently self-defeating. His sociological ethic was thus a latter-day version of Stoic philosophy in that virtuous conduct was more important than any notion of ultimate salvation in a this-worldly or otherworldly millennium—and only in this ethical sense was Weber a Machiavellian.

This anti-ideological insistence on *measure* has provoked the true believers in political panaceas, Left, Right, and Center. Accordingly, the ideological critiques of Weber have come mainly from three quarters: Marxism, Nazism, and Natural Law with its liberal and conservative wings. In the United States, advocates of moralistic liberalism, which is rooted in a strong natural rights tradition, have been especially provoked by Weber. Many of the other attacks, however, may seem at first sight to refer to another land and another time. Most of the participants in the extended debate were born in Germany; many left involuntarily, some on their own initiative; some returned; and some merely studied there. (In the course of this exposition it should become clear that more is involved than a mere quarrel between Germans, ex-Germans, Germanophiles and Germanophobes.)

The three ideologies are substantively opposed to one another, but they are all instances of an "ethic of good intentions" or "ultimate ends" (Gesinnungsethik) and, methodologically, they all resort to historical reductionism. To be sure, Marxism does not recognize the existence of absolute values in the sense of natural rights (a self-interested bourgeois postulate), but it adheres dogmatically to a correspondence theory of concept and object, maintaining that only critical, dialectical concepts can express the "truth." Nazism, in turn, was an "ethic of good intentions" only in the most formal sense.

Not surprisingly, the only Marxist critiques that warrant attention have come from writers who opposed Communist totalitarianism from the outside[2] or who eventually clashed with party orthodoxy from the inside. Among the latter, Georg Lukacs was the only writer on sociology in the Moscow of the Stalinist purges who approached serious scholarship. At the time he kept himself busy—and out of the way— with an attempt to construe German intellectual history as a road to irrationalism leading from Schelling to Hitler via Weber and all other major German sociologists.[3]

Despite important political and philosophical differences among these Marxist writers, their views on Weber appear very similar:

1. Weber refused to accept the dialectical idea of potentiality—he studied the facts of social life and tried to extrapolate future trends instead of measuring reality against the great possibilities postulated by Marx's theory of human nature.

2. Epistemologically, this was due to the fact that Weber was a Neo-Kantian, adhering to the belief that the phenomenal world can be conceptualized in many different ways.

[2] Prominent among Western spokesmen for a sophisticated "critical theory of society" are T. W. Adorno, who called for a critique of Weber's political philosophy in an address as president of the German Sociological Association at the 1964 annual convention in Heidelberg and Herbert Marcuse, who delivered the main attack at the same occasion. On Adorno's basic position, see Max Horkheimer and T. W. Adorno, *Die Dialektik der Aufklärung* (Amsterdam: Querido, 1947); specifically on Weber, see Horkheimer, *Eclipse of Reason* (New York: Oxford University Press, 1947), p. 6. For Marcuse's critique, see "Industrialisierung und Kapitalismus," Heidelberg address, April, 1964, and the critical rejoinders by Reinhard Bendix and Benjamin Nelson, forthcoming Proceedings. Marcuse has become the best-known representative of "critical social theory" in the U.S. through his books *Reason and Revolution* (1942), *Eros and Civilization* (1955, and the recent *One-Dimensional Man* (1963).

[3] See Georg Lukacs, *Die Zerstörung der Vernunft* (Berlin: Aufbau-Verlag, 1955); on Weber esp. 474–88.

Lukacs followed the Stalinist line before 1953 but joined the intraparty opposition before the Hungarian Revolution; after a period of banishment he recently emerged again with an appeal for a self-critical Marxism that can even accept Franz Kafka's bureaucratic nightmare. Cf. Melvin Lasky's perceptive review of two Lukacs translations in the *New York Times Book Review*, May 10, 1964, p. 4. especially his remarks on the "simple-minded thirties."

Less known in this country is Hans Mayer, who abandoned his professorship of modern literature at the University of Leipzig in 1963 and sought asylum in Western Germany. For Mayer's views on Weber, see "Die Krise der deutschen Staatslehre von Bismarck bis Weimar" (partly written before 1933), in *Karl Marx und das Elend des Geistes* (Meissenheim: Westkulturverlag, 1948), pp. 48–75.

3. Therefore, Weber postulated a universe of conflicting values among which no scientific choices are possible; this opens the way to irrationalism, leading directly to imperialism and ultimately to fascism. For if Weber denies the truth of Marxism and is too much of a secular relativist to subscribe to outmoded religious metaphysics he must perforce take the nationalist and militarist nation state as his major political and even moral reference.

4. Weber's mode of thinking was typically bourgeois, insensitive to the truth that capitalism has been the most extreme exploitation of man. In class defense, men like Weber and Georg Simmel—both capitalist rentiers and parasites, "objectively" speaking[4]—view social reality in formalized terms, conceiving of capitalism as a system of rational calculation based on the abstract medium of money. Significantly, Weber is also concerned with the "spirit" (*Geist*) of capitalism and its affinity to the Calvinist ethic. But in his most detached scholarly work, *Economy and Society*, an "orgy of formalism" in its casuistic definitions of types of action and modes of domination, Weber reveals the depravity, the *Ungeist*, of capitalist society.[5]

5. Weber's interest in a comparative study of social structure and ideology "reflects" the imperialist interests of the capitalist countries; it is "expansionist" sociology.

Most of these charges clearly apply to contemporary American social science as well. In spite of their basic optimism, most American social scientists are skeptical of the idea of potentiality, have been vaguely Neo-Kantian, and have focussed on the methodological and conceptual elaboration of their disciplines—hence have been guilty of "positivistic formalism." Moreover, American social science tends to appear as a defensive Cold War instrument, in view of its increasing interest in newly developing countries.

THE NAZI CRITIQUE

In general, the Nazi critique has been even less sophisticated than the Marxist critique, but there are also some striking parallels. Exceptions to the rule of ignorance and incompetence were Carl Schmitt, the renowned and notorious political scientist and constitutional expert, and the forgotten Christoph Steding, the unfulfilled hope of Nazi philosophy. Both men share two features with the Marxists mentioned above: they held substantially the same opinion of positivistic sociology—except for the race issue—and they were prominent but politically marginal ideologists. I shall limit myself to Steding, who was

[4] Lukacs, op. cit., p. 361.
[5] Cf. Marcuse, "Industrialisierung. . . .", op. cit., 2.

more direct and typical than the elusive and more capable Carl Schmitt.[6]

Steding made a limited effort to conform to some canons of scholarship in his Ph.D. dissertation of 1932 on "Max Weber's Politics and Science," in which he asserted their identity and found Weber's notion of charismatic leadership very congenial.[7] Steding's major concoction, begun on a Rockefeller Foundation grant in the early thirties, grew into a violent attack on the "disease of European culture."[8] Mixing historical fact and paranoic phantasy, he argued that this disease originated with the Westphalian Peace of 1648 when the Western European nation states established a balance of power which made an effective *Reich* impossible and hence vitiated a universalist political and cultural order that would have restored philosophic realism. The age of neutralism arrived and championed the liberal theory of the laissez-faire state, philosophical nominalism and value-free sociology.[9]

In vivid organic imagery, Steding showed that the "disease carriers" that threatened the *Reich* were located in the Rhine valley. Weber had suggested that terms like "nation," *"Nationalgefühl,"* or *"Volk"* were not really applicable to "neutralized" areas like Switzerland, Alsace-Lorraine, Luxemburg, and Lichtenstein, for which opposition to "militarist" Germany provided a strong basis of their sense of political community. The old Calvinist territories of Switzerland and the Netherlands became the cornerstones of the hostile wall of Rhenish cities which had been Free Imperial cities or anti-Prussian court resi-

---

[6] Carl Schmitt started from an authoritarian Catholic position. His major scholarly work is his *Verfassungslehre* (Munich: Duncker und Humblot, 1928, 3rd unchanged ed., 1957); on Weber, see pp. 286f., 307, 314, 335f., 341 and 347. Scholarly in substance too is his essay *Der Begriff des Politischen* (1927). See the text of 1932 with a defensive preface (Berlin: Duncker und Humblot, 1963). This essay contains his famous friend-foe distinction as the basic criterion of the political process. The Nazified edition of 1933 (Hamburg: Hanseatische Verlagsanstalt) differs only —but decisively—in tone, terminology, and omission. Weber, for whom Schmitt had high regard, is no longer mentioned, but Franz Oppenheimer is suddenly identified as a "Berlin-Frankfurt sociologist"—evoking the image of the two cities as citadels of liberalism-capitalism-bolshevism-Judaism-sociologism. Schmitt suffered quick decline after 1933, but he was one of the most effective opponents of the Weimar Republic and of sociology during the late twenties.

[7] Christoph Steding, *Politik und Wissenschaft bei Max Weber* (Breslau: Korn, 1932).

[8] *Das Reich und die Krankheit der europäischen Kultur* (Hamburg: Hanseatische Verlagsanstalt, 1938).

[9] Carl Schmitt also construed a theory of political decline from the 16th century to the liberal-bourgeois age of "neutral" and "unpolitical" attitudes and social spheres. See "Das Zeitalter der Neutralisierungen und Entpolitisierungen" (1929), reprinted in *Der Begriffe des Politischen*, op. cit. (1963), pp. 79–95.

dences. Basle was the preferred domicile of Jacob Burckhardt and Friedrich Nietzsche, the two most formidable intellectual enemies of the *Reich* in the last third of the 19th century; the old universities of Freiburg, Heidelberg, and Marburg excelled in "quasi-Calvinist" and "quasi-Jewish" Neo-Kantianism; the old court residence Darmstadt was the home of several figures of the charismatic George circle, which was suspect because of its esthetically refined vision of a Third *Reich*;[10] the trade and university centers of Frankfurt and Cologne, which pioneered institutes for economic and sociological research, provided the link to Amsterdam.

In this context Max Weber and Thomas Mann appear as the last two outstanding and personally admirable representatives of bourgeois civilization in its terminal stage of decadence and fatal disease—exactly as they did for the Marxists.[11] Their work is the last achievement of the bourgeois spirit: it is capitalist, urban, abstract, nominalist, neutralist, Neo-Kantian and, for Steding, of course, "Jewish" by association.

As in the Marxist perspective, there is no basic difference between Imperial Germany and the Weimar Republic: both are capitalist societies. The personnel and the personalities are largely the same: William II and Weber, his stormiest critic, appear akin in their haste, nervousness, and imperialist posturing, lacking a real power-drive. But Weber and Thomas Mann are also acknowledged to have been more perceptive than most other members of their class. Their support of parliamentary government made them ideological spokesmen or symbols of the Weimar Republic, the spirit of which, alas, was that of Locarno—another "neutralist" locality.[12]

[10] For Weber's own dead-pan references to George's charismatic exultation, see op. cit., pp. 142, 664.

[11] See, for example, Hans Mayer, *Thomas Mann: Werk und Entwicklung* (Berlin: Volk und Welt, 1950), and "Thomas Manns 'Doktor Faustus': Roman einer Endzeit und Endzeit eines Romans," in *Von Lessing bis Thomas Mann* (Pfullingen: Neske, 1959), pp. 383–404; Georg Lukacs, *Thomas Mann* (Berlin: Aufbau-Verlag, 1949); see also Hans Mayer's "revisionist" review essay, "Georg Lukacs' Grösse und Grenze," *Die Zeit*, July 24, 1964, p. 12.

Mann and Weber were impressed with Lukacs' pre-Marxist *Theory of the Novel* (written in 1914/15). The figure of Naphta in the *Magic Mountain* (1924) is said to have drawn on Lukacs' personality. On Lukacs' personal acquaintance with the Webers, see Marianne Weber, [*Max Weber* (Heidelberg: Schneider, 1959),] 508f., 511, 533, and his autobiographical statement of 1962 in *Die Theorie des Romans* (Neuwied: Luchterhand, 1963), pp. 5–9.

[12] In Locarno (Switzerland) in 1925, Belgium, France, England, Italy, and Germany concluded the famous treaty that guaranteed the existing frontiers and seemed to create the basis for lasting peace among the European nations. This was the era of the "Spirit of Locarno."

Christoph Steding and his Marxist counterparts read their sociologists with malicious care so as to use sociological insights as political weapons and turn the tables on Weber, Simmel, and other members of the Generation of 1890. Both Steding and the Marxists adhere to a vulgar sociology of knowledge, an all too easy and superficial notion of correspondence between ideas and social structure.[13] The facts are sometimes correct, but the political conclusions arbitrary. Thus, Steding points out that Weber became interested in Confucianism only after Germany took over Kiaochow in 1898. Weber wrote *Ancient Judaism* and some of his most passionate political essays in the midst of the turmoil of the First World War, when he felt like a lonely prophet.[14] Steding, the proud peasant son, also charged Weber with the inability of the decadent to finish their work and to defend their political interests successfully. Yet, ironically, he died at the age of 35 in 1938, before finishing his long and rambling work, and the two most notorious Nazi henchmen, Himmler and Heydrich, who considered his work as a major indoctrination text,[15] perished within a few years, eliminating for the time being this kind of threat to the social sciences.

THE NATURAL-RIGHT CRITIQUE

In reaction to the rise of totalitarian Nazism and Communism some prominent writers have urged a return to natural right, which posits a natural or rational hierarchy of values. Adherents believe that this hierarchy can be discovered by philosophic reflection or intuition, or that it has been revealed to man. However, because this latter-day revival of natural right is so obviously a reactive phenomenon, it has a strong instrumental or functionalist admixture. Those of Weber's critics who more or less fall back on natural rights have either stressed philosophical implications or they have been concerned primarily with political consequences, especially with the course of German history.

[13] This intellectual game of arguing by facile association or spurious correspondence has infinite variations. One latter-day version would consist in associating the meetings of the International Sociological Association in Liège, Amsterdam, and Stresa (where, in 1935, England, France, and Italy protested unsuccessfully against German rearmament) to the "neutralist" atmosphere of these localities, on the one hand, and the "neutralist" or, if need be, "instrumental" character of sociology on the other. For the 1962 meetings in Washington, D.C., other associations could easily be found ("Cold War stalemate," etc.).

[14] Cf. Steding, *Max Weber*, op. cit., pp. 108 and 31.

[15] See the letter of Heinrich Himmler to Reinhard Heydrich, February 1, 1939, in Leon Poliakov and Josef Ulf, eds., *Das Dritte Reich und seine Denker: Dokumente* (Berlin: Arani, 1959), p. 282.

Politico-philosophical Critiques

The attacks on this level have been carried in particular by Leo Strauss and Eric Voegelin.[16] For them, Weber is the greatest and most typical representative of modern social science. "No one since Weber," says Strauss, "has devoted a comparable amount of intelligence, assiduity, and almost fanatical devotion to the basic problem of the social sciences. Whatever may have been his errors, he is the greatest social scientist of our century." [17] But Weber helped lead social science into the "morass of relativism." According to Strauss and Voegelin, science should be understood no longer positivistically, but again ontologically as the search for *prima principia*. Whoever does not believe in the oneness of truth cannot help but succumb to a chaos of random values. Without the acceptance of natural rights, relativism and its dialectical counterpart, totalitarian absolutism, appear inevitable.

Like the Marxists and Steding, Voegelin develops a formula identifying the forces of evil in history. Instead of focusing on the capitalist spirit of inhuman rationality and neutrality, he attacks the whole "gnostic search for a civil theology," for a perfect order on earth.[18] For Voegelin, the Nazis' belief in the Third *Reich,* and the Marxists' hopes for a classless society after the Revolution, are gnostics' phantasies about the millennium. Their very attempt to create total goodness by their own definition is bound to turn government into a force of total evil. Furthermore, gnosticism is not just a matter of totalitarianism, but is typical of Westernization in general, a global process that is continuing in the United States and Western Europe.[19]

Positivistic gnosticism has destroyed political science proper: methods have subordinated relevance, useless facts are accumulated, objectivity is equated with the exclusion of value judgments. In this scheme Weber occupies a transitional position. He was a "positivist with regrets," who tabooed classic and Christian metaphysics. Voegelin finds it revealing that Weber neglected these two traditions in his vast comparative studies of the affinity between status groups and ethical ideas. If he had not shied away from them he would have discovered there "the belief in a rational science of human and social order and especially of natural law. Moreover, this science was not simply a

---

[16] Leo Strauss, *Natural Right and History* (Chicago: University of Chicago Press, 1953), ch. II; Eric Voegelin, *The New Science of Politics* (Chicago: University of Chicago Press, 1952), pp. 13–26.

[17] Strauss, op. cit., p. 36.

[18] Voegelin, op. cit., p. 163.

[19] Voegelin, op. cit., p. 164.

belief, but was actually elaborated as a work of reason." [20] Weber's positivism made him see history as a process of rationalization, whereas modern history was actually a downfall from the grace of reason—in the light of the *scientia prima*. Because Weber did not recognize natural right, he had to demonize politics. Only his ethics of responsibility was a rational counterforce. Voegelin concedes that Weber made a stronger effort than all other positivists to turn social science in a meaningful direction, but since Voegelin adopts a Christian dualism, he feels compelled to reject Weber in the end. [21]

For Strauss, too, the troubles of recent history have been due basically to the denial of natural right. Its rejection is tantamount to nihilism, and in Weber's case it led to "noble nihilism." Since American social science largely agrees with Weber's relativism, it has become something of a German aberration (says the German philosopher):

> It would not be the first time that a nation, defeated on the battlefield and, as it were, annihilated as a political being, has deprived its conquerors of the most sublime fruit of victory by imposing on them the yoke of its own thought. Whatever might be true of the thought of the American people, certainly American social science has adopted the very attitude toward natural right which, a generation ago, could still be described, with some plausibility, as characteristic of German thought. [22]

This is an extreme statement, which may have been advanced for its shock value. But Strauss is fair enough to denounce the *reductio ad Hitlerum*, [23] the assertion that Weber's thinking led to Fascism. This kind of reductionism has been typical of the historical critique associated with moralistic liberalism.

The Critique of Moralistic Liberalism

American liberals have traditionally shown exasperation with the reverses of democracy abroad. Moreover, their pragmatist background has made them especially skeptical toward German idealism and to a lesser extent toward historical materialism, another German product. [24]

---

[20] Op. cit., p. 20.

[21] As a young man, Voegelin was under Weber's spell and wrote an excellent analysis of Weber's rationalism, in particular, of the difference between the necessary resignation of the responsible political activist (Weber's theory) and that of the esthetic creator (Simmel's theory); see Eric Voegelin, "Über Max Weber," *Deutsche Vierteljahrsschrift für Literatur*, III (1925), 177–93.

[22] Strauss, op. cit., p. 2. By contrast, in the wake of the First World War some English scholars felt that one of its benefits had been the liberation from the yoke of "German" value-free science; see Voegelin, op. cit., p. 189.

[23] Strauss, op. cit., p. 42.

[24] Paradoxically, however, some liberals have been more sympathetic with the

Times have changed, however, since 1935 when Ellsworth Faris rejected Pareto from implied moralistic premises, without conceding any
utility whatever to Pareto's political sociology.[25] But many liberals
still tend to distrust the detached sociological study of power and of
non-democratic systems of government, except Communism and Nazism—as the most extreme negations of liberalism they fit into a
moralistic black-white scheme. At least until very recently, there were
few studies of the growing number of authoritarian governments not
just as variants of Fascism or Communism but as different types of
dominations, age-old or brand-new. This traditional mistrust may
also explain some of the uneasiness toward Weber's insistence on the
facts of power and toward his nationalism, which at best is regarded
as a characteristic that he shared with most scholars of his generation,
especially Durkheim. Moreover, the experience of Nazism provides a
powerful moral perspective on German history and makes it hard to be
fair to past generations.

The interest among American social scientists, first in Fascism and
then in totalitarianism in general, was shared and stimulated by German political exiles. In reflecting upon the rise of Nazism, some writers began to view Weber, not so much as a direct Nazi forerunner, but
as a symptom of things to come.[26] This concern has now been taken
up by a new generation of German scholars. Intent on understanding
the causes of the German catastrophe, some of them have been so
preoccupied with the political interpretation of Weber that they tend
to lose sight not only of his scholarly intentions and achievements but
also of the rationale of sociology. Weber, a major argument goes, emphasized too strongly the instrumental instead of the inherent value
of democracy—that is, democracy as decreed by natural law. He advocated charismatic leadership in the face of bureaucratization, and

---

extreme German left than with the convinced supporters of parliamentary government in the Social Democratic labor movement—after both 1918 and 1945—because
the former seemed to promise a utopian reconstruction. Cf. my study, *The Social
Democrats in Imperial Germany* (Totowa: Bedminster Press, 1963), pp. 323ff. For a
recent textbook illustration of this moralistic bias, see John E. Rodes, *Germany: A
History* (New York: Holt, Rinehart and Winston, 1964), preface.

[25] See Ellsworth Faris, "An Estimate of Pareto," *American Journal of Sociology*,
XLI (1935), 657–68.

[26] J. P. Mayer, who feels more at home with Tocqueville's older conservative
liberalism, wrote his reflections on Weber and German politics in the early thirties,
contemporaneous with the work of Lukacs, Hans Mayer, and Steding, and published them in war-time England. J. P. Mayer, *Max Weber and German Politics*
(London: Faber and Faber, 1943). Hans Kohn, life-long student of nationalism, recently echoed J. P. Mayer and placed Weber squarely into the ranks of narrow-
minded nationalists; see his *The Mind of Germany* (New York: Scribner, 1960), pp.
269, 278–87.

therefore favored the direct election of the President of the Weimar Republic, a constitutional provision that proved fatal in 1933. Hence the conclusion: Neither from the viewpoint of natural rights nor from that of pragmatic compromise does Weber's position provide reliable support for a pluralist system in which mundane group interests must continually be readjusted, a task that can be accomplished best with a minimum of charismatic excitement.[27]

Related to these arguments is another kind of historical reductionism, which assumes a downfall from the Age of Reason. A number of younger German writers, holding a natural rights position at least for polemical purposes, have construed an ideological line leading to Nazism which runs, for example, from Kant's formalistic Categorical Imperative, through Ranke's view of states and peoples as historical individualities, through the legal positivism since the 1860s, to Weber's sociological definition of politics and the state, and from there to Carl Schmitt's theory of politics as a friend-foe relationship—only one last step removed from Hitler's views and crimes.[28] In the same fashion,

[27] The most impressive study on this score, superseding J. P. Mayer, is Wolfgang Mommsen's *Max Weber und die deutsche Politik, 1890–1920* (Tübingen: Mohr, 1959); for Mommsen's implicit natural rights view, see p. 407. As a German historian, Mommsen is, of course, far removed from the interest of American sociologists in Weber, but his treatment becomes questionable to them at the moment in which he interprets Weber's sociological analyses as political ideology. Accordingly he was criticized on both historical and methodological grounds in a symposium by three American (formerly German) social scientists: Reinhard Bendix, Karl Loewenstein, and the late Paul Honigsheim in *Kölner Zeitschrift für Soziologie,* XIII (1961), 258ff. Mommsen replied at length against what he called the Weber orthodoxy in ibid., XV (1963), 295–321.

The facts on the presidential issue have now been uncovered in the excellent study by Gerhard Schulz, *Zwischen Demokratie und Diktatur: Verfassungspolitik und Reichsreform in der Weimarer Republik* (Berlin: Gruyter, 1963), I, 114–42. Schulz points out that far from taking a blunt position in favor of a "Caesarist" leader, Weber gradually shifted his opinions in response to the changing political situation and the diversity of opinion in committee meetings. Eventually he came to favor a popularly elected president as a mediator between the *Reichstag* and the States, between the unitary and the federative principle. Cf. Weber, *Gesammelte politische Schriften,* Joh. Winckelmann, ed. (Tübingen: Mohr, 1958), pp. 394–471, 486–89. Schultz also delivered the commemorative address on "Weber as a Political Critic" before the Friedrich-Naumann-Stiftung, Heidelberg, 1964.

[28] See Wilhelm Hennis, "Zum Problem der deutschen Staatsanschauung," *Vierteljahrshefte für Zeitgeschichte,* VII (1959), 1–23. For a similar construction making Schmitt a terminal point of a long development passing through Weber, see Heinz Laufer, *Das Kriterium politischen Handelns: Eine Studie zur Freund-Feind-Doktrin von Carl Schmitt* (Munich: Institut für politische Wissenschaften der Universität München, 1961. Identical with Ph.D. dissertation, University of Wurzburg, 1961.) For Mommsen's interpretation of Schmitt's "logical" elaboration of Weber, see Mommsen, op. cit., pp. 379–86. For a judicious assessment, in the wake of the

other writers have tried to trace the rise of totalitarian democracy from Rousseau's general will, through Saint-Simon's technocratic elite and Marx's theory of the class struggle, to Lenin's democratic centralism —only one last step removed from Stalin.[29]

The tracing of such ideological lineages is a challenging and fascinating task, but it is also very difficult, since the scholar must do justice to the individual's subjective intentions and to the complexities of historical reality; he must avoid a facile theory of antecedents, stepping stones and parallels, since it is in the nature of politics that differences of degrees in belief and action are critical (the rule of the lesser evil). With regard to "Max Weber before Fascism," Ernst Nolte has brilliantly balanced the account.[30]

SUBJECTIVE INTENT AND OBJECTIVE CONSEQUENCES

There is no effective protection against the misuse of ideas, against their deterioration into ideological coins and political weapons. The doctrine of natural rights, too, has been susceptible to political misuse, not least in this century.[31] Ideas always have unintended consequences, and sociology largely lives off this fact. Weber himself showed the possible relations between the Protestant Ethic and the spirit of capitalism. But he was never concerned with declaring Calvin or Baxter responsible for the materialism of the capitalist era, or Karl Marx, for the intransigence of the labor movement; his grasp of historical reality protected him from subscribing to any Devil-theory of history.

1964 Heidelberg convention, of the link and the difference between Weber and Schmitt, see Karl Loewith, "Max Weber und Carl Schmitt," a full-page essay in the *Frankfurter Allgemeine Zeitung*, June 27, 1964. Loewith also delivered the main address on "Science as a Vocation" at the Weber commemoration of the University of Heidelberg, April, 1964.

[29] In addition to Eric Voegelin, see Jacob L. Talmon, *The Origins of Totalitarian Democracy* (New York: Praeger, 1960), and *Political Messianism: The Romantic Phase* (London: Secker and Warburg, 1960); Georg Iggers, *The Cult of Authority: The Political Philosophy of the Saint-Simonians* (The Hague: M. Nijhoff, 1958), and id., ed., *The Doctrine of Saint-Simon: An Exposition* (Boston: Beacon Press, 1958), pp. ix–xlvii. For a critique of this approach, see Alfred Cobban, *In Search of Humanity: The Role of the Enlightenment in Modern History* (New York: Braziller, 1960).

[30] "Max Weber vor dem Faschismus," *Der Staat*, II (1963), 295–321; see also his major comparative study of French, Italian, and German Fascism, *Der Faschismus in seiner Epoche* (Munich: Piper, 1963).

[31] Cf. Ernst Topitsch, "Max Weber und die Soziologie heute," address before the 1964 Heidelberg convention.

Since my main interest is not an historical defense of Weber, I shall merely summarize some of the factors to be taken into consideration in this context:

1. Weber insisted on realism in politics because the politically dominant Right adhered to idealist and romanticist notions to provide motive and cover for irresponsible power politics.

2. Weber insisted on realistic politics also because for decades the sterile left-wing liberal opposition of Imperial Germany stuck to "principles" regardless of political feasibility.

3. He insisted that he was as patriotic as anybody else because (before 1918) he could not hope to exert any influence at all on the German Establishment unless he turned its own values against it by repeatedly pointing out that Imperial Germany and its ruling groups violated national ideals and national interest.[32]

4. He insisted on value-neutrality in the classroom because the nationalist historian Treitschke and similar "professors" of ideological creeds indoctrinated students from the rostrum.

5. He insisted it was the university's business to make the students face the logical consequences of their beliefs because most of his listeners were middle- and upper-class students predisposed to nationalist sentiments.

6. He insisted, finally, on an ethic of responsibility and of the politically possible (while conceding the abstract honorableness of an ethic of good intentions) because in 1919 the ideologists of the Right and the Left were interested in anything else but the creation of parliamentary government in Germany.

It is true that national welfare was Weber's ultimate *political* yardstick, since he considered himself a political man, not a theologian or philosopher—two very different types, who are not forced to operate within a given political unit. Constitutional problems were secondary to national welfare only in this abstract regard, not in the realm of practical politics or of sociological analysis. Weber gave much more thought to the instrumentalities of parliamentary government than almost anybody else, including the Left, during the last decade of the Empire. His only hope for public effectiveness lay in the persuasiveness of the *technical* arguments for parliamentary government;

---

[32] This is not to deny that Weber had a vociferously nationalist phase when he supported the extreme Conservatives, at about the age of 30, but he quickly moved on to the liberal Left, advocating the integration of the Social Democratic labor movement (cf. Roth, op. cit., chs. X and XI). See Weber's autobiographical statement on his shift of opinion in the preface to "Parlament und Regierung . . . ," *Politische Schriften*, op. cit., pp. 297f. Very useful for a historical judgment are the documents selected and commented on by Eduard Baumgarten in *Max Weber: Werk und Person* (Tübingen: Mohr, 1964).

the Empire's history had proven that ideological appeals for parliamentarianism were in vain.

Weber's references to national welfare were residual and did not imply any denial of the welfare of other nations. He never advocated colonialist or annexationist policies. But he was convinced that a great political power had special obligations—he called it a "miserable duty." He became ever more doubtful whether Germany was morally qualified to be a great nation, and he was prepared to let those obligations fall to the United States, where they have been affirmed in general by moralistic liberalism.

SOME IMPLICATIONS

*   *   *

Political critiques of Weber can to some extent be considered merely the price a scholar must be prepared to pay for entering the political arena and exposing himself to the crude vehemence of political controversy. Most social scientists since Weber's time have refrained from playing the dual role of scholar and political man, but the critiques reviewed here illustrate that this does not guarantee protection. On the one hand, adherents of Marxism, Nazism, and Natural Law have not only refused to recognize any dividing line between ideology and sociology, but they have also shown a common tendency toward an historical reductionism which is a challenge to serious scholarship; on the other, political sociologists are liable to provoke political opposition by dealing with the facts of national power and domestic group interests. This makes them controversial in their professional roles and ultimately makes it impossible for them to avoid taking an explicit political stand. Weber's scholarly canons and his sociological ethic were a major attempt to cope with this potential tension. . . .

The insights of political sociology can benefit both friend and foe of a pluralist society, but only such a society can provide the requisite freedom of intellectual inquiry. This gives political sociology a vested interest in its preservation. The growing involvement of political sociology in problems of political, economic, and social development, an involvement which to opponents appears as a result of Yankee imperialism, neocolonialism, or even fascism affirms this interest. At the same time the political prospects of social science, and especially of political sociology, have become less and less hopeful in many of the newly developing or newly independent countries. Until a few years ago most American social scientists hoped for the spread of their disciplines to many of these countries. But at this point one cannot put

much faith in the reception of certain research techniques in Communist countries, particularly the Soviet Union; and recent events in
Cuba,[34] Burma, and Africa have increased the possibly that society
science will remain a Western institution linked to the general fate
of the Western world, the unique history and uncertain future of
which were Weber's dominant political and scholarly concern.

[33] Cf. Heinz Hartmann, "Sociology in Cuba," *American Sociological Review,*
XXVIII (August, 1963), 624–28.

SELECTED BIBLIOGRAPHY

WORKS BY MAX WEBER

WEBER'S WORKS IN GERMAN

I have not listed early editions or several anthologies of writings that are included in the larger collections.

Die römische Agrargeschichte in ihrer Bedeutung für das Staats- und Privatrecht. Stuttgart: Ferdinand Enke, 1891.

Die Verhältnisse der Landarbeiter im ostelbischen Deutschland. Schriften des Vereins für Sozialpolitik, Vol. LV; Berlin: Duncker and Humblot, 1892.

Gesammelte Aufsätze zur Religionssoziologie, 3 vols. Tübingen: J. C. B. Mohr, 1920–21.

Gesammelte Aufsätze zur Soziologie und Sozialpolitik. Tübingen: J. C. B. Mohr, 1924.

Gesammelte Aufsätze zur Sozial- und Wirtschaftgeschichte. Tübingen: J. C. B. Mohr, 1924.

Gesammelte Aufsätze zur Wissenschaftlehre, 2nd edition revised and expanded by Johannes Winckelmann. Tübingen: J. C. B. Mohr, 1951.

Gesammelte Politische Schriften, 2nd edition revised and expanded by Johannes Winckelmann with an introduction by Theodor Heuss. Tübingen: J. C. B. Mohr, 1958.

Staatssoziologie: Soziologie des rationalen Staates und der modernen politischen Parteien und Parlamente, revised by Johannes Winckelmann. Berlin: Duncker and Humblot, 1956.

Wirtschaftgeschichte. Abriss der universalen Sozial und Wirtschaftsgeschichte, 2nd edition revised and expanded by Johannes Winckelmann. Berlin: Duncker and Humblot, 1958.

Wirschaft und Gesellschaft. Grundriss der verstehenden Soziologie, 2 vols., 4th edition revised and arranged by Johannes Winckelmann. Tübingen: J. C. B. Mohr, 1956.

ENGLISH TRANSLATIONS

General Economic History, translated by Frank H. Knight. London and New York: Allen and Unwin, 1927; paperback reissue, New York: Collier Books, 1961.

The Protestant Ethic and the Spirit of Capitalism, translated by Talcott Parsons with a foreword by R. H. Tawney. New York: Charles Scribner's Sons. First published, London, 1930.

From Max Weber: Essays in Sociology, translated, edited, and with an introduction by H. H. Gerth and C. Wright Mills. New York: Oxford University Press, 1946.

The Methodology of the Social Sciences, translated and edited by Edward A. Shils and Henry A. Finch. Glencoe, Ill.: The Free Press, 1949.

The Religion of China: Confucianism and Taoism, translated and edited by H. H. Gerth. Glencoe, Ill.: The Free Press, 1952.

Ancient Judaism, translated and edited by H. H. Gerth and Don Martindale. Glencoe, Ill.: The Free Press, 1952.

The Religion of India: The Sociology of Hinduism and Buddhism, translated and edited by H. H. Gerth and Don Martindale. Glencoe, Ill.: The Free Press, 1958.

The Rational and Social Foundations of Music, translated by Don Martindale, Johannes Riedel, and Gertrud Neuwirth. Carbondale: Southern Illinois University Press, 1958.

Economy and Society. An Outline of Interpretive Sociology, 3 vols., edited, revised and partially translated by Guenther Roth and Claus Wittich with an introduction by Guenther Roth. New York: Bedminster Press, 1968.

The following titles represent earlier translations of parts of *Economy and Society* which have been incorporated into the Roth-Wittich edition, but which include important introductions by the editors, translators, or other scholars and are still available in paperback editions.

The Theory of Social and Economics Organization, translated by A. M. Henderson and Talcott Parsons, edited and with an introduction by Parsons. New York: Oxford University Press, 1947.

Max Weber on Law in Economy and Society, translated by Edward A. Shils and Max Rheinstein, edited, annotated, and with an introduction by Rheinstein. Cambridge: Harvard University Press, 1954.

The City, translated and edited by Don Martindale and Gertrud Neuwirth. Glencoe, Ill.: The Free Press, 1958.

The Sociology of Religion, translated by Ephraim Fischoff with an introduction by Talcott Parsons. Boston: Beacon Press, 1963.

CONTRIBUTORS

DENNIS H. WRONG, the editor of this volume, is Professor of Sociology at New York University. He studied at the University of Toronto and Columbia, from which he received the Ph.D. degree in 1956. He is the author of *American and Canadian Viewpoints, Population and Society,* co-editor (with Harry L. Gracey) of *Readings in Introductory Sociology,* and has written extensively for scholarly journals as well as for *Commentary, Partisan Review,* and *Dissent,* of which he is an editor.

CARLO ANTONI was before his retirement Professor of Philosophy at the University of Rome. He was previously Professor of German Literature at the University of Padua. His *From History to Sociology,* a study of German historical thought, has been published in English translation.

RAYMOND ARON is Professor of Sociology at the University of Paris (Sorbonne). Among his many books that have been translated into English are *German Sociology, The Opium of the Intellectuals, Main Currents in Sociological Thought* (two volumes), *The Industrial Society,* and *Progress and Disillusion.*

REINHARD BENDIX is Professor of Sociology at the University of California at Berkeley and current president of the American Sociological Association. He is the author of *Higher Civil Servants in American Society, Social Science and the Distrust of Reason, Work and Authority in Industry, Social Mobility in Industrial Society* (with Seymour Martin Lipset), *Max Weber: An Intellectual Portrait,* and *Nation-Building and Citizenship,* and editor of *Class, Status and Power* (with Seymour Martin Lipset) and *The State and Society.*

PETER M. BLAU is Professor of Sociology at the University of Chicago. He is the author of *Dynamics of Bureaucracy, Bureaucracy and Society, Formal Organizations* (with W. R. Scott), *Exchange and Power in Social Life,* and *The American Occupational Structure* (with Otis Dudley Duncan).

KARL LOEWITH was until his retirement Professor of Philosophy at Heidelberg and taught in the United States during the Nazi period. He is the author of numerous books and articles published in Germany and his *Meaning in History* and *From Hegel to Nietzsche* have been published in English translations.

HERBERT LUETHY is a Swiss historian who has lived for many years in Paris. His book *France Against Herself* is available in English translation. He is also the author of *La Banque Protestante en France de la Révocation de l'Édit de Nantes à la Revolution* (two volumes) and of numerous articles on contemporary politics and culture in such English-speaking journals as *Commentary* and *Encounter*.

WOLFGANG MOMMSEN is Professor of History at the University of Cologne and author of *Max Weber und die deutsche Politik, 1890–1920.*

BENJAMIN NELSON, historian and sociologist, is Professor of Sociology on the Graduate Faculty of the New School for Social Research. He is the author of *The Idea of Usury* and editor of *Freud and the Twentieth Century.*

TALCOTT PARSONS is Professor of Social Relations at Harvard University and a former president of the American Sociological Association. His major books are *The Structure of Social Action, Essays in Sociological Theory, The General Theory of Action* (with Edward A. Shils), *The Social System,* and *Sociological Theory and Modern Society.*

GUENTHER ROTH is Professor of Sociology at the University of California at Davis and author of *The Social Democrats of Imperial Germany,* and co-editor and co-translator of the three-volume English edition of Max Weber's *Economy and Society.*